Unfortunately, She Was a Nymphomaniac

Unfortunately, She Was a Nymphomaniac

A New History of Rome's Imperial Women

Joan Smith

WILLIAM
COLLINS

William Collins
An imprint of HarperCollins*Publishers*
1 London Bridge Street
London SE1 9GF

WilliamCollinsBooks.com

HarperCollins*Publishers*
Macken House,
39/40 Mayor Street Upper,
Dublin 1, D01 C9W8, Ireland

First published in Great Britain in 2024 by William Collins

2

Copyright © Joan Smith 2024

Joan Smith asserts the moral right to be identified as the author of this work
in accordance with the Copyright, Designs and Patents Act 1988

A catalogue record for this book is available from the British Library

ISBN 978-0-00-863880-1 (Hardback)
ISBN 978-0-00-863881-8 (Trade paperback)

All rights reserved. No part of this publication may be reproduced, stored in a retrieval system, or transmitted, in any form or by any means, electronic, mechanical, photocopying, recording or otherwise, without the prior permission of the publishers.

This book is sold subject to the condition that it shall not, by way of trade or otherwise, be lent, re-sold, hired out or otherwise circulated without the publisher's prior consent in any form of binding or cover other than that in which it is published and without a similar condition including this condition being imposed on the subsequent purchaser.

Typeset in Adobe Garamond Pro by Palimpsest Book Production Ltd, Falkirk, Stirlingshire

Printed and bound in the UK using 100% renewable electricity at CPI Group (UK) Ltd

This book contains FSC™ certified paper and other controlled sources
to ensure responsible forest management.

For more information visit: www.harpercollins.co.uk/green

For Andrea Wakefield

CONTENTS

Dramatis Personae	ix
Introduction	1
1. The *I, Claudius* Effect	11
2. Surviving Augustus	28
3. Unfortunately, She Was a Nymphomaniac: Part I	54
4. Women Without Men	88
5. The Woman Who'd Had Enough	115
6. The Misogynist's Apprentice	138
7. Unfortunately, She Was a Nymphomaniac: Part II	160
8. The Last Woman Standing	193
9. The Serial Killer	227
10. The Long Shadow of Roman Misogyny	252
Acknowledgements	257
Endnotes	259
List of Illustrations	281
Index	285

DRAMATIS PERSONAE

Augustus, Roman general, conventionally known as Octavian until he became first emperor of Rome

Claudia Pulchra, first wife of Augustus

Scribonia, second wife of Augustus

Julia, known as the elder, daughter of Scribonia and Augustus, the emperor's only child, wife of Marcellus, Agrippa and Tiberius

Marcus Claudius Marcellus, son of Octavia, nephew of Augustus, first husband of the elder Julia

Marcus Vipsanius Agrippa, Roman general, second husband of the elder Julia

Gaius and Lucius, first and second sons of the elder Julia and Marcus Vipsanius Agrippa, designated heirs of Augustus

Julia, known as the younger, first daughter of the elder Julia and Agrippa

Lucius Aemilius Paullus, half-cousin and husband of the younger Julia

Agrippina, known as the elder, second daughter of the elder Julia and Agrippa, wife of Germanicus

Agrippa Postumus, third (and youngest) son of the elder Julia and Agrippa, born after his father's death

Livia Drusilla, third wife of Augustus, first empress of Rome

Tiberius Claudius Nero, first husband of Livia

Tiberius, first son of Livia and Tiberius Claudius Nero, third husband of the elder Julia, second emperor of Rome

Vipsania Agrippina, daughter of Marcus Vipsanius Agrippa, first wife of Tiberius

Drusus, known as the elder, second son of Livia and Tiberius Claudius Nero, brother of Tiberius

Drusus, known as the younger, son of Vipsania Agrippina and Tiberius

Mark Antony, Roman general, colleague and rival of Octavian, defeated in the civil wars

Fulvia, third wife of Mark Antony

Antyllus, first son of Fulvia and Mark Antony, betrothed to the elder Julia in childhood

Iullus Antonius, second son of Fulvia and Mark Antony, friend and alleged lover of the elder Julia

Octavia, younger sister of Augustus, mother of Marcellus, fourth wife of Mark Antony

Cleopatra VII, queen of Egypt, fifth wife of Mark Antony

Antonia, second daughter of Octavia and Mark Antony, wife of the elder Drusus

Livilla, daughter of Antonia and the elder Drusus, sister of Germanicus and Claudius, wife of Gaius (son of the elder Julia) and the younger Drusus

Julia Livia, *Tiberius* and *Germanicus Gemellus*, children of Livilla and the younger Drusus

Lucius Aelius Sejanus, Praetorian prefect, lover of Livilla

Apicata, divorced wife of Sejanus

Germanicus, first son of Antonia and the elder Drusus, brother of Livilla and Claudius, husband of the elder Agrippina

Nero and *Drusus*, first and second sons of the elder Agrippina and Germanicus

Caligula (real name Gaius), third son of the elder Agrippina and Germanicus, third emperor of Rome

Agrippina, known as the younger, first daughter of the elder Agrippina and Germanicus, fourth wife of Claudius, empress of Rome

Julia Drusilla, second daughter of the elder Agrippina and Germanicus

Julia Livilla, third daughter of the elder Agrippina and Germanicus

Junia Claudilla, first wife of Caligula

Livia Orestilla, second wife of Caligula, empress of Rome

Lollia Paulina, third wife of Caligula, empress of Rome

Milonia Caesonia, fourth wife of Caligula, empress of Rome

Claudius, second son of Antonia and the elder Drusus, brother of Germanicus and Livilla, fourth emperor of Rome

Pallas, *Narcissus and Callistus*, freedmen (freed slaves) of Claudius, powerful ministers in his regime

Plautia Urgulanilla, first wife of Claudius

Aelia Paetina, second wife of Claudius, mother of Claudia Antonia

Valeria Messalina, third wife of Claudius, empress of Rome

Domitia Lepida, mother of Valeria Messalina

Domitia, elder sister of Domitia Lepida and Gnaeus Domitius Ahenobarbus, aunt of Messalina and the emperor Nero

Gnaeus Domitius Ahenobarbus, brother of Domitia and Domitia Lepida, first husband of the younger Agrippina

Gaius Sallustius Passienus Crispus, friend of Caligula, second husband of the younger Agrippina

Nero, son of the younger Agrippina and Gnaeus Domitius Ahenobarbus, fifth and final Julio-Claudian emperor

Acte, freedwoman (freed slave) and lover of Nero

Claudia Octavia, daughter of Messalina and Claudius, younger half-sister of Claudia Antonia, first wife of Nero, empress of Rome

Britannicus, son of Messalina and Claudius, younger half-brother of Claudia Antonia

Poppaea Sabina, second wife of Nero, empress of Rome

Marcus Salvius Otho, friend of Nero, previous husband of Poppaea Sabina, emperor in AD 69

Claudia Antonia, daughter of Aelia Paetina and Claudius, elder half-sister of Claudia Octavia and Britannicus, sister-in-law of Nero

Statilia Messalina, third wife and widow of Nero, empress of Rome

INTRODUCTION

> Femicide is generally understood to involve intentional murder of women because they are women . . . [It] is usually perpetrated by men, but sometimes female family members may be involved. Femicide differs from male homicide in specific ways. For example, most cases of femicide are committed by partners or ex-partners, and involve ongoing abuse in the home, threats or intimidation, sexual violence or situations where women have less power or fewer resources than their partner.
>
> World Health Organization, 2012[1]

When you emerge from Rome's central railway station, Termini, there is an imposing Renaissance palace to your left. The Palazzo Massimo looks out of place in this run-down area of the city, where charities distribute food and second-hand clothes to the growing numbers of homeless people who live on its margins. But the palace, now a museum, houses an outstanding collection of sculpture from ancient Rome, including leading members of the Julio-Claudian dynasty. In the first century BC, two great families, the Julians and the Claudians, joined together and provided Rome's first five emperors, from Augustus to Nero. Its leading members are amply represented on the lower floors, where one of the prized exhibits is a typically self-aggrandising statue of Augustus in the robes of a priest. There are also busts of women from the dynasty, including heads that are believed to represent Augustus's sister, Octavia, and his niece, Antonia. The Julio-Claudian women are among the first in western history whose names, faces and histories have been recorded, even if what we 'know' about them turns out to be problematic.

But the most celebrated exhibit in the Palazzo Massimo is not a piece of sculpture. A grand marble staircase leads to the room on an upper floor which is now home to a set of frescoes known as 'Livia's Garden' (*il giardino di Livia*). Livia was Augustus's third wife and Rome's first empress, a position that had never previously existed. The wall paintings come from her country house at Prima Porta, a small town 14 kilometres north of Rome, where they once adorned the walls of an underground dining room (*triclinium*). The frescoes are as fresh today as when they were painted more than 2,000 years ago, creating the illusion of being in a garden where birds perch in trees heavy with fruit. The colours are ravishingly beautiful, smoky blues and greens, designed to lighten the atmosphere in the subterranean room where the family would have taken refuge from the fierce summer heat. It isn't hard to imagine Livia and Augustus dining on fruit grown in the villa's extensive gardens, while the flickering light from torches offered glimpses of the painted forest in the background. It's a rare insight into their private life, and their guests would have included Augustus's daughter, Julia, and Livia's sons, the future emperor Tiberius and his younger brother Drusus.

The Julio-Claudian family tree is famously tangled, with frequent marriages between close relatives creating a web of connections that's hard to follow; Drusus was the husband of Augustus's niece, Antonia, while Julia was briefly and unhappily married to her stepbrother, Tiberius. Julia was one of the most beautiful, literate and popular women in ancient Rome, but her separation from Tiberius would have drastic consequences, leading to her exile on a distant chain of islands off Italy's west coast. She would also become a magnet for some of the most salacious gossip that circulated in the city, gleefully recorded by Roman authors who couldn't resist the opportunity to denigrate one of the most famous women in the ancient world. It's a tradition that's been carried on by later writers, who've found the stories about adultery, wild parties and prostitution irresistible. They're still being repeated to tourists in the twenty-first century, as I discovered during a visit to the Palazzo Massimo while I was writing this book.

An English-speaking Italian guide brought a party of visitors into the room where I was admiring Livia's frescoes. He spoke loudly and with confidence, describing the history of the paintings and the origins of the Julio-Claudian dynasty. He explained that Augustus and Livia were married for many years but never had children together. Then things took an unexpected turn.

'Augustus only had one child, with his first wife,' he told the tourists, 'and unfortunately his daughter was a nymphomaniac.'

Julia was a nymphomaniac? I could hardly believe what I was hearing.

'Excuse me,' I said, interrupting his spiel. 'Julia's mother was not Augustus's first wife. And Julia was *not* a nymphomaniac.'

The guide turned to me with a smirk. 'It's in the sources, *signora*,' he said.

'I'm familiar with the sources,' I said. 'I assume you're referring to Seneca's essay *De Beneficiis*? Where he claims that Julia, despite being one of the most instantly recognisable women in Rome, went down into the forum at night and had sex with every passing barman and gladiator. Do you really think women behave like that?'

I pointed out that Julia was young and famously fertile. She had given birth to six children when she is supposed to have made this startling change to her lifestyle, yet she never became pregnant again, despite allegedly having unprotected sex (as though there *were* any other kind in ancient Rome) with dozens of paying customers.

'How did she manage that?' I asked.

'Maybe the sources exaggerated,' the guide said through gritted teeth.

They did, and it's hard to think of a better illustration of why this book is needed. Ancient authors made up pornographic fantasies about the Julio-Claudian women which have been accepted as fact by generations of commentators. Lucius Annaeus Seneca was a philosopher and senator in the first century AD, and his sneering portrait of Julia obsessively seeking sex with strangers is the foundation for the most damaging claims about her. The satirist Decimus Junius Juvenalis (universally known as Juvenal), who died in the early second century, invented an entire second career working in a brothel for the empress Messalina. She too has been accused of 'nymphomania', a word not even used in English until the early eighteenth century, and popularised by a French doctor who had some very bizarre ideas about the female half of the human race.[2] He believed that some women suffered from a 'horrible distemper' called *furor uterinus*, a kind of madness originating in the womb that led to excessive sexual desire. His pseudo-scientific diagnosis has been seized on with glee, turning Roman women who had sex with men other than their husbands into insatiable 'whores'. That's before we even get started on the accusations of greed, incest and murder, the latter often made about deaths that were more than likely due to accidents or natural causes.

I have loved Latin since I was fortunate enough to attend one of the few state schools that continued to offer it. For a working-class girl who lived on a council estate, it opened up a vista of another world, where literature, art and architecture were highly valued. I loved Roman authors, especially the historians Tacitus and Suetonius, but I couldn't help noticing the ugly misogyny that portrayed patrician women as wilful, ambitious and sexually incontinent. I went on to do a degree in Latin and included a chapter on Roman women in my book *Misogynies*, but the idea of a whole book lingered in the back of my mind.

Three or four years ago, when I began rereading texts I'd first encountered as an undergraduate, the misogyny of ancient authors was just as overt as I remembered. One thing did surprise me, however. I began the research assuming that sceptical modern attitudes would have led to a re-evaluation of sources so obviously hostile to Roman women. There were honourable exceptions but I kept finding the same old slurs, treating the emperors' wives, daughters and mothers as little more than wilful children and deserving of everything that happened to them. The double standard was astonishing: I was often told, while I was writing this book, that Roman sources for the reigns of the Julio-Claudian emperors were hostile and shouldn't be trusted. Stories showing them in a bad light have been dismissed as malicious gossip, repurposing Augustus as a statesman, Tiberius as an outstanding administrator, Claudius as a misunderstood intellectual, and so on.

This process reached its nadir in 2021, with the opening of the British Museum's *Nero* exhibition, devoted to the fifth and final emperor in the dynasty.[3] The museum's website described the purpose of the exhibition as 'question[ing] the traditional narrative of the ruthless tyrant and eccentric performer, revealing a different Nero, a populist leader at a time of great change in Roman society'. When I first read the announcement, I assumed it was a marketing device; exhibitions on this scale involve huge expense, including insurance for priceless objects, and obviously the museum needed to sell tickets. When I visited the exhibition, however, it turned out that they meant every word. A caption aimed at visiting schoolchildren displayed a flavour of the apologetics on offer:

> Nero's mother and wives were powerful. Ancient writers said that Nero had them killed. Nero said his mother and first wife betrayed him.
> Who would you believe?

Since few thirteen-year-olds are familiar with the accounts of Roman historians, it's hard to know how they were supposed to judge. More to the point, the museum was regurgitating the defence offered by just about every abuser who has killed a current or former wife: 'She made me do it.' This excuse has been called out many times by experts on domestic violence, who know that a woman's murder by a male relative is usually preceded by long periods of abuse and plenty of warning signs. That was certainly true in the case of Nero, who would eventually be implicated in the murders of five women – his aunt, his mother, two of his wives and his sister-in-law – yet no one at the British Museum seems to have challenged a caption making light of serial murder.

It's the most dramatic example I've encountered of the excuses currently being made for the Julio-Claudian emperors, but also the victim-blaming that goes with it. Ancient historians are said to have embellished accounts of the ruling men to suit a hostile political agenda, gleefully repeating anecdotes such as the emperor Caligula making his favourite horse, Incitatus, a consul, and yet, at the same time, they told the unvarnished truth about their wives, mothers, sisters and daughters. We're supposed to believe that the Julio-Claudian women were truly *awful*, so much so that some of the people vehemently expressing this view wondered why I was bothering to write about them at all. The reason is simple: Roman history is immensely popular, inspiring books, exhibitions and TV series, yet few contemporary commentators on the period know anything about violence against women. Stories of the Julio-Claudian women are still being told by institutions, academic historians and popular biographers who don't know the first thing about domestic abuse. They repeat lazy tropes about emperors being driven beyond endurance by unfaithful wives or promiscuous daughters, while minimising and excusing serious crimes committed by the men themselves.

My reading of the sources is different, informed by a lifetime's work researching and writing about violence against women. For eight years, from 2013 to 2021, I advised two mayors of London, Boris Johnson and Sadiq Khan, on strategies to tackle domestic and sexual violence in the capital; I worked with senior police officers, lawyers, and organisations that provide services for women who've suffered psychological, sexual and physical abuse at the hands of male relatives. And what I saw when I began to look more closely at the Julio-Claudian dynasty was a pattern of behaviour that amounts to extreme abuse: child marriage, serial rape, house arrest, exile on distant islands, forced suicide and murder. One of the most striking forms of cruelty was contempt for mothers, whose value plummeted as soon as they produced the heirs imperial men wanted above all else. Separation from children is one of the themes of this book, reflecting an assumption that even young children belonged in their fathers' households, regardless of the impact on mothers or the infants themselves.

Attempts to re-evaluate periods of history are often accused of 'presentism', applying modern standards to cultures with very different values, but it's not even as though mine is an exclusively twenty-first-century view; we know that ordinary people in Rome recognised how badly women in the dynasty were being treated *at the time* and poured onto the streets to protest. It happened in 2 BC, when crowds heard that Julia had been exiled and demanded her return, continuing their demonstrations when Augustus responded furiously. It happened again in AD 62, when Nero divorced his first wife, another woman called Octavia, and an angry mob invaded the imperial palace.

Indeed, one of the most remarkable texts to have survived from the ancient world, a play written not long after the empress Octavia's murder, lists some of the women in the dynasty who had suffered terrible abuse over several generations. The list is by no means definitive but it mentions the murders of Nero's grandmother Agrippina, Claudius's sister Livilla, her daughter Julia Livia, Octavia's mother Messalina, and Nero's mother, also called Agrippina. It includes a catalogue of the punishments imposed on some of the women: 'exile, flogging, cruel chains, grief, bereavement and finally death after years of suffering' (*exilium, verbera, saevas passa catenas, funera, luctus, tandem letum cruciata diu*).[4] The fact that the women's brutal mistreatment was recognised as long ago as the first century AD makes the willingness of some modern historians to overlook it all the more culpable.

This is not to argue that the women always behaved well, especially towards the end of the dynasty when only the most single-minded managed to survive. It's vital to bear in mind that by the middle of the first century AD the Julio-Claudian women had experienced half a century of femicide. Some readers may not be familiar with the word but it has a specific meaning, applying to the killing of women *because* they are women. And while it's true that many men were executed during the Julio-Claudian period, the murders of female members of the dynasty were inspired by an extraordinary degree of personal animosity. They were also unnecessary: the emperors were absolute monarchs, who exercised unlimited power over their wives, mothers and daughters. If they wanted to get rid of annoying female relatives, they could have sent them to live on a country estate outside Rome, guarded by soldiers, or on islands from which escape was impossible. Exile *was* the fate of around half the women in this book, but it was more than mere banishment and usually the precursor to a very unpleasant death. It is clear that the emperors *wanted* these women to suffer, imposing the cruellest imaginable punishments on mothers or wives they once claimed to love.

The figures speak for themselves: in this book, I tell the stories of twenty-three women closely associated with the Julio-Claudian emperors, and fewer than half a dozen can be said with any confidence to have died of natural causes. The others were savagely beaten, suffered multiple stab wounds or perished from starvation, either deliberately denied food on the orders of an emperor or because they could no longer bear to live, an outcome all too familiar to modern experts on domestic violence. The fate of the sixteen women who married men who were or became emperors is particularly telling: nine were divorced, while seven were eventually murdered even if they survived the marriage. There was even an attempt, in some cases, to obliterate them from history, leading to the wholesale destruction of statues, friezes and inscriptions. It didn't always work, but we have few verified images of some of the most significant women in the dynasty, including Augustus's daughter Julia, whose direct descendants included the emperors Caligula and Nero.

These absences are frustrating, but they are a sign of what the Julio-Claudian women have become, tantalising figures glimpsed in the shadows of the biographies of their male relatives. In this book, I've tried to piece together their stories, using my own translations from the Latin, to show how they struggled for control of their lives at a time when both the law and culture were stacked against them. It is not a conventional history but an interpretation of the original texts informed by what we know now about the mechanics of domestic abuse. There are no 'nymphomaniacs' here; the picture that emerges is one of spirited, inspiring and sometimes reckless resistance to male authority. The way these women have been misrepresented for 2,000 years speaks volumes not just about ancient misogyny, but the origin and persistence of attitudes that continue to blight women's lives today.

1

The I, Claudius *Effect*

First, some background. The Julio-Claudian dynasty ruled Rome from 27 BC to AD 68, although Augustus had effectively been in charge since he defeated his great rival, the Roman general Mark Antony, at the battle of Actium four years earlier. The switch from a republican form of government to one-man rule was seismic, causing festering resentment among the patrician class whose ancestors had, for the most part, ruled Rome for centuries. They were the most privileged of the city's three social classes, the others being knights (*equites*) and plebeians. Patrician families were often able to trace their ancestors back for several centuries and they were used to a political system where two of their number were elected as consuls, the highest political office in Rome, each year and served (usually) for twelve months. It was more an oligarchy than a democracy, distributing power among a number of prominent families. Now, though, power was concentrated permanently in the hands of a single man, something that had happened in the past but only as a temporary measure – and one of the effects was to give the emperor's female relatives a prominence never previously enjoyed by Roman women.

The wives of consuls had not been public figures under the republic and historical women, as opposed to mythological figures, were rarely memorialised with statues. Augustus changed all that, making a deliberate decision to put his relatives at the heart of imperial propaganda. His extended family was celebrated on one of the most famous monuments in Rome, the Ara Pacis Augustae, or Altar of Augustan Peace, where they appeared in processions on the north and south sides of what is in effect a small temple. Begun in 13 BC to celebrate the emperor's military successes in Gaul and Spain, it represents a startling break from the Roman republic in terms of public representations of women. Men still outnumber women, but a veiled female figure in the south procession probably represents Julia, standing next to her husband, the Roman general Marcus Vipsanius Agrippa, their eldest son, Gaius, hanging on to his father's toga.[1]

The prominence of women in public life was by no means universally welcome, however, and not just because it was such a departure from tradition. The Romans had a profoundly conservative view of the roles of the sexes, believing that women belonged firmly in the domestic sphere. One of the most startling indicators of their lack of status is the fact that girls did not have first names in the republic and early empire. A Roman man traditionally had three names: a first name (*praenomen*), a surname (*nomen*) and a nickname (*cognomen*) that indicated which branch of the family (*gens* in Latin) he belonged to. Girls had two names, the feminine versions of their father's surname and nickname; the names we know them by, Julia or Agrippina, are actually surnames, a bit like referring to them as Jones or Brown, and in large families there were sometimes several girls with the same name. Mark Antony had three daughters called Antonia and would very likely have had a fourth if his final wife, Cleopatra, had not put her foot down (her daughter with Antony was called Cleopatra Selene). Families must have used nicknames to get round the problem of having several girls in the same household with the same name, possibly based on birth order – the girls' name Tertia, for instance, means 'third'. Some female names are very clearly diminutives, signalling their lesser status; Drusilla is not just the daughter of a man called Drusus but a 'little' version of her father, for instance. It's also the case that girls in patrician families were married at such an early age that sisters born years apart didn't always overlap for long.

The fact that female children were not considered important enough to have their own personal names creates problems for anyone writing about successive generations of the same family. The Julio-Claudian family tree contains a daunting number of women with the same names, with far too many girls called Julia, Agrippina and Claudia for comfort. It's baffling even to those of us who are immersed in the period, and I have occasionally started awake in the early hours, trying to remember which of Mark Antony's daughters called Antonia was the mother of the emperor Claudius (it was the younger of his two daughters with Augustus's sister, Octavia). The conventional way to distinguish between identically named women is to call them 'the elder' and 'the younger', but it's an unwieldy device when repeated many times. No system is ideal, but where it isn't clear from the context, I've added a couple of words about an individual's role in the family or her position in the dynasty – Augustus's daughter Julia, as opposed to his granddaughter of the same name, for instance.

What needs to be stressed from the outset is that the early Roman empire was a period of dramatic change for upper-class women. Under the republican system of government, which lasted for several centuries, the ideal Roman matron had been an intensely private person. She left her sons' education to their father, taught her daughters traditional pastimes such as spinning and weaving, was rarely seen in public and would be praised for her undemanding existence on her tombstone. Some women did step out of line and have affairs, providing an abundance of material for Roman poets who complained endlessly about their cruel mistresses. These women were often what are euphemistically known as 'courtesans', to distinguish them from prostituted women who sold sex in brothels, but they belonged to a class of females who would be indulged as long as it suited their lovers and then abandoned without further obligation. (I don't use the ideological neologism 'sex worker' in this book because prostitution is a form of abuse, not a job like any other.) Others were married women or widows who risked being shamed and ostracised by their families if their affairs became public knowledge.

The equation of female pleasure with prostitution was deeply imbued in the psyche of Roman men – ironically, as it happens, because most women in the commercial sex trade were slaves or former slaves, often of Greek origin, who certainly weren't in it for the sake of enjoyment. It was a prejudice that had existed for years when the Julio-Claudian women began to emerge from the shadows towards the end of the first century BC (and, indeed, still exists today, when religious conservatives equate sexual autonomy in women with being available to all men). The censorious attitudes women in the imperial family would encounter are vividly illustrated by one of the most notorious court cases of the late Roman republic.

It took place in 56 BC, two years after the birth of the future first empress, Livia. A well-connected woman called Clodia Pulchra accused a dissolute young man called Marcus Caelius Rufus, who had been her lover before they fell out, of trying to poison her. Caelius was also accused of involvement in a plot to murder an ambassador, Dio of Alexandria, who had been poisoned in Rome by agents acting on behalf of the king of Egypt. Clodia's brother, Publius Clodius Pulcher, was a populist politician who had changed the family's name to minimise its connection to the aristocratic *gens Claudia*, changing hers at the same time. He was also a mortal enemy of one of Rome's greatest orators, Marcus Tullius Cicero, whom Caelius engaged as his defence counsel. Clodia was a widow, around forty years of age at the time of the trial, and Caelius was one of several younger men who were supposed to have been her lovers. One of them was the poet Catullus, who disguised her under the pseudonym 'Lesbia' when he wrote some of the finest love poems in the Latin language (and the most vituperative, when the affair ended). Clodia's marriage to a cousin had been unhappy and she evidently relished her freedom as a wealthy widow, owning houses in Rome and the fashionable seaside resort of Baiae, on the bay of Naples.

Cicero pretty much ignored the charges against Caelius, homing in on Clodia's lifestyle like a defence barrister in a modern rape trial. A sexually active single woman was no different from a prostitute in Cicero's eyes and he repeatedly characterises Clodia as exactly that; he describes her as living like 'a self-willed prostitute' (*libidinosa meretricio more*) and portrays her dinner parties in Rome and Baiae as orgies.[2] In an early example of the short-skirt defence, he attacks her clothes (*ornatu*) and goes on to criticise the way she looks men in the eye, speaks without hesitation, and her affectionate behaviour towards male friends. (There are shades here of the accusations that would be made against Augustus's daughter Julia half a century later, when her friendships with personable young men would be turned into charges against her.) Without a shred of evidence, and no doubt to the delight of Caelius's cronies, Cicero condemns Clodia as 'not just a prostitute but also a shameless and impudent prostitute' (*non solum meretrix sed etiam proterva meretrix procaxque*).[3] He even uses her address in Rome, on the fashionable Palatine hill, as a stick to beat her with, calling her a 'Medea of the Palatine' (*Palatinam Medeam*) after the fabled figure from Greek mythology who was accused of a series of murders including those of her brother and her children.[4]

Onlookers might have been forgiven for thinking it was Clodia who was on trial, not the man accused of trying to poison her, and the impact of the speech must have been devastating. Caelius was acquitted and Cicero was so proud of his efforts on the wastrel's behalf that he published his defence. In a testament to the invisibility of Roman misogyny, the *Pro Caelio* (*In Defence of Caelius*) is regarded as one of Cicero's greatest speeches, even though the historian Michael Grant, who translated it for the Penguin Classics series in 1969, acknowledged that Caelius was almost certainly guilty of the murder of Dio of Alexandria and several other people as well. Clodia disappeared from history after her ex-lover's acquittal, erased so thoroughly that we don't even know when or how she died.

This was the context in which the Julio-Claudian women would find themselves scrutinised and judged when Augustus became emperor in 27 BC. Events of the period were extensively documented, providing an extraordinary record of one of the most fascinating periods of European history. But the men who wrote about it – and they *were* all men – were the inheritors of misogynistic attitudes that had underpinned Roman culture for centuries. The 'sources' are often quoted without any acknowledgement of the fact, so it's worth having a look at who they were – and why their work should come with a health warning.

One of the few contemporary accounts we have of the reigns of Augustus and his successor, Tiberius, was written by a career soldier called Velleius Paterculus. He was born around 19 BC, during the first years of the Roman empire, and he not only served in the army under Tiberius but regarded his former commander with something close to hero-worship. His usefulness as a historian is compromised by his hostility to Tiberius's ex-wife Julia, whom he loftily condemns as 'a woman whose womb was fortunate neither to herself nor to the state' (*feminam neque sibi neque rei publicae felicis uteri*).[5] His bias is by no means confined to Julia and is typical of Roman men of his generation, illustrated by his damning aside about Mark Antony's wife Fulvia. She had outraged an earlier generation of Roman men by involving herself in the civil wars that followed the assassination of Julius Caesar, and Velleius can't even bring himself to admit she was a woman; he sneers that she had 'nothing womanly about her except her body' (*nihil muliebre praeter corpus gerens*).[6] Velleius offers useful information about chronology but he is not remotely in the same league as Tacitus, the next and greatest Roman historian of the period.

Publius – or Gaius – Cornelius Tacitus (we don't know his first name for certain) was born during Nero's reign but wrote in the early second century AD, long after the dynasty ended. He was himself prominent in Roman politics as a senator, consul, and eventually governor of Asia (the western part of modern-day Turkey). His *Annals* are a year-by-year account, stylistically brilliant and full of mordant wit, of the period from the death of Augustus in AD 14 to the end of Nero's reign in 68. Crucial sections, including the reign of Caligula and the two years before Nero's enforced suicide, are missing. But Tacitus was well informed, growing up at a time when older people had vivid memories of significant events such as the death of the emperor Claudius and the murder of Nero's mother, Agrippina. He had read (and sometimes quotes from) books that no longer exist, such as the work of the historian Marcus Cluvius Rufus, who lived in the reigns of Caligula, Claudius and Nero. He had even read one of the great lost works of ancient history, the empress Agrippina's autobiography, of which no copies survive. (No doubt she would have had a great deal to say about the men in her family, and it is perhaps not surprising that such an explosive document was destroyed.)

The *Annals* are generally regarded as a reliable, if partisan, version of events, greatly influenced by Tacitus's own experience during the reign of the deeply unpleasant emperor Domitian (AD 81–96). It left him with a lasting hatred of tyranny that undoubtedly colours his account of the Julio-Claudian emperors, but what is even more striking is his distrust of women, one of the few things he has in common with Velleius. In the *Annals*, they operate as the classic power-behind-the-throne, their influence even less legitimate than that of their male relatives. Tacitus is ambivalent even when they do something he can't help admiring – Julia's daughter Agrippina rallying her husband's mutinous troops in Germany, for example – because it's not how Roman women are supposed to behave.

Tacitus's near-contemporary, Gaius Suetonius Tranquillus, adopted a more straightforward approach in his biographies of the first Roman emperors, *De Vita Caesarum*, usually known in English as *The Twelve Caesars*. Suetonius was about a dozen years younger than Tacitus and he became the emperor Hadrian's private secretary, which gave him access to the imperial archives; he was able to quote from the correspondence he found there, including letters written by Mark Antony, and Augustus's private papers. His focus is very much on the emperors, whose lives he covers according to an eccentric, non-chronological method of his own devising. His physical descriptions are often entertaining – Nero's body was 'spotty and smelly' (*corpore maculoso et fetido*), for instance[7] – and he's less personally hostile towards women than Tacitus. When he's rude about them, it sounds more as though he's repeating received wisdom than offering a passionately held opinion, which suggests that his observations were common currency at the time he was writing.

Suetonius and Tacitus are both a great deal less garrulous than our third important source, the Roman senator Cassius Dio, whose history of Rome stretches to eighty volumes. Dio was born around the year AD 165 in Nicaea, a Greek city in north-western Turkey, and he wrote in the early third century, more than 200 years after the founding of the Julio-Claudian dynasty. (Like many educated Romans he spoke, and indeed wrote, in Greek.) Dio is an inveterate gossip and his account of the Julio-Claudian period often includes longer versions of anecdotes told by other writers, with additional information he appears to have found in histories that have not survived. He is turgid, however, even in translation, and the inclusion of long, made-up speeches in his text does not encourage confidence in his credibility as a historian.

Between them, Tacitus, Suetonius and Dio offer an impressively detailed account of the early Roman empire, but their verdicts on women certainly shouldn't be taken at face value. That warning applies even more dramatically to authors such as Seneca and the poet Juvenal, whose *Satires*, written in the early second century, include a diatribe against women. Astonishingly, Juvenal's misogynist fantasy about the empress Messalina has been treated as fact by commentators who should know better, doing incalculable damage to her reputation, as we shall see later in this book. Disapproval of the conduct of the Julio-Claudian women is the default position of all these authors, none of whom acknowledges the limitations they were struggling against. They ignore a crucial circumstance, which is the fact that the emergence of patrician women onto the public stage in the late first century BC was accompanied only by gradual improvements in their legal position – and indeed some additional restraints. They mistake the *appearance* of power for its reality, even though it makes a nonsense of applying the same critical standards to the women's behaviour.

There is one more, perhaps surprising 'source' for what we know, or think we know, about the Julio-Claudian women, and its impact has been incalculable. Writing almost 2,000 years later, the poet Robert Graves seized on the material left behind by Roman authors and turned it into two best-selling novels, *I, Claudius* and *Claudius the God and His Wife Messalina*. His idea to write the 'autobiography' of the emperor Claudius, despised by everyone including his own mother, was a masterstroke, appealing to the popular imagination in a way that few historical novels have managed to do. To this day, people who haven't read the original ancient texts have got their impressions of early imperial Rome either from the novels or, more likely, from the various films and spin-offs of Graves's historical fiction.

When I was researching this book, friends' eyes would light up when I said I was writing about Livia, Julia and Messalina, and more often than not they would mention *I, Claudius*. It is true that Graves was a classical scholar and intimately acquainted with the work of Roman historians, but few people know more than that. The problem is what he did with the sources, interpreting and embellishing them to produce a hugely influential – and profoundly misogynist – version of events in early imperial Rome.

Graves's novels were published to great acclaim in 1934. But they really achieved prominence when the BBC turned them into a TV series in 1976, written by the highly regarded screenwriter Jack Pulman, which won numerous awards. The series is still being shown and talked about half a century later, often referred to as one of the BBC's crowning achievements. It created an appetite for Roman 'history' that's never gone away, even though the results are sensationalised and have little connection with reality. An eight-part TV series called *Domina*, made by Sky Atlantic in 2021, had the empress Livia as its main character and relished its portrayal of her as a villain; the series devoted an entire episode to her 'murder' of Augustus's nephew Marcellus, who actually died in an outbreak of fever in Rome in 23 BC that killed thousands of people. It prompted the *Daily Mail* to describe Livia as 'the real Wicked Witch of Rome', salivating over her 'real-life lust for power that saw her kill her grandsons, exile her daughter and poison her husband'.[8]

None of this is true but it's directly traceable to Siân Phillips's stellar performance as Livia in *I, Claudius*, glowering at the other characters as she schemes to put her son Tiberius on the throne. Phillips's empress is a steely matriarch who sends her own doctor to a military camp in Germany to finish off her gravely injured younger son, Drusus, who has hinted that he would like to restore the Roman republic. The purpose of the scene is to demonstrate her ruthlessness but it's a complete invention; Drusus's death was caused by injuries sustained in a fall from a horse, most probably when his wounds became infected with gangrene. In another early episode, Augustus – played by a hopelessly miscast Brian Blessed – enters a room where men who have slept with his daughter Julia have been lined up to give evidence against her; the actors appear to have been chosen for their unprepossessing appearance, confirming that she's so promiscuous that she doesn't care what her lovers look like. It's another fabrication, based on a scene in Graves's first novel in which Claudius blames Julia's insatiable appetite for sex on a 'love-philtre', consisting of the notorious Spanish fly and given to her by Livia, thus condemning both women in the same breath.[9]

The underlying misogyny of the novels *and* the TV series is exposed by the fact that both make use of a myth beloved by men's rights activists, namely that women often make false claims of rape to conceal their own bad behaviour. Julia's youngest son, Agrippa Postumus, is lured to her bedroom by Claudius's sister, Livilla, who screams and accuses him of rape to cover up the fact that they've had an affair.[10] Livilla is one of the most tragic figures in the Julio-Claudian dynasty, wrongly accused of murdering her husband and starved to death by her own mother, but neither Graves nor Pulman hesitated to damage her reputation even further with this sordid and entirely fictitious anecdote.

The cover of the Penguin Modern Classics edition of *I, Claudius* tacitly acknowledges the novel's distance from historical reality; it shows a seventeenth-century painting by Benedetto Gennari the Younger of a voluptuously naked Cleopatra, who killed herself

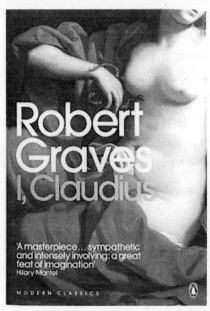

twenty years before Claudius was born, applying a snake to her breast. Graves's motive for writing the novels was an acute financial crisis, prompted by scarcely credible events in his own life. It was in his interests to make the books as sensational as possible and the strategy worked, earning him the equivalent of around £350,000 in today's money. The damage done to the historical record by the *Claudius* novels has rarely been recognised, something that's all the more remarkable because Graves projected so much of his own chaotic life onto the early Roman empire.

When Graves began writing the books, he was still very much affected by his horrific experiences during the First World War, when he suffered severe injuries on the Somme. He made a slow and painful recovery, recording what he went through in the trenches in his autobiography, *Goodbye to All That* (1929), but he was left with troubling symptoms which would now be diagnosed as PTSD. His attitudes to women were confused and ambivalent, leading him to marry a feminist, Nancy Nicholson, in 1918. His account of the marriage in *Goodbye to All That* is curiously detached but with intimations of resentment; Graves claims that Nicholson 'ascribed all the wrong in the world to male domination and narrowness', dismissing his wartime experience as insignificant compared to the sufferings of millions of working-class married women.[11] Sex was a bone of contention, with Nicholson apparently regarding Graves's expectations as 'excessive', but they managed to have four children before he began an affair with another unconventional woman, an American poet called Laura Riding.

In 1927, Graves and Riding moved to a top-floor flat in a Georgian house in St Peter's Square in Hammersmith, while Nicholson and the children were installed on a houseboat on the nearby Thames. At this point, an Irish poet called Geoffrey Phibbs appeared on the scene and seems to have become involved with the others in an unstable *ménage à quatre*; when Graves imagined Julia and Messalina rushing from one bed to another, the origin surely lies here, in his tumultuous private life, but the consequences were devastating. One evening in April 1929, Phibbs announced that he was returning to his wife, and the four principals in the tangled relationship argued and pleaded with each other long into the night. Eventually, around dawn, Riding balanced on the sill of the open top-floor window at the back of the house and threatened to jump. The other three seem to have assumed she was bluffing but Riding plunged fifty feet into the back garden. Graves ran down a flight of stairs, threw up another window and jumped into garden, landing beside or on top of her.[12] Whatever his motive, whether his intention was to help Riding or make himself part of the drama, it was not the action of someone who was thinking rationally.

Riding's injuries were serious. She had broken her pelvis and four of her vertebrae, and damaged one of her eyes. She underwent several bouts of surgery and was eventually able to walk again, but she suffered recurring pain for the rest of her life. Graves suffered only minor injuries and separated from Nicholson the following month, leaving the children with his soon-to-be ex-wife. Later that year, he moved to Majorca with Riding, where the couple's financial problems were so pressing that Graves embarked on writing *I, Claudius*. When the novel was published and won prizes, a significant parallel between ancient Rome and the period after the First World War went unnoticed. Graves was writing at a time of social upheaval, when an early generation of feminists was carrying on the work begun by the suffragettes and challenging traditional ideas about femininity. Like the Julio-Claudian women, they had emerged from a period of conflict to find social change happening at a rapid pace, something Graves evidently found exciting and threatening at the same time. (He would eventually split up with Riding and marry for a second time, producing four more children.) It would be crazy to treat his Roman fiction as anything remotely resembling history, but that's what happened. The *Claudius* novels are a misogynist's fever dream, written by a man obsessed with and fearful of female desire. The Julio-Claudian women deserve better, not least because modern research allows us to get a clearer idea of the abuse they were subjected to – and the way it influenced their behaviour.

Ancient Rome was a patriarchal society. Women couldn't hold public office and were, in theory at least, under the authority of a male guardian throughout their lives. That power might be exercised by a father or, in his absence, the nearest male relative, who would make crucial decisions about matters such as marriage and property. When Augustus became emperor, he made significant changes to family legislation, introducing severe penalties for adultery, including exile and loss of property, but the law did not affect men and women equally. Sex with a prostituted woman did not count as adultery and men who had mistresses were unlikely to face consequences, but a father was allowed to kill his daughter if he caught her with a lover; such draconian penalties were rarely imposed, but Roman women knew they were operating under different expectations from their husbands. One piece of Augustan legislation worked in women's favour, however, due to the emperor's anxiety about the falling birth rate among the aristocracy. Keen to encourage large families, Augustus changed the law to allow wives who had given birth to three children (four if the mother was a freed slave) to be released from male control. Ironically, in light of the emperor's pro-natalist policies, neither he nor his successors were proficient at producing sons. Out of the five Julio-Claudian emperors, only Claudius had a son who outlived him, and he was displaced from the succession by his stepbrother, the future emperor Nero. The dynasty survived as long as it did thanks only to the extraordinary fertility of the women, whose ability to bear children impressed even the ancient Romans (Julia's daughter Agrippina gave birth to nine infants, six of whom survived to adulthood). The women were rewarded with titles, and some were even deified after death, but statues and temples did not signal equality.

The material reality of patrician women's lives included experiences that would be regarded unequivocally as abuse today, and the most damaging was child – which is to say forced – marriage. When ancient and modern authors fantasise about patrician Roman women's sexual habits, they completely overlook the fact that girls were taught to satisfy the appetites of older men from a cruelly young age. Child marriage was sanctioned by the Roman state in the form of a minimum age of twelve for girls. (In another example of institutional discrimination against women in ancient Rome, it was fourteen for boys.) The Romans were either uninterested in or oblivious to the harmful effects of becoming sexually active at such a young age, which included a very much increased risk of dying in childbirth.

Perinatal mortality was high in ancient Rome, with around one in fifty mothers dying in labour, but it was even higher among teenage girls.[13] The bodies of girls in their early to middle teens are not fully developed and an immature pelvic girdle makes giving birth at this age very dangerous. The impact was visible in terms of numbers: Dio makes the startling admission that there was a shortage of women in the upper classes in Augustan Rome, but it didn't interest him enough to speculate on the cause.[14] The classicist Sarah B. Pomeroy, who was one of the first modern authors to write specifically about women in the ancient world, suggested that the most likely explanation was the shorter lifespan of girls once they reached child-bearing years.[15] Girls from the imperial family were as vulnerable as anyone else and Junia Claudilla, first wife of the emperor Caligula, died in childbirth along with her baby, possibly when she was as young as sixteen (the exact dates of her birth and death were not even recorded, an indignity suffered by numerous women who were not considered important in dynastic terms).

But the damage caused by child marriage isn't limited to premature death. Forcing a girl of thirteen or fourteen to marry a man in his thirties, forties or fifties creates a perverted version of a father–daughter relationship, while forcing female children to behave in ways appropriate to adult women. It teaches girls to relate to men primarily through sex, habituating them to think of themselves as having little power unless they anticipate and accede to male sexual demands. In the twenty-first century, the harmful effects are so widely accepted that the United Nations' children's agency, UNICEF, campaigns to raise the legal age of marriage to eighteen around the world, six years older than the legal age in ancient Rome.

There is no reason to imagine it was any less damaging for girls born into the Julio-Claudian dynasty 2,000 years ago, who were traded between their fathers and sexually experienced adult men like pieces of meat: Claudius's sister Livilla was only twelve when she was married for the first time, while Augustus's daughter Julia was married at fourteen, widowed just before her sixteenth birthday and married to her father's best friend, who was almost a quarter of a century older, at eighteen. When Julia's granddaughter Agrippina was accused of seducing her uncle, the emperor Claudius, to persuade him to marry her, she was only doing what she had been taught when she was married to a much older man at the age of thirteen. Many of these 'brides' would not even have begun to have periods because the menarche happened later in the ancient world than it does today, probably around the age of fourteen.[16]

There's no evidence to suggest that the husbands of these teenage brides held back from sexual relations with the children they had just married; on the contrary, the fact that very young girls were expected to have sex is confirmed by records that show them becoming mothers at the age of fifteen or sixteen. Marriageable girls were valuable assets and a teenage wife whose husband died, whether on a military expedition or of natural causes, would quickly be found another by her father. There was no question of girls being asked to consent to these marriages, and while some of the couples managed to get along, some would have been trapped in relationships that amounted to nothing less than serial rape. The historian Guy de la Bédoyère, who is more sympathetic than most modern commentators to the situation of women in ancient Rome, argues that 'the brutalization of women was a very real part of Roman society'.[17] How early that brutalisation started, and the lifelong impact of premature sexualisation on generations of patrician girls, will become evident in this book.

2

Surviving Augustus

Claudia Pulchra (*c.*57/56 BC–DoD unknown): first wife of the emperor Augustus. **Cause of death unknown**

Scribonia (*c.*70 BC–*c.*AD 16): second wife of the emperor Augustus, mother of Julia. **Died of natural causes**, aged around 86

Livia Drusilla (58 BC–AD 29): first Roman empress, third wife of the emperor Augustus, mother of the emperor Tiberius. **Died of natural causes**, aged 86

The Julio-Claudian dynasty began with a squalid deal between two men. One was the general who would eventually emerge as the victor in the civil wars that followed the assassination of the dictator Gaius Julius Caesar in 44 BC. The other was an officer who had fought on the other side and spent years as a fugitive with a price on his head. The general was Caesar's great-nephew, the future emperor Augustus, who is usually referred to as Octavian in the period before he accepted the title in 27 BC. The other man was Tiberius Claudius Nero, a member of a minor branch of the Claudian family, who had just been allowed to return to Rome following an amnesty for Octavian's opponents.

Tiberius Nero was in a precarious position in 39 BC, having spent the last couple of years on the run in Italy and Greece, but he would turn out to have a priceless bargaining chip in the shape of his much younger wife, Livia. She was now nineteen and pregnant with the couple's second child. She had shared her husband's hair-raising experiences as a fugitive, dodging soldiers who would have killed him without a second thought, and she had endured unimaginable privations. No doubt she was hugely relieved that the threat had been lifted, although there was some uncertainty about what kind of reception the couple would get on their return to Rome. Tiberius Nero didn't need to worry: in an entirely unexpected turn of events, Octavian was introduced to Livia and decided instantly he wanted to marry her, regardless of the fact that they were both married to other people. Her husband, far from being dismayed, was quick to realise he could trade his young wife for an extremely comfortable existence in Rome. Livia's father was dead and Tiberius Nero agreed not only to divorce his wife but to give her away at her remarriage to Octavian.

The wedding took place in January 38 BC, only three days after Livia had given birth to her second son, Drusus, when she was still recovering from labour; she would have been bleeding, quite possibly in pain, and may even have had some perineal tearing, given how common it is in new mothers.[1] The marriage scandalised Rome, shocking even the serving boys employed to amuse guests at the wedding feast. Seeing Livia sitting next to Octavian, one of the boys pointed out Tiberius Nero, who was lounging on a couch on the opposite side of the room. 'What are you doing here, madam?' he asked. 'Your husband is reclining over there.'[2] Livia's response is not recorded, and neither are her feelings in the matter. It may be that she felt the wisest course was to stay silent, after witnessing her new husband's studied cruelty towards her predecessor. Octavian's second wife, Scribonia, was also expecting a child in 39 BC, although her pregnancy was three months ahead of Livia's. The marriage was in theory an obstacle to his plans but he removed it with clinical efficiency, divorcing Scribonia on the very day she gave birth to their daughter, Julia, in October that year. He promptly evicted the exhausted mother from the marital home and installed Livia in her place, three months before their wedding. His motive, Tacitus says bluntly, was his eagerness to have sex with her (*cupidine formae*) before the birth of Drusus.[3]

This sequence of events is as shocking now as it was in the first century BC. Unusually, and to their credit, even Roman historians saw the marriage for what it was, the brutal abduction of a pregnant woman from her husband. They make no pretence of Livia being in love with Octavian or of her wishes being considered by either man. Suetonius uses blunt language, stating that Octavian 'seized Livia Drusilla, wife of Tiberius Nero, even though she was pregnant' (*Liviam Drusillam matrimonio Tiberi Neronis et quidam praegnantem abduxit*).[4] Tacitus describes the marriage as literally an abduction, characterising it as 'the kidnap of Nero's wife' (*abducta Neroni uxor*).[5] Both authors use parts of the same Latin verb, *abducere*, which means to 'carry off' or 'take away'; it is derived from the verb *ducere*, which has an explicitly sexual meaning in Latin, relating to a man 'taking' a woman for sex.[6] Neither writer leaves any doubt about the forcible nature of the transaction. Even as inveterate a womaniser as Mark Antony, who was himself used to exchanging one wife for another in a pretty brutal fashion, thought that the marriage was conducted with 'indecent haste'.[7] It is hard to believe that anyone familiar with the Latin texts could imagine that this was a romance; indeed, it's clear from Tacitus, who says Livia's 'abduction' was still causing gossip when Augustus died more than fifty years later, that Antony's view was widely shared. Ignoring the unequivocal evidence of the ancient texts, modern authors – the male ones, at any rate – divide into two camps, either portraying Livia as a chilly, calculating female who 'snared' an unsuspecting Octavian, or depicting the relationship as a passionate romance. Robert Graves is in the first camp in *I, Claudius*, suggesting that Octavian was so much in awe of Livia that he wasn't even able to consummate the marriage (more evidence, if any were needed, that Graves was terrified of strong women).[8] So is the contemporary historian Tom Holland, who has Livia arriving back in Rome in a sour mood, already on the lookout for another husband.[9] Firmly in the other camp is the popular historian Anthony Blond, whose sensational account of the Julio-Claudian emperors asserts that Octavian fell in love with Livia, married her and lived happily ever after.[10] Even Augustus's biographer, the military historian Adrian Goldsworthy, believes that Octavian was in love with Livia's beauty and mind, while she was just as enthusiastic about him.[11] It's what we might call the Mills & Boon version of Roman history but all these authors, hostile or otherwise, have made the same error, assuming that Livia – a pregnant and penniless teenager, burdened with all the disadvantages of a first-century Roman woman – had as much agency as Octavian.

A more down-to-earth view, proposed by Elaine Fantham, is that 'political interest, rather than any personal affinity' brought the couple together.[12] Fantham is a welcome female voice amid the hubbub of commentators mansplaining Livia's marriage to Octavian, and the author of a rare biography (I'm not aware of any other) of Augustus's daughter, Julia. She believes Tacitus is telling us that public opinion in Rome regarded Livia's second marriage as 'a virtual rape', a suggestion supported by the obvious absence of any question of consent – and Tiberius Nero's enthusiastic collusion.[13] His shameful conduct at the wedding is almost our final glimpse of him, although we know he was allowed to keep both his sons, three-year-old Tiberius and the newborn Drusus, in his own home; Livia was not allowed to have them live with her until five years later, when her ex-husband died of natural causes. In this and other respects, she had as little say in her second marriage as she had in her first. Glib commentators often forget or gloss over the fact that when she was targeted by Octavian, she had already been a victim of child marriage – and it was only four years since her first experience of being forced into a sexual relationship with a man she had not chosen.

Livia Drusilla celebrated her fourteenth birthday in January 44 BC, a momentous year for Roman politics. Just over six weeks later, Caesar was assassinated, dividing Rome into supporters and opponents of the tyrannicides. It is not obvious from her name that she was a Claudian, something that would play a significant role in both her marriages, but that is because her father, Appius Claudius Pulcher, had been adopted by a childless politician, Marcus Livius Drusus. Livia's father took the name Marcus Livius Drusus Claudianus to reflect his changed status – a smart move, because he ended up inheriting his adoptive father's huge fortune. His daughter was given the name Livia Drusilla, but we know little about her mother, apart from the fact that she was called Alfidia and came from a town called Fundi (modern-day Fondi), halfway between Rome and Naples. Being connected to two aristocratic families, the *gens Livia* and the *gens Claudia*, was no bad thing but it was Livia's Claudian blood that mattered, so much so that it would be hard to overestimate the importance of her ancestry. She was one of the most eligible girls in Rome at the time of Caesar's assassination, regarded at fourteen as more than ready for marriage, but politics intervened.

Livia's father, Claudianus, had been a praetor, one rung down from a consul, six years before the assassination and he favoured a return to the republican form of government overthrown by Caesar. He sided with the assassins, led by Brutus and Cassius, and did not get round to arranging his daughter's marriage until 43 BC at the earliest. She was by now fifteen and Claudianus decided to keep things within the family. Tiberius Claudius Nero was a distant relative, a member of a junior branch of the *gens Claudia*, and he was more than twice Livia's age. (His *cognomen* 'Nero' was a Sabine word meaning 'strong and brave', indicating his descent from a tribe that lived to the north of Rome.) He had almost certainly been married before, having unsuccessfully proposed marriage to the daughter of the orator Cicero some years earlier, but we don't know whether any previous marriages ended in death or divorce. He would have been delighted to marry a girl with Livia's distinguished pedigree and there was more good news when she became pregnant early in 42 BC, with the birth expected in the winter months. By then, however, her father Claudianus was caught up in an exceedingly dangerous conflict with Octavian and Caesar's former second-in-command, Mark Antony. However commendable it was in political terms, Claudianus's decision to join Brutus and Cassius as they prepared for battle with Caesar's self-appointed avengers put him on the losing side.

Octavian was only nineteen when his great-uncle was murdered but he been adopted as Caesar's heir in his will. He divided up the Roman empire with Mark Antony and another outstanding general, Marcus Aemilius Lepidus, forming what's known as the second triumvirate in November 43 BC. (The first, an informal alliance between the generals Gnaeus Pompeius Magnus, otherwise known as Pompey the Great, Marcus Licinius Crassus and Julius Caesar, was formed in 60 or 59 BC when the three men were trying to push legislation that favoured their interests through the Senate.) Whatever sympathy had attached to Octavian because of his adoptive father's assassination rapidly evaporated as the three men embarked on an orgy of revenge, ruthlessly using their power to settle personal and political scores. Anyone suspected of supporting Caesar's assassins or plotting to restore the Roman republic was 'proscribed' – exiled, stripped of their possessions and at imminent risk of execution. Livia's father Claudianus was one of them and it's very likely that he forfeited his substantial assets, marking a dramatic change in the family's fortunes. The effect on Livia's mother, Alfidia, who was transformed overnight from being the wife of a wealthy ex-praetor to the spouse of a wanted man, must have been dramatic. Did she stay in Rome? Did her own family in Fondi take her in? No author, ancient or modern, has ever shown much curiosity about her, even though she would become the ancestor of four Roman emperors.

Livia, at least, wasn't homeless; she was living in her husband's house on the Palatine hill by now, looking forward to the birth of her first child. Even at the age of sixteen, Livia knew what was expected of her, trying age-old methods to discover whether her unborn child was a boy or a girl. The one she chose involved taking a recently laid egg from beneath a hen and warming it in her own hands and those of her attendants; when the shell cracked, a fine male chick with a fully formed comb (*pullus insigniter cristatus*) is supposed to have emerged, confirming that Livia's unborn child was male.[14] There are obvious reasons to take this story with a pinch of salt, but it shows that the youthful Livia understood her role in the Claudian dynasty. She did, indeed, give birth to a boy on 16 November 42 BC, called Tiberius after his father. But by then a series of catastrophes had overtaken her family.

A month earlier, Octavian and Mark Antony faced Brutus, Cassius and their armies at Philippi, in what is now modern-day Greece. Cassius killed himself after being defeated in the first battle, but Brutus fought on until his army was crushed later in the month. Brutus then committed suicide and so did Livia's father Claudianus, who was widely praised for following a noble Roman tradition of displaying courage in defeat. News of the battle's outcome would have reached Rome by the time Tiberius was born, although it isn't clear when Livia heard about her father's suicide. Her husband, Tiberius Nero, had fought on the same side as Caesar in the past but his Claudian ancestry overrode his loyalty to the dictator; following the assassination, he had made a brave but foolhardy stand, becoming a lone voice in the Senate who proposed honours for the assassins. He had managed to survive his expression of support for Brutus and Cassius, but their defeat at Philippi, and his father-in-law's suicide, were major blows. Fortunately for him, the triumvirs were now arguing among themselves. Octavian and Mark Antony would spend the next decade fighting for supremacy, forging and breaking alliances and enlisting foreign monarchs, most famously Cleopatra of Egypt. Tiberius Nero tried to take advantage of this volatile political position by joining forces with Mark Antony's wife Fulvia, who was representing his interests in Italy while her husband was occupied overseas, the latest in a series of poor decisions that would impact severely on his young wife and her infant child. It is not clear whether Tiberius Nero was ever formally proscribed but he certainly behaved as though he was, marking the beginning of a period in which the couple were almost constantly on the move. They were in so much danger that they kept to back roads and Livia was accompanied by only one servant, in the hope of avoiding drawing attention to themselves.[15]

Towards the end of 41 BC, when Tiberius was just a year old, Tiberius Nero joined Fulvia and Mark Antony's younger brother, Lucius Antonius, who had retreated to the hilltop city of Perusia (Perugia) with Octavian's forces in hot pursuit. What happened next was a brutal siege: Livia would spend her eighteenth birthday in the city at the beginning of the following year as the desperate inhabitants ran out of food. When Octavian's troops finally entered Perugia in the spring of 40 BC, they slaughtered 300 of the city's leading citizens before burning it to the ground. Octavian was not yet ready for all-out war with Mark Antony, however, and he allowed Fulvia and Lucius Antonius to escape with their lives.

Tiberius Nero managed to escape as well, taking his family with him on yet another fraught journey. They sought refuge in Neapolis (Naples), intending to find a ship to take them to Sicily where Sextus Pompeius, son of Caesar's onetime ally and later bitter rival, Pompey the Great, was in charge of what was effectively an independent kingdom. With Octavian's forces about to break into Naples, the little family tried to slip down to the port in total secrecy, only to have their flight almost given away by the cries of the infant Tiberius.[16] The family arrived safely in Sicily, by no means a certain outcome at a time when shipwrecks were common, but Tiberius Nero received a chillier reception than he had hoped. Proscribed men were flocking to Sicily in droves, so perhaps Sextus Pompeius didn't think Tiberius Nero was anything special, but it was too much for a proud Claudian.[17] Soon he was on the move again, this time heading for Greece, where the family found temporary refuge in Sparta, which had historical ties with the Claudians. Even then, another terrifying experience awaited them: leaving Sparta by night, under cover of darkness, the family walked into a sudden outbreak of forest fire. The flames leapt from tree to tree, completely surrounding them, and came so close that part of Livia's robe and her hair were scorched (*ut Liviae pars vestis et capilli amburerentur*).[18] How they escaped the conflagration is not recorded, but it was another close brush with death for the young mother and her son.

The impact of these terrifying events on Livia can hardly be overestimated, teaching her to focus on survival above all else – a useful lesson given what was lying in wait for her when she finally got back to Rome. They also had a catastrophic effect on Tiberius, however, shaping his character in a way that would one day impact severely on generations of Julio-Claudian women. Suetonius describes the future emperor's infancy as 'arduous and demanding' (*laboriosam et exercitatam*) and it's clear that he spent his formative years in a state of heightened anxiety, his infant brain flooded with stress hormones.[19] He knew no stability until he was almost three years old, when the treaty negotiated between Octavian, Mark Antony and Sextus Pompeius finally opened the door for his parents' return to Rome. By then it was too late; Tiberius would grow up to be a morose, suspicious individual, never fully recovered from his childhood fears.

In the summer of 39 BC, Livia's situation was improving, though still far from stable. The world she knew as a child was gone, her father dead and disgraced, her mother's whereabouts unknown. She was not yet twenty, and married to a man in his forties whose political decisions had repeatedly put her life at risk. If Tiberius Nero's willingness to hand her over to another man seems a tad ungrateful, after all he had put her through, it also suggests he was not strongly attached to her or concerned about her welfare. It would be comforting to believe that Livia's second husband was an improvement on her first – something that was almost true at least in material terms – but it is an impulse that has led many commentators into a species of wishful thinking. Even Suetonius does it, sugar-coating his account of the involuntary nature of Livia's second marriage by claiming that Octavian 'loved and valued her extravagantly and steadfastly' (*dilexitque et probavit unice ac perseveranter*) for the rest of her life.[20] Nothing could be further from the truth, as we shall see in a moment.

Gaius Octavius, as he was originally known, was just over four years older than Livia. He changed his name to Gaius Julius Caesar after being adopted in his great-uncle's will, but modern historians tend to refer to him as Octavianus or Octavian, a diminutive that indicates he previously belonged to another *gens*, to avoid confusion with the dictator. His immediate family was nothing like as grand as Livia's, hailing from the provincial town of Velitrae (Velletri), 40 kilometres south-east of Rome. Many people believed he was born there, in a house owned by his grandfather, although the actual place of his birth in Rome was marked by a shrine. He was a relentless social climber, conscious that he was a Julian more by adoption than by birth, and his eagerness to marry up is demonstrated by the fact that two of his three wives were members of the Claudian family. Statues and sculpted heads suggest he was a handsome man with even features, but also the possessor of a short chin, a characteristic he would pass on to his descendants. Suetonius says he was unusually good-looking (*forma fuit eximia*) with fair, slightly curly hair (*capillum leviter inflexum et subflavum*) and eyebrows that met in the middle. His eyes were bright but his sight failed in his left eye as he got older and his teeth were in poor condition.[21] His health was not robust, and there were several scares during his time as emperor when he seemed to be on the verge of succumbing to one of the fevers that periodically swept through Rome. The problem, however, was his character. He was coming up to twenty-four when he met Livia in 39 BC and had already achieved so much that he could have appeared glamorous and charismatic, had his vengeful character not been so apparent.

Octavian had a reputation as an impulsive young man, personally violent on occasion, who showed little mercy to his enemies. During the proscriptions that began when the second triumvirate was formed in 43 BC, he applied himself to the task of condemning rivals with enthusiasm, ignoring pleas for mercy from members of the most distinguished families in Rome. Despite his youth, he quickly became a hate figure with a multitude of enemies, fearing assassination during every encounter with the public. One day, when he was addressing a group of soldiers, he spotted a civilian, Pinarius, taking notes. Thinking he was a spy, he ordered him to be stabbed to death. On another occasion, he was approached by a magistrate, Quintus Gallius, who wanted to speak to him about some trifling matter. Octavian panicked, thinking he could see a weapon concealed under Gallius's clothes, and ordered him to be arrested and tortured. When the 'sword' turned out to be a harmless writing tablet, Octavian hurled himself at the unfortunate man and gouged out his eyes with his own hands.[22] Some historians excuse these outbursts of violence, suggesting they happened at a time when Augustus was young and rash, but there are plenty of examples from later in his life. After the death of his grandson, Julia's eldest son Gaius, he lashed out by having the boy's tutor and servants thrown into a river with weights tied round their necks, claiming they had taken advantage of their master's illness to enrich themselves. Even members of his inner circle had good reason to fear his temper; he once broke the legs of a secretary, Thallus, who had taken a bribe to reveal the contents of a letter.[23]

It is his treatment of women, however, that indicates the abuse Livia would have to endure over the fifty-odd years of their marriage. Octavian's first wife, Claudia Pulchra, was from another branch of the *gens Claudia*. She was the teenage daughter of Publius Clodius Pulcher, the rabble-rousing politician we met in Chapter 1, and hence the niece of the Clodia who was publicly shamed by Cicero. Clodius was dead by now and Claudia's widowed mother, Fulvia, had married Mark Antony, making the teenage Claudia a stepdaughter of Octavian's fellow triumvir. The union had everything to recommend it, in both social and political terms, and it went ahead in or around 43 BC, even though Suetonius describes Claudia as 'barely old enough for marriage' (*vixdum nubilem*).[24] It is a curious observation, because while Claudia was certainly very young, thirteen or fourteen, she wasn't much younger than other patrician girls when they were married for the first time. Suetonius may be hinting that she was too young to bear children, making an excuse for the childless state of the marriage when Octavian divorced Claudia a couple of years later. He blamed the divorce on his mother-in-law Fulvia, claiming he could not bear her temper, and sent Claudia back to her mother with a sneering remark that he had never had sex with her.[25]

Fulvia was infuriated by this insult to her family and it was one of the causes of the siege of Perugia, but Octavian's claim that the marriage was unconsummated is unconvincing. Few people believed him at the time and Octavian was so annoyed that he swore an oath that he had not slept with Claudia, which failed to dispel near-universal scepticism. That's hardly surprising, because Octavian was notoriously keen on sex, showing off to his friends about whom he had slept with, and the idea that he would keep his hands off an attractive teenager who was living in his own house defies belief. Mark Antony describes an occasion at a dinner party thrown by an ex-consul when Octavian took a fancy to his host's wife; he got up and took her into a bedroom, returning her to the dining room some time later with her hair in disarray and her ears burning with shame or embarrassment.[26] What's being described here is not remotely consensual sex and Mark Antony went even further, claiming that Octavian's friends were given the task of procuring women on his behalf, acting like slave-dealers as they forced mothers and unmarried women to strip as if they were being put up for sale. There were (presumably) consensual affairs as well, and Mark Antony listed some of the women by name in a letter quoted by Suetonius, while using coarse language to mock the notion that Octavian was faithful to Livia. 'Do you only screw Drusilla?' (*Tu deinde solam Drusillam inis?*)[27]

Few men had ever enjoyed so much power in Rome and this species of institutionalised abuse of patrician women and their husbands appears to be one of Octavian's innovations. To modern eyes, it also suggests he had something to hide; Octavian was keen to parade his virility, or the appearance of it (no one knows how a man performs in his bedroom), but his fertility was another matter. The lack of a male heir would plague his reign as emperor and it would have felt like a very personal failure; elite Roman men expected (and were expected) to have as many children as possible. Throughout history men have blamed their female partners for failing to conceive, even though the medical problem often lies with them; there was little or no knowledge in the ancient world of subfertility, a condition that affects one in twenty men, resulting in a low sperm count or defective sperm.[28] If Octavian tried and failed to get Claudia pregnant, it would explain his very public rejection of her *and* his insistence that they had not had sex. His failure would have been all the harder to bear in comparison to other leading men of the period, notably Mark Antony, who already had at least three children and would go on to have several more.

Indeed, Octavian's next choice of wife attests to his eagerness to have an heir, his choice lighting on a woman in whom he seems to have had no personal interest. She was, however, a relative of Sextus Pompeius, with whom Octavian wanted to keep on good terms, and had already demonstrated her fertility. Scribonia was seven or eight years older than Octavian and had been married twice – she was almost certainly still married, in fact, when he decided to make her his second wife. She came from a plebeian family and had two children, a daughter and a son, by her previous marriages. In 40 BC, she was forced to divorce her second husband while the unfortunate Claudia disappeared from history, so much so that Scribonia is, as we have seen, sometimes erroneously referred to as Octavian's first wife. (No doubt the oversight would have pleased Octavian, who was keen to erase his first marriage from people's memories as quickly as possible.) He would have been delighted when Scribonia became pregnant at the beginning of 39 BC, thus fulfilling the only function required of her.

If Scribonia expected the pregnancy to bring the couple together, she was to be bitterly disappointed. The birth of their daughter Julia marked the end of the marriage, and Octavian was churlish enough to denigrate his now ex-wife in the private papers Suetonius read in the imperial archives. In another nod to ancient misogyny, Scribonia has gone down in history as a shrew, a tradition exemplified in the historical novel *Augustus* (1986) by the highly regarded Scottish author Allan Massie, where he wrongly claims she was twenty years older than the future emperor and describes her as a 'gap-toothed, big-breasted scold'.[29] This is pure invention: there are no images of Scribonia and the only clue to her appearance lies in the fact that her daughter Julia was regarded as one of the most beautiful women in Rome. Tom Holland is only slightly less rude, describing Scribonia as 'a woman of frigid dignity'.[30] The Penguin Classics edition of Suetonius's life of Augustus, published in 1957 and still the most widely available translation for readers who don't understand Latin, is the source of much of this disdain for Octavian's second wife. 'I could not bear the way she nagged at me,' the English text reads, although that is not what Suetonius actually wrote.[31] His direct quote from the private papers of Augustus is *pertaesus, ut scribit, morum perversitatem eius*.[32] There is no mention of 'nagging' here, and a more accurate translation would go something like this: Augustus was 'disgusted, as he himself wrote, by her unreasonable behaviour'. *Morum* is the genitive plural of *mores*, which means 'habits' or 'behaviour', but the key word is the Latin noun *perversitas*. It is the origin of the English word 'perversity' and indicates a kind of stubbornness or refusal on Scribonia's part to go along with her husband's wishes – the age-old complaint of entitled men, in other words.

So why has Scribonia been treated so harshly by modern writers? The answer lies in the identity of the author of the Penguin Classics translation, who is none other than Robert Graves. His casual mistranslation has done untold damage to Scribonia's reputation, even though we know from Mark Antony what form her so-called 'unreasonable behaviour' took. Scribonia was no slip of a girl; she was a mature woman and had a clear idea about the respect her young husband owed her, especially when she was carrying his child. When he turned his attention to another woman – possibly Livia, although we don't know for certain – she was understandably upset. Once again quoting private papers, Suetonius credits Mark Antony with the observation that Scribonia was 'greatly distressed by the excessive influence of one of Octavian's mistresses' (*liberius doluisset nimiam potentiam paelicis*).[33] The Latin is clear: Scribonia was distressed, not angry, which is the implication behind the 'nagging' accusation. If anyone was angry it was Octavian, who didn't like having his behaviour questioned by a mere woman; his remark about 'perversity' implies that Scribonia was a rare Roman woman who didn't suffer in silence. Maybe that had something to do with the fact that she didn't come from a patrician family, where obedience to male authority would have been drummed into her from childhood. But Scribonia's feelings about the divorce, whether she regretted being ejected from the marriage or was glad to escape her petulant young husband, were not recorded. She did not remarry and she would defy Augustus again many years later, when he exiled their daughter, Julia. We will meet Scribonia again in the next chapter, but for now she disappears into the shadows like Octavian's first wife, Claudia Pulchra.

Livia, meanwhile, had learned the lessons offered by her new husband's behaviour towards her predecessors. She knew she was fertile and no doubt expected to have a child or children with Octavian, which might go some way towards securing her position. But her sole pregnancy during the marriage ended in a premature birth (*immaturus est editus*) and the infant did not survive.[34] Livia was as dispensable as Octavian's previous wives, in theory at least, but she was smart enough to think of other ways to make herself useful. Many years later, according to Dio, she explained the strategy she had adopted to avoid becoming another casualty of her capricious husband. It is one of the rare occasions when we get an insight into Livia's interior life and it hardly casts the marriage in a romantic light:

> When someone asked her how and by what course of action she had obtained such a commanding influence over Augustus, she answered that it was by being scrupulously chaste herself, doing gladly whatever pleased him, not meddling with any of his affairs, and, in particular, by pretending not to hear or notice the favourites that were the objects of his passion.[35]

In this passage, Livia sounds like a 'surrendered wife', the sad creature who appears in a 2001 self-help book of the same title by an American author, Laura Doyle, but it was a strategy that required iron self-control.[36] Around the year 16 BC, when Livia had been married to Augustus for more than twenty years, his affair with a married woman called Terentia, wife of his friend Gaius Maecenas, became public knowledge. Maecenas was one of the emperor's most trusted advisors and a noted patron of poets such as Virgil, yet there is evidence to suggest that the relationship had been going on for years. Revelation of the affair caused such a scandal that Augustus left Rome for a time, amid rumours that he was running away with Terentia, but not before he had forced the two women to take part in a beauty contest (the outcome of this humiliating spectacle is not recorded).[37] This is not to underestimate Livia's eventual influence over Augustus, especially later in the marriage, when she was one of the few people he trusted, but it shows the humiliations she had to put up with time and time again. Whether being consulted on family matters – Suetonius quotes from letters Augustus wrote to her, discussing the problem of her disabled grandson, Claudius – was sufficient compensation is impossible to know. Some ancient authors suggest that she tried to temper her husband's cruelty, with Dio inventing a long speech in which she pleads with Augustus to show mercy to a grandson of Pompey the Great, Gnaeus Cornelius Cinna Magnus, who had been caught plotting against him in or around the year 16 BC. This event is shrouded in mystery, with some historians doubting whether it ever happened, but the point of the speech is to show how discreetly Livia exercised her influence over Augustus. It is not a view of her character that has appealed to posterity, however, which has heaped a whole series of far-fetched 'crimes' onto the ones implied in the ancient texts.

* * *

On the second floor of the British Museum, in a room devoted to objects from the early Roman empire, there is a stunningly beautiful marble head of Livia. Its exact date is not known, but she appears to be in her early thirties. Her hair is pulled back in the simple style known as the *nodus*, or Roman knot, with a roll of hair above the forehead, giving her the look of a 1930s film star. It's a serene portrait, like most heads of the period, but it would have looked quite different 2,000 years ago, when it would have been painted in brilliant colours. Livia's head stands on a plinth next to one of her husband, portraying him as a handsome young man even though it was probably made after his death in AD 14.

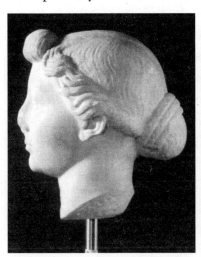 

Both objects have been provided with short captions and the contrast between them is a lesson in the way ancient and modern prejudice affects even scholarly summaries of women's lives. Augustus is described neutrally as the first emperor of Rome and 'very much the hub of the new political order'. There is no reference to his role in how that order came about: the brutal civil wars that followed Caesar's assassination, the proscriptions he ordered during the second triumvirate, his own occasional outbursts of violence. Livia is correctly described as his empress and third wife, but then the caption swerves into conjecture: 'She was very influential and some said that she played a part in the untimely deaths of Augustus' potential heirs.' This is true in a narrow sense, because Livia has been accused of involvement in the deaths of her husband's adopted sons, but the caption is simply repeating malicious gossip. Why is Augustus presented as a statesman while dubious stories about his wife, repeated by authors known to be hostile to her, are singled out for use in a one-paragraph summary of her long life?

It is clear that hindsight colours history's view of Livia: through her sons Tiberius and Drusus, who were not blood relatives of Augustus, she would become absolutely central to the continuation of the Julio-Claudian dynasty. But it was far from clear at the outset that that would be the case, as it was the continued absence of a hoped-for son that prompted her husband into a series of adoptions. Livia and Tiberius would have been also-rans if any of these schemes had succeeded, but they were propelled to the front rank of history by a series of illnesses and accidents. Few of these deaths were suspicious, given that infectious diseases were rife in Rome and military careers were often cut short by accidents or in battle, but they presented an irresistible opportunity to hostile commentators.

For Tacitus, Livia was the first in a series of ambitious women who schemed and manipulated behind the scenes, using authority stolen from men to advance their own and their sons' interests – and he was more than happy to use 'her' failure to provide Augustus with an heir against her. One of his most famous aphorisms characterises Livia as 'a weight on the state as a mother, and a weight on the house of the Caesars as a stepmother' (*gravis in rem publicam mater, gravis domui Caesarum noverca*).[38] This is Roman misogyny in full flow, blaming Livia for the accession of her gloomy son Tiberius to the principate (the form of government instituted by Augustus, who designated himself *princeps* or 'first citizen' to avoid any suggestion he was a king) and characterising her role in the dynasty as the wicked stepmother, implying that she systematically cleared out her husband's chosen heirs. Tacitus chooses his words carefully, attacking Livia's reputation through hints and asides, but never quite accusing her outright; he uses distancing mechanisms such as 'some people said' to suggest she was responsible for a whole series of murders in her husband's family. Tacitus was writing more than a century later and it isn't clear whether such accusations were taken seriously in Livia's lifetime or existed merely as dinner-party gossip, circulating among members of patrician families who yearned for the return of the Roman republic.

As the conduct of the Julio-Claudian emperors became more notorious, however, the temptation to look back and identify Livia as the dynasty's evil matriarch was hard to resist. Her great-grandson, the emperor Caligula, sneered that she was 'Ulysses in a dress' (*Ulixem stolatum*), comparing her unfavourably with the cunning Greek hero whose adventures are described in the *Odyssey*.[39] The most damaging anecdotes about her were picked up and amplified by authors writing after the dynasty came to an ignominious end, such as Tacitus, and culminating in Robert Graves's libellous portrait of her in *I, Claudius*.

Who were these supposed victims? The first, Augustus's nephew Marcus Claudius Marcellus, has already been mentioned. Augustus seems to have been in two minds about this nephew, never formally adopting him, but in 25 BC he married Marcellus to his daughter Julia. The marriage was childless when Marcellus died at the age of nineteen, becoming the first of Augustus's potential heirs to meet an untimely end. There is very little material in the ancient texts to justify an accusation of murder; Velleius, who was born shortly after these events and moved in the highest circles, doesn't mention any suspicion attaching to Marcellus's death, and neither does Suetonius. By the early third century, Dio was ready to claim that suspicion fell on Livia, but even he admits that the accusation was flimsy, given how many people died from a highly infectious disease that year and the next.[40] Tacitus describes the young man's death as an example of the bad luck that attached to popular members of the imperial family, but he is less cautious when reporting the deaths of Augustus's grandsons, Gaius and Lucius.[41]

They had been groomed more or less from birth as the emperor's likely successors, adopted in 17 BC when Lucius was a newborn and Gaius was three. They began their military careers in their teens, sent to different parts of the empire to gain the experience considered necessary for the emperor's heirs. Such expeditions were always risky, however, and so they proved on this occasion. Lucius was on his way to Spain in AD 2 when he became ill and died in Massilia (Marseille), aged nineteen. Gaius was in the eastern provinces at the time of his brother's death and within eighteen months he too would be gone, dying from a protracted illness caused by injuries sustained in an ambush in Armenia. He was twenty-four and his death meant that Augustus had lost both his heirs in the space of two years. Tacitus once again acknowledges the imperial family's bad luck but can't resist a sneaky aside, suggesting that the deaths might have been caused by 'the treachery of their stepmother Livia' (*novercae Liviae dolus*).[42]

After the deaths of Gaius and Lucius, Augustus had only one grandson left, a boy called Marcus Agrippa Postumus (his last name signifies that he was born after the death of his father, Agrippa, in 12 BC). He was not obvious emperor material – he is said to have had a volatile character and his main interest was fishing – so Augustus hedged his bets, adopting Postumus and his stepson Tiberius at the same time in AD 4.[43] Two years later, Augustus lost patience with Postumus, revoked his adoption and exiled him to a villa near Surrentum (Sorrento), denying him the inheritance left to him by his father, Agrippa. Postumus does not seem to have had political ambitions but he was furious about the loss of his inheritance and complained bitterly about it. Augustus responded with characteristic spite, having Postumus removed from Sorrento and exiled to an island called Planasia (Pianosa), where he was placed under armed guard.

He spent the next few years on the island, pretty much forgotten until Augustus became ill and died in AD 14. Postumus was twenty-five by now and put up a ferocious fight when he was ambushed by a centurion sent to kill him, even though he had been taken by surprise and was unarmed (*ignarum inermumque*).[44] Dio says Tiberius gave the order himself, later denying it and threatening to have the perpetrators punished, although he didn't do anything about it.[45] Tacitus blames the death squarely on Tiberius, calling it 'the first crime of the new regime' (*primum facinus novi principatus*), and claiming that the new emperor was terrified that Postumus would challenge his right to the throne. But the historian can't resist dragging in Livia, suggesting that she had a hand in the murder because of 'a stepmother's malice' (*novercalibus odiis*).⁴⁶ It's not even clear that Livia would have been able to issue such an order, but Tacitus's choice of words is deliberate, repeating his characterisation of her as an evil stepmother.

The most sensational accusation against Livia, however, is that she murdered her husband after more than half a century of marriage. Augustus died on his estate at Nola, 30 kilometres from Naples, on his way back to Rome from a visit to Capreae (Capri), where he owned a palace. He had been suffering from recurrent stomach trouble for several weeks and his final words, according to Suetonius, betray no suspicion of foul play: 'Don't forget our marriage, Livia, and goodbye' (*Livia, nostri coniugii memor vive, ac vale!*).⁴⁷ Whether Augustus actually uttered these words – they sound rather too formal for someone about to expire – is impossible to know, but there is no suggestion in the text that his death

was anything but natural. Augustus was a month short of his seventy-seventh birthday and it seems unlikely that the historian who was writing his semi-official biography would have omitted any such suspicion, had it been taken seriously. Tacitus can't resist pointing the finger at Livia but puts the accusation in the mouths of other people, claiming that 'some suspected his wife of a crime' (*quidam scelus uxoris suspectabant*).⁴⁸

A direct accusation doesn't appear until two centuries after Augustus's death, when Dio specifies the method Livia supposedly used to murder her husband (he says she smeared poison on some figs she had picked from his favourite trees on the estate and handed them to him herself).[49] Dio suggests her 'motive' was the discovery that Augustus had recently made a secret trip to reconcile with Postumus, putting Tiberius's position as his heir in doubt. The story is out of character for a man as unforgiving as Augustus, who had spent years verbally abusing Postumus, but the accusation fits a familiar pattern: in the first place, suspicion is cast on what was regarded as a natural death at the time, then more detail is added, including a sensational claim about the 'method' used.

There was ample material here for later authors to work with. By the time Robert Graves came to write *I, Claudius*, Livia's reputation as a cold-blooded poisoner was already established and he saw no reason to question it. With his usual disregard for evidence or accuracy, he added even more murders to her tally, not just her younger son Drusus, but her first husband, Tiberius Nero. Graves invents a conversation between Claudius and his cousin Postumus, in which the latter adds a completely new accusation: that Livia poisoned his father, Agrippa. The fictional Postumus even claims to have confronted Livia, cheekily asking whether she preferred to use slow- or fast-acting poisons.[50]

If Livia really had got away with killing eight members of her own and her second husband's family, it would make her one of the most successful serial killers in history. But she wasn't: only one of her 'victims' was murdered, not by her, and the others died of natural causes or as a consequence of military life. Yet it is Livia who has gone down in history as the dynasty's evil matriarch while her husband, who caused the deaths of thousands of people as he slogged his way to supreme power, is presented as a thoughtful ruler who created a golden age in Rome. One of the reasons is that Livia's deliberately chaste sexual conduct could not be used against her, unlike other women in the dynasty, so she was smeared with baseless accusations of murder instead.

Her survival was extraordinary, given how close she came to death as a teenage refugee, and how profoundly she was affected by the arbitrary decisions of the men close to her. She outlived Augustus by fifteen years and his death should have ushered in a gratifying old age, releasing her from a difficult marriage and allowing her to enjoy her elder son's reign as Rome's second emperor.

But it was not to be. Her later years were blighted by slights and insults from Tiberius, who complained bitterly that his mother expected to rule alongside him. He avoided private meetings with her, refused to listen to her advice and responded furiously when the Senate proposed to honour him with the title 'son of Livia'. He revealed himself to be as rigid as previous generations of Roman men, warning her to 'keep out of matters unbecoming to a woman' (*nec feminae convenientibus negotiis abstineret*). He resented anything that redounded to her credit, reacting angrily when he discovered she had gone to the scene of a fire near the temple of Vesta – a goddess often identified with Livia – and directed rescue operations, even though she was in her seventies by then.[51] He eventually removed her from involvement in public affairs altogether, even suggesting that she was the reason for his eventual retirement to Capri where he spent the final decade of his reign.⁵² He saw Livia only once in the final three years of her life and refused to return to Rome when she fell sick with her final illness. She was around eighty-six when she died in AD 29 and Tiberius delayed so long in leaving Capri to travel to Rome that her corpse began to decompose. Thanks to her son's heartless behaviour, Rome's first empress was denied a proper funeral and had to be hastily buried, in defiance of tradition.⁵³

3

Unfortunately, She Was a Nymphomaniac: Part I

Julia (39 BC–AD 14): daughter of Scribonia and the emperor Augustus, stepdaughter of the empress Livia. **Starved to death**, aged 52

The Pontine islands lie in the Tyrrhenian Sea, off the west coast of Italy, halfway between Rome and Naples. There are six islands in the archipelago and one of them, Ventotene, is the summit of an extinct volcano. It's 53 kilometres from the mainland and the journey from Rome by modern transport takes about five hours, starting with a train to the port of Formia on the Gulf of Gaeta. It's advisable to go in the summer when the fast ferry takes about ninety minutes, heading into open sea and rapidly losing sight of Formia; even today, nothing but water is visible for more than an hour until the low-lying island of Ventotene comes into vision. The ferry anchors in a modern harbour built on the far side of the little Roman port, disgorging tourists and local people who've returned with essential supplies; the island is small, 3,000 metres by 800 metres, and not much grows here apart from lentils. Around 750 people live permanently on Ventotene, catering to the tourists who stay in spa hotels or hire diving equipment to explore the azure waters that surround it. Picturesque houses in pastel colours straggle up the hillside, but it's an unsettling location for anyone who knows that Ventotene functioned as a prison – and a place of execution – for some of the most famous women in Roman history.

In the late first century BC, Augustus built a palace on the northern tip of the island, which was then called Pandateria, but there's no evidence that he ever visited it. The extensive archaeological site where it stood is closed to visitors and barely signposted; when I visited Ventotene during the writing of this book, my question about how to get there was repeatedly met with shrugs. After walking out of town, I was finally directed to the site by a woman who was hanging out her washing. She pointed up some rickety steps next to a hand-painted sign to what's known locally as the Villa Giulia, and I found myself peering over a fence at the ruins of the farm that once supplied the inhabitants of the palace with food.

Its most famous resident was Augustus's daughter Julia, who was imprisoned in the palace for five years after she was disgraced and exiled in 2 BC. Julia was eventually moved to the mainland, but three more Julio-Claudian woman would be imprisoned here and, unlike Julia, they would all die here. Lovely as the island appears today, its history is overshadowed by the fate of these women, who were forced to undertake the long journey from Rome in closed litters, listening to the clanking swords of the soldiers preventing their escape; we know that at least one of them, Julia's daughter Agrippina, was brought here in chains. They would have been tormented by fear and despair as they were rowed across to the rocky island, the many hours in a boat a warning of how far from the mainland their prison would turn out to be. It was still being used as a dumping ground for inconvenient women in AD 95 when the emperor Domitian exiled his niece Flavia Domitilla to Pandateria, allegedly for converting to Judaism.[1]

Julia was thirty-six or thirty-seven when she was exiled to Pandateria. She had five children from her marriage to Agrippa: two daughters, Julia and Agrippina, as well as the three boys. They were aged between ten and eighteen, and she would never see any of them again. The scale of her disgrace is hard to imagine: she had been accused of adultery and plotting against the regime, denounced in a letter by her own father which was read aloud to the Senate. Her estranged husband Tiberius had been ordered to divorce her and four of her alleged lovers were exiled to other parts of the empire; a fifth, she would later learn, had either been executed or forced to kill himself. Accusations of immorality were often a distraction from alleged political offences that were an embarrassment to the regime, especially if they involved close relatives of the emperor – and few were closer than his own daughter. Augustus was astonished by the popular reaction in Rome, where angry crowds gathered to protest against her banishment, but he refused to change his mind; some ancient sources even suggest that he seriously considered having her executed.[2] Instead, he decided to

Unfortunately, She Was a Nymphomaniac: Part I

make sure her conditions of imprisonment were as harsh as possible, banning her from drinking wine and eating anything but the plainest food, a prohibition that hardly seems necessary, given the island's limited resources. Julia's sole consolation was the presence of her mother Scribonia, who voluntarily accompanied her into exile. She was approaching seventy by now and it was no small matter to give up her existence in Rome – where her adult son from an earlier marriage may still have been alive and she had at least six grandchildren – to share Julia's disgrace on the windswept island. But Scribonia had already lost her elder daughter, Cornelia, whose death in 18 BC was recorded by the poet Propertius; he wrote an elegy addressed to Cornelia's widower, Paullus Aemilius Lepidus, in which the dead woman tries to console her grieving mother.[3] Sixteen years later, Scribonia didn't want to lose another daughter, but even so her decision to accompany Julia into exile was a leap into the unknown.

Nothing like Julia's exile had happened before in Rome and the two women may have heard reports of the demonstrations from gossip passed on by sailors on the ships that brought supplies, raising their hopes of a reprieve. If anything, however, the protests backfired: Augustus was furious, calling on the gods to curse the defiant crowds with similarly disobedient wives and daughters. The protesters were not cowed; when Augustus declared that fire would mix with water before he would recall Julia to Rome, they mocked him by tossing burning torches into the Tiber.[4] Julia's popularity shocked him, but no one could have guessed that the emperor's vendetta against his lovely, kind and cultured daughter would last until his death – and beyond.

The summer of 2 BC was a significant milestone for the emperor. It was twenty-five years since he had accepted the title of Augustus and earlier that year he had been awarded another, *Pater Patriae* (Father of the Nation), by the Senate. He stuck to the conceit that he had restored the republic, but no one doubted that he was in charge, or that a member of his family would succeed him as sole ruler of Rome. He was sixty-one that summer, Livia around fifty-six, and he celebrated the anniversary with grand building projects, finally finishing the Forum of Augustus. The scandal that erupted over his daughter could not have been more unwelcome, but it had been brewing for a long time – and he had only himself to blame. No daughter could have behaved more impeccably than Julia in terms of the succession, marrying men chosen by her father and producing the male heirs that Augustus had not been able to provide himself.

But her marriage to Livia's son Tiberius had broken down years earlier, and she found herself uncomfortably exposed. Tiberius left Rome altogether in 6 BC, moving to the island of Rhodes and leaving Julia in a species of limbo. It is important to bear in mind at this point that the daughter of the first emperor was the nearest thing in the ancient world to a celebrity, attracting attention and gossip on a scale no Roman woman had ever experienced (Cleopatra is probably the nearest comparison). Technically she was still married, but any pretence that the marriage was intact was destroyed when her husband decamped to Greece.

Julia's situation after 6 BC was not unlike that of Princess Diana after she separated from the Prince of Wales, subject to endless speculation and the age-old assumption that an attractive single woman must be having sex with somebody. Julia tried to resolve the situation by asking for a divorce, denouncing Tiberius's behaviour in an angry letter to her father, but Augustus would not hear of it (so much for the idea that mothers of three or more children, let alone one with five, were free to decide for themselves). If Julia were allowed to divorce Tiberius, she wouldn't want to remain on her own for long and any future husband would become stepfather to Augustus's adopted sons, giving him a status the emperor would find intolerable.

Julia thus found herself in an impossible situation: still of marriageable age but neither a wife nor a widow, and denied the opportunity to find a more amenable husband. It's likely that she was denied the company of her elder sons, Gaius and Lucius, who had been adopted by their grandfather, while her daughter Julia the younger was married around this time and would have been living in her husband's household. Julia herself relied on a coterie of high-spirited male friends from well-connected families to avoid being lonely, becoming a magnet for gossip. Whether these men *were* just friends, or lovers and would-be conspirators against the regime, is hard to establish, but it's obvious that the situation was open to being misconstrued; in the years after her divorce, Princess Diana only had to be seen with a man for rumours of an affair to start flying, whether or not they were justified. But Julia's position in the dynasty meant that her behaviour was, or appeared to be, a threat to the established social order.

The pursuit of extramarital sex by Roman men was tolerated, even expected, but it was a very different matter when the rumours related to the emperor's daughter. The situation gained added piquancy from the fact that everyone knew about Augustus's disapproval of adultery, his own excepted, of course. The emperor's liaisons were mostly short-lived, with no constitutional implications, but he would have regarded a serious, long-term relationship involving his daughter as a dangerous development. Opposition to the principate was muted but widespread, particularly among patrician families, and Julia's lover or lovers might easily become the foundation of a party of dissent. Whether or not she was aware of the political implications of an affair, it is a more likely scenario than lurid claims about her supposed promiscuity – and might account for her father's implacable rage towards her.

Roman historians are pretty much unanimous in condemning Julia's conduct. The template they established has been followed to a large extent by modern scholars, who, as Julia's biographer

Elaine Fantham has observed, 'have found it far easier to believe in her loose living than even the debauchery of Augustus' other propaganda victim, Mark Antony'.[5] To be fair, some modern commentators give the impression that they're uncomfortable with the wilder allegations, but that doesn't stop them reverting pretty rapidly to the nymphomaniac stereotype. Mary Beard speculates that Julia's arranged (forced, to be more accurate) marriages 'had something to do with her notoriously rebellious sex life'.[6] Augustus's biographer, Adrian Goldsworthy, casts doubt on the most lurid stories but blames the emperor for failing to prevent his daughter's behaviour 'from getting as bad as it did'.[7] Tom Holland acknowledges that the rumours were 'fetid and unsourced' but repeats them, claiming that Julia was 'as wilful as she was bold'.[8] Anthony Blond goes completely overboard and describes Julia as 'arrogant, stubborn, insolent, defiant, libidinous and deeply tricky'.[9] Even Guy de la Bédoyère describes Julia as 'turning out to be the worst daughter Augustus could possibly have had'.[10]

Rebellious, wilful, defiant: these are all adjectives that infantilise women, reducing them to naughty children or sulky teenagers. They are harsh judgements on a woman whose principal offence, if we leave aside political considerations for a moment, was to try to take control of her own body. But it's also worth remembering, as the empress Agrippina's biographer Anthony A. Barrett has pointed out, that 'the borderline between immorality and conspiracy is a fine one' in terms of accusations against the Julio-Claudian women.[11] When women were regarded as their father's or husband's property, the act of having sex with another man was a challenge to the social order. It's one of the reasons why it's so hard to disentangle accusations of sexual impropriety and treason in Julia's case, with the latter lurking in the background of sensational stories about orgies in the forum.

Rumours about Julia's infidelity had begun to circulate as far back as her marriage to her second husband, Agrippa, which took place in 21 BC. Tacitus claims she had already started an affair with a senator called Sempronius Gracchus, whom he describes as a man notable for his smart intelligence and vicious wit.[12] There was gossip about other affairs as well, but what isn't in doubt is Julia's fertility, which should have been a matter of congratulation in a society where women's primary function was bearing children. Sex and maternity are uncomfortable companions in patriarchal cultures, however, and there's no doubt that Julia's supposedly uninhibited sex life sat uneasily with her essential role in the continuation of the Julio-Claudian dynasty, not least because of husbands' perpetual fear of another man's child being covertly introduced into the family. Observers of her behaviour couldn't understand how Julia had avoided becoming pregnant by one of her lovers, if the rumours were true, and it prompted one of the most famous ripostes from antiquity.

According to the fifth-century philosopher Macrobius, Julia was once asked to explain how her sons resembled Agrippa when she was sleeping with other men. 'I never allow a passenger on board until the hold is full,' she is supposed to have replied (*numquam enim nisi navi plena tollo vectorem*).[13] It's quoted by Macrobius as an example of Julia's ready wit, but he was writing 400 years later. He got the story from a first-century collection of sayings by famous people, now lost, but his own book appeared at a time when Julia's reputation as an adulteress had long been established. The possibility that it was an *ex post facto* invention to account for the annoying absence of any actual evidence for her affairs has to be considered. All we can say for certain is that Agrippa never questioned his children's paternity, but dinner-party gossip from those years set the scene for much more malicious slanders after his death.

This is not a version of events even considered in the ancient texts. There are several accounts of Julia's alleged transgressions, varying in tone from disgusted to pornographic. What's striking is how short they are on detail, while siding with Augustus against the largely unspecified things his daughter is supposed to have done. The scandal that ruined her life is portrayed as a tragedy for the *emperor*, with scant sympathy for the half-dozen prominent people (more, if you count their families and friends) who lost everything as a result. Velleius sets the tone, describing Julia's disgrace as a storm (*tempestas*) in the emperor's household that he finds almost too horrible to describe or remember (*foeda dictu memoriaque horrenda*). The Latin is so bristling with disgust that it's not easy to translate, but this is more or less what it says:

> For his daughter Julia, with no thought for her great father and her husband, did not refrain from any disgusting deed tainted with extravagance or lust that a woman could be guilty of, whether screwing or being screwed, and measured the extent of her status by the liberty she had to sin, justifying whatever she wanted to do by the fact that she got away with it.[14]

Yes, but what did she actually *do*? Once he's got this tirade off his chest, Velleius names five men who supposedly debauched (*violassent*) Julia, necessitating her removal from the sight of her country and her parents (*patriaque et parentum*). The assertion is not even accurate because Julia's mother Scribonia volunteered to go into exile with her, as Velleius himself admits. But his account is the first to list her alleged lovers, recycling the old story about Sempronius Gracchus and adding Iullus Antonius, Quinctius Crispinus, Appius Claudius and Cornelius Scipio (Iullus is the key figure, as we shall see in a moment, but they were all scions of great republican families and could easily have been seen as a threat by Augustus). Dio is more specific, claiming that Julia 'was so dissolute in her conduct as actually to take part in revels and drinking bouts at night in the Forum and even upon the rostra', the platform from which some of Rome's most celebrated orators had made speeches.[15] There is an implication here that Julia was sticking two fingers up at her father, because the rostra was where Augustus had announced some of his laws, including his legislation imposing severe penalties for adultery.

Suetonius is another source who takes the side of the emperor, claiming that the scandal affected him so profoundly that he couldn't bear to receive visitors for a long time afterwards, but his account, like that of Velleius, is notably short on detail. He bundles together Julia and her daughter of the same name, declaring that Augustus found them both 'polluted by every type of vice' (*omnibus probris contaminatas*), without saying what they were.[16] Augustus even expressed a wish that his daughter would kill herself like one of her friends, a freed slave called Phoebe who hanged herself after Julia's disgrace. The anecdote is supposed to show that even Julia's closest associates were horrified by her behaviour, but it could equally have been the case, as Elaine Fantham points out, that Phoebe was terrified of being tortured; the anecdote implies that other members of Julia's household had been interrogated, raising the possibility that some of the 'evidence' against her was obtained under torture.[17] It's striking that Tacitus is a lone voice of dissent, describing Julia's offence as no more than 'shamelessness' (*impudicitia*) and suggesting that Augustus overreacted to cases of adultery by imposing excessively harsh penalties.[18]

So far, the allegations are all pretty similar, amounting to not much more than affairs with prominent men and outdoor parties (not so unusual on hot summer nights in Rome). Seneca's account is different, amounting to a Roman version of a tabloid headline: 'Emperor Stunned after Daughter Sells Body in Midnight Sex Orgies'. He claims to be quoting from the letter of denunciation written by Augustus himself and read on his behalf to the Senate:

> The divine Augustus exiled his daughter, who was shameless beyond the curse of shamelessness, and placed the scandals of the imperial family in the public domain: he said she had

committed adultery with scores of men; that she had roamed the city at night in search of thrills; that she had enjoyed using the forum itself for her debauchery, and the speaker's platform where her father had announced his law against adultery; that she went daily to the statue of Marsyas where, exchanging adultery for prostitution, she claimed the right to indulge herself with complete strangers.[19]

Seneca's account reads like a fantasy, enjoying the contrast between Julia's exalted status and her lewd behaviour, and expressing the idea that a 'whore' exists inside every woman. We don't know whether it's a faithful summary of what was in Augustus's letter or an embroidered version of it, adding details that existed only in Seneca's fevered imagination; it's worth remembering at this point that conservative Roman men made no distinction between a woman who had sex outside marriage and a prostitute. If the source *was* Augustus's letter, it seems unlikely that he was describing something he'd seen for himself, unless Julia was not the only member of the imperial family who had taken to wandering through the forum – effectively Rome's red light district – at night. So who is supposed to have witnessed and reported this behaviour? Someone who wanted to cause trouble for Julia, evidently, and tailored the accusations to cause maximum outrage, siting her supposed misconduct in a location that amounted to a deliberate insult to her father's beliefs about women. But why would a wealthy Roman woman, who lived in a comfortable house and had supposedly chosen some of the most personable men in Rome as her lovers, suddenly take the risk of having sex with complete strangers in one of the most exposed areas of the city? Leaving aside the likely reaction of her father, the risks attendant on engaging in prostitution in ancient Rome – disease, pregnancy, being beaten up by a drunk, violent man – would have been enormous.

The question of why Augustus believed the accusations, turning so violently against his daughter, has rarely been addressed, even though it has to be seen in the context of a longstanding (and accelerating) conflict between them. The fact that Julia was the loser doesn't make the accusations true, and it's clear that she had become a scapegoat for growing anxieties about female behaviour at this time; she was the most conspicuous, but by no means the only, victim of a very unpleasant moral panic, fuelled by the increasing visibility of women in ancient Rome. In a jaw-dropping development, Julia's disgrace resulted in a rush of patrician men accusing their own wives of adultery, airing all sorts of suspicions and seizing the opportunity to get rid of inconvenient spouses. Augustus was taken aback by the volume of the allegations, which led to dozens of other women being accused of similarly shameful sexual conduct, and he refused to act on all the charges.[20] Maybe he realised that many were spurious. But he couldn't be persuaded to forgive Julia, even though there are compelling reasons to challenge Seneca's lurid summary of his letter.

One of the most obvious is the previously mentioned issue of Julia's fertility. By the time the scandal broke, she had been pregnant six times in the course of two marriages. She married Tiberius

in 11 BC, a year after the death of Agrippa, and was soon pregnant again. Around this time, Tiberius was given a provincial command in Pannonia, an area that comprises part of the modern-day

Balkans, Austria and Hungary, replacing his new wife's late husband, who had died as he was returning to Rome from Campania. Julia travelled with Tiberius as far as north-east Italy, even though she was pregnant. She went into labour in a town called Aquileia, where their son was born, but the infant didn't survive long.[21] The loss of the child would have been desperately upsetting for both parents and it's evident from Suetonius's account that the impact on the marriage was catastrophic; he says the couple had been on good terms until the child died and broke the bond between them (*intercepto communis fili pignore*).

Not long afterwards, the accidental death of Tiberius's brother Drusus had a profound effect on his already gloomy character; Tiberius hurried to Germany, arriving just before Drusus died in 9 BC, and walked all the way back to Rome, carrying his ashes. Around this time, Tiberius withdrew emotionally and even insisted on sleeping apart from Julia (*ut etiam perpetuo secubaret*) for the rest of their marriage.[22] The sequence of events is clear from Suetonius's account: within a couple of years, the couple were miserable together and had stopped having sex. The animosity between them reached such a point that Tiberius's departure from Rome in 6 BC was said to have been motivated by disgust towards his wife (*uxorisne taedio*), whom he could no longer endure.[23]

This was a low point, perhaps the lowest, in Tiberius's career, which explains why he behaved with uncharacteristic magnanimity when Julia was exiled four years later, asking that she be allowed to keep all the gifts he had given her;[24] he was out of the country, out of favour, and had nothing to gain by adding to his ex-wife's troubles. But the rapid breakdown of the marriage is significant, suggesting that the period when Julia had a husband in name only might have been as long as six or seven years. If she was as dependent on sex as her critics suggested – and what they describe is close to an addiction, if such a thing exists – it is striking that there are no reports of further pregnancies.

Unfortunately, She Was a Nymphomaniac: Part I 67

Roman contraception was not exactly reliable, not least because doctors in the ancient world misunderstood the menstrual cycle, giving women diametrically wrong advice about when they were least likely to conceive. Medical texts suggested ineffectual methods such as having a cold drink before sex, squatting or sneezing afterwards to dislodge sperm, and using crude plant-based pessaries or swallowing herbs that were believed to prevent conception. One of the most outlandish is recommended by Pliny the Elder, who advises cutting open the head of a hairy spider, removing two little 'worms' and tying them to a woman's body with a strip of deer hide.[25] (A modern thesis highlights the difficulty of 'understanding exactly what kind of spider' Pliny is referring to, but I suspect that's not the main obstacle to its use as an effective contraceptive.[26])

Julia may have employed one or other of these methods, and it's just possible that she had a miscarriage during her lengthy separation from Tiberius, but nothing of the sort has been recorded. Tacitus implies that she was sleeping with Gracchus when she was first married to Tiberius, yet the risk would have been great; her new husband was hardly the forgiving type and he was most unlikely to accept a child he knew he hadn't fathered.[27] If Julia had become pregnant *after* Tiberius disappeared to Rhodes, the scandal would been enormous – and ancient authors would have been all over it.

One possible answer is that Julia was careful and didn't start having regular unprotected sex with Gracchus, Iullus or anyone else until she believed her fertility had begun to decline. Another is the revolutionary suggestion that she was able to have male friends, like her stepmother Livia, without feeling the need to sleep with them. Macrobius recounts an anecdote that's extremely revealing in this regard, describing how Augustus once slipped a note to his daughter at a gladiatorial contest, unfavourably contrasting the dignified older men who had accompanied Livia to the event with the exuberant male friends with whom Julia surrounded herself.²⁸ She may well have been fed up with his constant carping but she restrained herself, making the point that her friends were the same age as her. 'They will grow old with me,' she added (*et hi mecum senes fient*). If the friends included Iullus, she would be proved tragically wrong. But it's telling that no one has ever suggested that Livia was having wild sex with the senators and upper-class men who accompanied her to public events, and perhaps we should extend the same consideration to Julia.

There is reason to think that something else was going on in 2 BC. The reference to the statue of Marsyas, while intended to place Julia's shameful conduct in a location as instantly recognisable as Nelson's Column, puts a different complexion on the scandal. Marsyas is best known as a mythological figure, a satyr who lost a musical contest with the god Apollo and was flayed alive as a punishment. But he had another function in ancient Rome, where he was regarded as a symbol of the republic and free speech, and the statue mentioned by Seneca had long been a focal point for opposition to one-man rule.²⁹ The fact that Julia and her friends are accused of hanging a garland on the statue lends weight to the idea that it was an act of defiance, carried out by a group of people who chafed at Augustus and the fact that he was effectively a dictator. It may even have been a jokey gesture, like students placing a traffic cone on the head of Winston Churchill in Parliament Square, but Augustus was clearly determined to believe the very worst of his daughter.

Whether there was a serious conspiracy against the emperor is impossible to determine, but some ancient authors certainly thought so. Dio accuses Iullus of having 'designs upon the monarchy'.³⁰ Pliny the Elder is even more explicit, saying that Augustus accused Julia of adultery *and* of planning to kill him (*consilium parricidae*).³¹ Tacitus believes that Augustus was exaggerating, being so full of himself that he treated personal slights as though they amounted to sacrilege or treason (*violatae maiestatis*).³² Augustus was certainly egotistical enough to regard any sign of defiance on his daughter's part as tantamount to treachery. But what if he meant it literally?

One of the reasons behind this theory is the identity of the man named as Julia's lover and principal co-conspirator, Iullus Antonius. He was a striking figure, a published poet who was said to be as attractive and irresistible to women as his father, Mark Antony. He was the principal casualty of the scandal, aside from Julia, although we don't know whether he killed himself or was executed (the sources differ). Iullus certainly had reasons to hate Augustus: his mother, Fulvia, and his half-sister, Claudia Pulchra, had both been treated with contempt by Octavian, as Augustus was known at the time, while his father had killed himself after being defeated by Octavian at the battle of Actium. It would not have been surprising if Iullus wanted revenge; indeed, he might well have attracted popular support in Rome, where Mark Antony's memory was regarded with warmth.

Whether Julia was involved in a conspiracy, assuming one even existed, is impossible to know; it may be that Julia and Iullus had quite different intentions, that he was motivated as much by ambition as passion, but it's hard to think of a liaison that would have been more intolerable to her father. It was almost as if Iullus's father had returned to haunt him, a point grasped by Seneca, who wrote that, for the second time in his life, Augustus was confronted by a woman in an alliance with a man named Antony (the first, of course, was Cleopatra).[33] It's also possible that the 'plot' amounted to little more than wild talk and high spirits getting out of control in the forum. But Julia had causes of resentment that stretched back to her childhood, and perhaps she found a receptive ear in Iullus.

From birth, Julia's relationship with her father was characterised by his desire for control of her body. She was a victim of both child and forced marriage while still a teenager, and the consequences were clear: when Augustus chose her husbands, he was deciding who could have sex with her and father her children. His behaviour was not out of the ordinary among patrician Roman men, but his rage when he exiled Julia reveals something close to paranoia; if she had slept with men who weren't chosen by him, she had allowed unauthorised access to herself, and his response was to place her under his complete control. As well as restricting her diet, he announced that no man could visit her on Pandateria without his permission and first submitting to a strip search; Augustus wanted a record of height, skin colour and every distinguishing mark, including brands and scars (*notis vel cicatricibus*).[34]

One of his intentions was to deter potential visitors but there's also an irrational fear here, as though Julia was so sexually incontinent that she might have sex with – and get pregnant by – any male visitor who made the arduous journey to the island. Any child of Julia's would be a threat to the succession and Augustus wanted to be able to identify the guilty party, not that such an eventuality was remotely likely. (He was evidently vague about which physical characteristics were hereditary and which weren't.) There is no record of *any* visits to Pandateria, and, in any case, most of Julia's supposed lovers were exiled or dead. Her shock at being publicly shamed and separated from her children, family and friends surely would have meant that sex was the last thing on her mind – though not, evidently, on her father's.

Augustus's behaviour in 2 BC appears beyond reason, an implacable outpouring of fury, but he had never treated Julia as a human being with wishes and needs of her own. He did not show much interest in her at all at the time of her birth in 39 BC, given that she was a girl and what he wanted was sons. He would have been intent on having children with Livia at the beginning of their marriage, and it is likely that he allowed Julia to live with Scribonia for months or even years after her divorce. The fact that Julia's mother bought a highly educated Greek slave, a grammarian who wrote a treatise on spelling,[35] suggests there were children living in her household who needed instruction in reading, writing and grammar, and Julia may have got to know her elder half-sister Cornelia through these lessons.

But Octavian never lost sight of his daughter's usefulness in forming political alliances; she was only two when he betrothed her to Mark Antony's eldest son and official heir, Antyllus. The boy was eight years older than Julia and it's likely that they actually never met; Antyllus had a typically disrupted civil-war childhood, living in Greece with his stepmother, Octavian's sister Octavia, after his own mother, Fulvia, died suddenly. Later he joined Mark Antony and Cleopatra in Egypt. The engagement was broken off when Octavian fell out with Mark Antony, and the boy met a gruesome end shortly after the suicide of his father, dragged from a temple in Alexandria by Roman soldiers and beheaded, despite his pleas for mercy. Julia was not yet nine at the time, too young perhaps to understand what had happened, but she would have heard about Antyllus's fate as she got older.

Augustus's disappointment over the absence of children in his marriage to Livia changed his priorities, leading him to take a closer interest in Julia. Elaine Fanthan suggests she was around five when he took her away from her mother, moving her into Livia's house, opposite his own on the Palatine, where she received an unusually good education for a girl, learning Greek as well as Latin.[36] Julia developed a love of reading and was regarded as scholarly for a woman (*litterarum amor multaque eruditio*), although it's impossible to know whether she was allowed reading matter while she was in exile.[37] Such accomplishments in a woman were not universally admired in ancient Rome and a vignette in Juvenal's Sixth Satire, where he complains about a woman who has barely sat down to dinner when she starts comparing the merits of Virgil and Homer, is sometimes taken as a sneer against Julia.[38] One of Augustus's affectations was that the imperial family avoided extravagance and Julia was taught spinning and weaving, encouraged to make her own and her father's clothes. She was also forbidden to say anything that was not suitable to be recorded in the daily diary kept by Livia's household.[39]

In light of her later history, it's striking that Julia's social circle was small and she knew most of the men she would later be associated with from childhood. She grew to early adulthood with Livia's sons, her stepbrothers Tiberius and Drusus; and she would almost certainly have known Iullus Antonius, who was four years older and brought up in Rome by his stepmother, Julia's aunt Octavia. Her first husband, Octavia's son Marcellus, was part of the same household. The fact that Julia would marry two of these childhood playmates and have an affair with a third speaks to the incestuous atmosphere within the imperial family. But it's also clear that her father's preoccupation with her chastity, to use an old-fashioned but accurate word, began early. Augustus went to great lengths to prevent her meeting strangers and once told off a young man, Lucius Vinicius, who had dared to visit Julia without first getting permission when she was on holiday in Baiae.[40]

As she reached her teens, Julia was the regime's premier asset, expected to please men from an early age – but only those selected by her father. It is not surprising to discover that she took great care over her appearance, but harder to establish what she looked like. There is an image of her on a coin issued by her father long

before her disgrace, a profile portrait in which Julia is flanked by her sons, Gaius and Lucius, but it does little more than confirm that she wore her hair in the *nodus* style of the period. A bust in the Musée Saint-Raymond in Toulouse very likely represents Julia, not least because it belongs to a family group of heads, including those of her second husband, Agrippa, and several of her children, that were all found together. It shows a woman with regular features, deep eye sockets and lips in a cupid-bow, who bears a striking resemblance to the veiled female figure identified as Julia on the Ara Pacis. Her expression appears to convey sadness, but that may be no more than an absence of animation familiar in Roman sculpture – or, indeed, an assumption based on her tragic history. But Julia's disgrace was spectacular enough to lead to a hasty rethink about the wisdom of displaying images of someone so roundly condemned by the emperor, ensuring the near-complete disappearance of her statues and reliefs.

Anxiety about ageing is not a modern phenomenon and Julia worried about losing her looks. To this day, women are victims of double standards, expected to go to extreme lengths to be attractive to men and simultaneously accused of vanity. When Julia's hair began to lose its colour when she was only in her thirties, she was as upset as any modern celebrity. Macrobius tells a touching anecdote about Augustus arriving unannounced at Julia's house and finding her hairdressers quietly plucking grey hairs from her scalp. Augustus had no time for such trivial anxieties, demanding to know whether she would rather be grey or bald (*cana . . . an calva*). When Julia admitted she would rather be grey, he seized on her answer. 'So why are these women trying so hard to make you bald?' he asked (*quid ergo istae te calvam tam cito faciunt?*).[41] A slew of anecdotes confirms that he was an incredibly controlling father, endlessly criticising her clothes and friends, warning her that she should be less extravagant in her appearance and choose less conspicuous companions.[42]

Julia, to her credit, did not take any of this lying down. She once visited him in an outfit he considered too revealing, leading him to compliment her the next day when she appeared in a much more conservative style of dress – much more suitable for the daughter of Augustus, he told her smugly. He got what he deserved: Julia retorted that today she had dressed to please her father, while the day before she had dressed to please her husband (*hodie enim me patris oculis ornavi, heri viri*).[43] Frustratingly, we don't know which husband she was referring to, although she sounds more like a woman in her twenties than the adolescent Julia would have been during her brief marriage to Marcellus. Such quick thinking is unlikely to have gone down well with Augustus, but it shows that Julia understood that an important part of her role as a wife was to please her husband sexually.

In 23 BC, following the death of Marcellus, Julia had become available once again to further her father's schemes. Two years later, Augustus decided to marry her to his close friend and contemporary, Agrippa, who had played a key role during the civil wars, commanding Octavian's fleet at the battle of Actium in 31 BC. Julia was not quite eight at the time of the two men's victory over Mark Antony and Cleopatra, but she could hardly have been unaware of Agrippa's importance to her father. In 21 BC, Agrippa was still married to his second wife, Julia's cousin Claudia Marcella Major, who was the sister of Julia's recently deceased husband Marcellus, but powerful Roman men did not allow such minor obstacles to stand in their way. Like Julia, Claudia was much younger than Agrippa, and she would soon find another husband, her cousin's future alleged lover, Iullus Antonius; how the women felt about being put in competition with family members for husbands they had not chosen is never considered by ancient authors, nor modern ones either. While Marcellus was alive, Agrippa had gone to live in Greece, angry because he felt he was being overlooked in favour of the much younger man, but he came back soon enough when Marcellus's demise was announced. It put him in an extraordinarily powerful position as Augustus's most likely successor, so much so that the emperor's friend Maecenas warned him that he must make Agrippa his son-in-law or have him killed.⁴⁴ The emperor opted for the former, even though Agrippa came from a plebeian family and was not, in social terms, anything like Julia's equal.

The marriage went ahead in or around 21 BC when the widowed Julia was eighteen and her new husband forty-two. Their first son, Gaius, was born in 20 BC, but Agrippa was often away from Rome, on military campaigns or as governor of the eastern provinces. (It may be that it was during Agrippa's absences that Julia began to surround herself with witty, handsome young men, giving rise to the gossip that would do so much damage later.) Julia sometimes accompanied Agrippa on his travels, giving birth to their daughter Julia in Gaul in or around 19 BC (the exact date is disputed). The couple were back in Rome for the birth of their second son, Lucius, in 17 BC, the year Agrippa was appointed governor of the eastern provinces for a second time. Julia travelled to join him, almost dying in a flash flood at Troy, a misfortune that angered Agrippa so much that he fined the inhabitants an exorbitant amount (he later cancelled the fine after Herod, king of Judaea, intervened on their behalf).[45] The couple's fourth child, Agrippina, was born in Greece in 14 BC, and Julia was pregnant again in 12 BC when Agrippa died suddenly in southern Italy.

Augustus never wasted an opportunity where Julia was concerned and he now decided to marry her to his stepson Tiberius, despite the massive complications that caused in the family tree. The rapidly overlapping roles in the dynasty are jaw-dropping: Tiberius was married to a woman called Vipsania Agrippina, who was Agrippa's daughter by an earlier marriage, which meant that his proposed bride, Julia, was his current wife's stepmother; even more remarkably, Agrippa had been Tiberius's father-in-law, which meant that Julia was his former mother-in-law. Mary Beard has observed that 'only rarely does any hint survive of the personal cost' of all these forced divorces and remarriages – and she could have added that when it does, it's the *men's* feelings that are recorded.[46] Tiberius was very reluctant to give up Vipsania, and when he caught sight of her accidentally after the divorce, he followed her down the street with tears in his eyes (*umentibus oculis*), displaying so much distress that measures were taken to avoid their ever meeting again.[47]

Vipsania lost the child she was expecting at the time of the divorce, who is never mentioned again in the ancient sources, but she went on to marry a senator called Gaius Asinius Gallus. He had several children with Vipsania and made the mistake of casting doubt on the paternity of the son she had had with Tiberius a couple of years earlier, called Drusus, implying that he was the boy's real father. Tiberius had a rare capacity for nursing a grievance and he got his revenge many years later, as we shall see in a later chapter, but Gallus would not be the only victim of Tiberius's rage over the divorce. The long-term effect on Julia, her daughters and her grandchildren was disastrous, suggesting that Tiberius's enforced separation from one of the few people he loved – and the loss of two infants in such a short time frame – turned a habitually bleak character into one who was deeply vindictive.

It was a dreadful start to Julia's third marriage, made worse by Tiberius's conviction that she had wanted to have an affair with him while Agrippa was still alive.[48] Suetonius says this was widely believed, but it is not an easy story to credit if we compare Tiberius with the party animals Julia spent time with by choice. Tacitus tells a very different version, portraying Julia as a snob who despised Tiberius as inferior to her (*spreveratque ut inparem*), even though, as a Claudian, he was a great deal more aristocratic than Agrippa.[49] Both of these assertions – that Julia wanted an affair with Tiberius and that she regarded him with contempt – cannot be true, yet the habit of presenting her in the worst possible light is so ingrained that her unlikely passion for Tiberius is usually asserted as fact. The marriage was never likely to succeed, but Augustus wouldn't have worried about that, caring nothing about what he was putting her through.

Like her mother, however, Julia had a sense of what she was entitled to. 'He may forget that he is Caesar,' she once said of her father, 'but I remember that I am Caesar's daughter' (*ille obliviscitur Caesarem se esse, ego memini me Caesaris filiam*).[50] The trouble with that, of course, was that her father held all the cards – and his daughter had very few, aside from her name and her looks. Her mother, Scribonia, had paid for refusing to turn a blind eye to Octavian's affairs, as her husband was then known, by being divorced and thrown out of his house. Julia would pay a much higher price for defying Augustus, including the loss of almost everything she held dear – and eventually her life.

* * *

Very little is known about Julia's existence on Pandateria. Suetonius says she was moved to the mainland after five years (*post quinquennium*), but the precise date is uncertain.[51] Her circumstances on the island could not have been more different from the glamorous round of dinners, athletic contests and gladiatorial shows she was used to in a cosmopolitan city like Rome. Opportunities for walks and exercise would have been limited by the island's size, while Augustus's spiteful restrictions on her diet meant that she did not even have meals to look forward to. She may have been banned from sending and receiving letters, although such rules could hardly have applied to her mother, who was not technically a prisoner at all. But we can assume that news from Rome arrived on the island, either via Scribonia's correspondents or gossip brought by the crews of ships. The two women would have been eager for every morsel, no matter how trivial or stale it was by the time it arrived; Julia would have heard, for example, that her eldest son, Gaius, was now married to his second cousin Livilla, a bizarre turn of events given that she was the niece of Julia's disgraced lover, Iullus Antonius.

By AD 2, Julia had not seen any of her children for four years. They were growing up fast, their ages now between twenty-two and fourteen, and she must have found the fact of missing milestones in their lives exquisitely painful. It seems likely that they would have been curious in turn about this glamorous mother who had disappeared overnight from Rome, although it's impossible to know how much the younger children knew or understood about the cause of her disgrace. Their grandfather – officially the father of the eldest boys, of course – had never been in robust health and there was a real possibility that he might die in a year or two, allowing Gaius to succeed him. Such a turn of events could result in a dramatic reversal of Julia's fortunes, allowing her to return to Rome as the new emperor's mother (and cutting her miserable ex-husband Tiberius out of the line of succession for good). Julia was around forty and could reasonably look forward to living for another couple of decades, judging by her mother's continuing good health.

This is how things stood that summer, four years into Julia's exile, when the worst imaginable news arrived: Julia's second son, Lucius, had died suddenly in Gaul. Maybe she heard by letter

although there is no record of Augustus sending a message; the maternal bond was not valued in ancient Rome and he would have been too consumed by his worries over the succession to give any thought to his estranged daughter's feelings. Of course Lucius had been the 'spare' rather than the heir, functioning chiefly as insurance against unexpected events, such as the sudden demise of Marcellus a quarter of a century earlier. His body was brought back to Rome, where his ashes were placed alongside those of his father, Agrippa, in the Mausoleum of Augustus.

Now everything rested on Gaius, and Dio implies there were already concerns about his fitness for office, making the curious suggestion that he was 'not robust to begin with and the condition of his health had impaired his mind'.[52] It's the first intimation of a strain of mental instability or illness in the Julian side of the dynasty – Gaius had no Claudian blood – but it would surface again in later generations, notably when Gaius's nephew (and namesake) became known as the 'mad' emperor Caligula. If Gaius's mental health was precarious, it can hardly have been helped by the huge scandal surrounding his mother, and it seems as though steps were taken to keep him away from direct involvement in military engagements. Even so, the sudden demise of his brother Lucius was a reminder of the risks involved in the military education deemed necessary for Augustus's heirs. If Julia knew that Gaius was currently in Armenia, a perpetual trouble spot for Roman generals, she would have had good reason to be worried.

Gaius was young, inexperienced and eager to make a name for himself. He faced a revolt in Armenia after installing a new king there, and less than three weeks after Lucius died, he was wounded in an ambush. The details are murky: Gaius was lured into a trap in the town of Artagira, barely escaping with his life, but it didn't seem at first as though the injuries he had received would prove fatal. It may be that the version of events that filtered back to Julia on the island was initially optimistic, suggesting that Gaius was expected to recover, but worse news was to follow. Gaius did not get better and Dio hints, as mentioned above, that his illness, which was presumably caused by an infection, was exacerbated by his pre-existing mental condition. Velleius says something similar, suggesting that the decline in Gaius's physical condition was accompanied by something that sounds like a nervous breakdown.[53]

Instead of returning to Rome, where he could at least be treated by Augustus's own doctor, Gaius lingered in the eastern provinces. It's not clear whether his physical or mental condition was the most pressing problem, but he eventually petitioned Augustus to allow him to give up his public role and live as a private citizen. Gaius had by now been sick for eighteen months and Augustus reluctantly agreed, but urged him to return to Rome before making a final decision. Gaius endured an arduous overland journey and boarded a cargo ship, but only got as far as Lycia in modern-day Turkey where he died in February of AD 4, evidently in agony. His body was taken back to Rome, where his ashes joined those of his father and brother in the Mausoleum of Augustus.

The impact on Julia and Scribonia, when news of Gaius's death finally reached them, must have been shattering. Julia had lost both her eldest sons within two years, and she was not even allowed to return to Rome to take part in the extravagant funeral laid on for Gaius. She and the boy's grandmother were left to grieve on their own, but Julia was such a non-person in elite circles by now that no one in the ancient world even mentions the devastating double blow she had suffered. Dio suggests she had at least been moved to the mainland, a concession he attributes to continuing pressure on Augustus from the Roman people, who clearly hadn't forgotten her.[54]

Julia's feelings, as she left the island of Pandateria for the last time, must have been tumultuous; during her stay, she had had to grieve the deaths of her presumed lover, Iullus, and her son Lucius, and she now had Gaius's injuries to worry about. Her destination, Rhegium (Reggio di Calabria), was a provincial town close to Sicily, and certainly not somewhere a patrician Roman woman would have chosen to live; Reggio di Calabria had been founded by the Greeks and was an important commercial centre, as well as being home to thousands of retired veterans who had served Augustus in naval engagements. But if it lacked the kind of stimulating company Julia had been used to in Rome, maybe that was the point, driving home the fact that she was neither trusted nor forgiven. (If anyone has ever wondered why Julia's stepmother, Livia, took such care not to challenge Augustus, his treatment of his only daughter is surely one of the answers.)

The conditions of her exile were relaxed somewhat, allowing her to walk around the town, and she seems to have had a substantial household, owning slaves, including a father and son whom she eventually freed. She would have been able to eat a more varied diet now that she could send her slaves to food shops or visit them herself; she may even have had a hairdresser who could dye her hair, which is likely to have been fully grey after all the privations she had endured. Julia was in her early forties by now and she would have looked very different from the stylish woman expelled from Rome half a dozen years earlier. Was she able to exchange letters with her surviving children, Postumus, Julia and Agrippina? Her elder daughter, Julia, had been married before her mother's exile, but Agrippina's marriage in or around AD 5 to Tiberius's nephew and adopted son, the popular general Germanicus, was one of many family events Julia missed. She had grandchildren via both marriages, and the fact that she met only one of them, Julia's daughter Aemilia, who was born before her grandmother was banished, would have been hard to endure. And if she hoped that her transfer to the south of Italy signified a softening in her father's attitude towards herself and her surviving children, she was badly mistaken.

Over the next few years, Augustus waged a pitiless vendetta against two of his grandchildren (only Agrippina was spared, for reasons we shall discover in the next chapter). Postumus's banishment to the island of Pianosa was followed in AD 8 by the exile of his sister, Julia's elder daughter of the same name, to a chain of islands on the other side of Italy on a single charge of adultery (plenty of people, including historians, were quick to say 'like mother, like daughter'). It's striking that Augustus had so little sympathy for his once beloved daughter, ignoring her bereavements and heaping punishments on her youngest son and elder daughter; on the contrary, his abusive behaviour was escalating as he wallowed in self-pity. Like many men who mistreat family members, he regarded himself as the victim, railing against Julia and expressing a spiteful wish that he had remained childless. He used to complain, before her disgrace and exile, that he had to put up with two spoiled daughters (*filias delicatas*), the state and Julia.[55] Now he began referring to his daughter and her exiled children as his 'three ulcers and three sores' (*tris vomicas ac tria carcinomata sua*).[56] It was dehumanising language – and, as history demonstrates, terrible things happen to people who have been dehumanised.

The extent of Augustus's animosity towards his only daughter would be revealed in his will, which made no provision for her. Indeed, it extended beyond her death, in the form of an instruction that neither she nor her elder daughter were to be interred in the family mausoleum facing the Tiber. In the will, which he wrote in the year before his death, the emperor divided his property between Livia and Tiberius, while the annual allowance he had made to pay for Julia's living expenses was not mentioned, allowing her ex-husband to claim that she should not continue to receive it.[57] It meant she would be left destitute, dependent on whatever money Scribonia had or on handouts from her stepmother, Livia. Augustus may have tried to persuade himself that he had provided for his daughter by suggesting she was 'worthy to receive gifts', inadvertently turning her into a charity case.[58] But Julia faced an even bigger threat than Augustus's meanness, in the shape of the return to favour of Tiberius. Dio makes the surprising suggestion that Julia had actually lobbied her father to adopt her ex-husband in AD 4, after the conditions of her exile had been relaxed somewhat. With her sons Gaius and Lucius both dead, Julia knew that Augustus was running out of options and it was all but inevitable that Tiberius would succeed him, in which case advocating on his behalf might have been a desperate attempt on her part to lessen his hostility towards her.[59] It suggests she was an astute politician, but if she feared for her life once Tiberius gained supreme power, she was right to do so. Julia and her surviving son, Postumus, would be dead within months of Tiberius becoming emperor in AD 14.

It is possible that Tiberius regarded Postumus, who was Augustus's only living grandson, as a threat, fearing that someone hostile to the new regime might try to stage a rescue and displace him as emperor. While Augustus was still alive, there had been a half-hearted attempt to do just that, planned by a man called Lucius Audasius, whom Suetonius dismisses as elderly, feeble and a convicted fraudster. But the plot was discovered at an early stage and there is no evidence that Postumus or his mother had anything to do with it.[60] If Tiberius genuinely believed that someone might use them in a coup, he could have moved them to a more secure location and increased the number of soldiers keeping them under guard. But he did not, and the fact that Tiberius saw his accession as an opportunity to settle scores is demonstrated by his treatment of his ex-wife's rumoured lover, Sempronius Gracchus. He had been exiled in 2 BC, at the same time as Julia, and he had endured sixteen years on the island of Cercina (Kerkennah), off the coast of Tunisia. Tiberius had waited a long time for revenge on Gracchus, whom he suspected of helping Julia to write the letter to her father asking for a divorce twenty years earlier. Now he sent soldiers to Kerkennah, where Gracchus was staring out to sea from a promontory, evidently expecting Tiberius's death squad. Gracchus faced his murderers calmly, asking to be allowed to write a last letter to his wife, Alliaria (a woman never previously mentioned in all the excited allegations about his supposed affair with Julia). Then he bravely stretched out his neck and was hacked to death on the spot.[61] Tacitus says Tiberius tried to blame the 'scandal of the assassination' (*famam caedis*) on someone else, just as he did in relation to the murder of Postumus.[62]

The new emperor then turned his attention to his ex-wife. It's hard to avoid the assumption that he approached the situation with anything but relish, immediately revoking the 'privileges' – walking around the town, for example – she had been granted by Augustus. The late emperor's final punishment of his daughter had been to deliver her into the hands of her abusive ex-husband, something that amounted to a death sentence. Tiberius put Julia under house arrest and forbade visitors, refusing to restore the allowance she needed to live. Even ancient historians, not usually sympathetic to the Julio-Claudian women, are in no doubt that his intention was the physical and mental destruction of his ex-wife. To put it bluntly, Tiberius starved her to death. Here is Dio's account of Julia's final days, followed by that of Tacitus (the italics are mine):

> Tiberius did not recall his wife Julia from the banishment to which her father Augustus had condemned her for unchastity, but even put her under lock and key *until she perished from general debility and starvation*.⁶³
>
> Once he became emperor, [Tiberius] destroyed her – exiled, disgraced and, after the killing of Agrippa Postumus, deprived of all hope – by *cutting off supplies and leaving her to waste away* (*inopia ac tabe*), assuming that her slaughter (*necem*) would not attract attention because she had been exiled for so long.⁶⁴

The picture that emerges from these accounts is horrific: Julia, who was shocked and despairing after hearing about the murder of her only remaining son, was deliberately denied food until she starved to death. This wasn't an unintended event, caused by the cessation of her allowance, because her mother Scribonia survived. It is hard to imagine Scribonia's anguish, prevented by armed guards from taking meals to the room where her daughter was suffering, and forced to listen to her anguished cries. Starvation is a slow and painful death, amounting to torture, involving the gradual erasing of a human being until the emaciated body can no longer sustain life. It's clear from the ancient sources that Julia – witty, charming and one of the loveliest woman of her generation – was the victim of a profoundly personal femicide ordered by her ex-husband. Tiberius's murder of his former wife was a horrifying act of domestic violence, long planned, and carried out more than two decades after their marriage broke down. Through the pitiless collusion of her father and ex-husband, Julia's struggle to take control of her own body was punished with its literal destruction.

Scribonia, who was now in her eighties, somehow managed to survive witnessing this obscenity and returned to Rome, where her former son-in-law was now lording it over the Senate. She had been absent from the city for sixteen years, demonstrating a loyalty to her daughter that shamed her ex-husband, and we know that she lived for at least two more years. It can't have been an easy homecoming: her grandsons via Julia were dead, one of her granddaughters in exile, and only Julia's youngest girl, Agrippina, was both alive and living in Rome (Her great-granddaughter Aemilia Lepida had recently married and given birth to her first child, which may have provided some comfort). Scribonia had no way of knowing that the devastation wrought on her family by her former husband and son-in-law was only the beginning; worse was to come, but she did not live to see it. Tiberius was prepared to bide his time – and it would be several years before his campaign of vengeance against his ex-wife's family was complete.

4

Women Without Men

Julia (*c.*19 BC–AD 29): elder daughter of Julia and Agrippa. **Starved to death**, aged around 47

Agrippina (14 BC–AD 33): younger daughter of Julia and Agrippa, wife of Germanicus, mother of the empress Agrippina and the emperor Caligula. **Blinded, starved to death**, aged 46

It is hard to think of two sisters who have been treated more differently by history than Julia's daughters. Following tradition, they were given the feminine version of their father's name, Marcus Vipsanius Agrippa, which meant they were both called Vipsania Agrippina. There was already a woman with that name, their half-sister from their father's first marriage, but fortunately there is a way of differentiating them. The eldest of the three, who was born around 36 BC and became Tiberius's first wife, has always been known as Vipsania. Perhaps because she was the first granddaughter of a Roman emperor, the second Vipsania Agrippina was given an extra name, Julia, to emphasise her connection to the family Augustus had been adopted into. She is the Julia referred to in this chapter, while her younger sister is always referred to as Agrippina, sometimes called 'the elder' to distinguish her from her daughter of the same name. The two sisters were born around five years apart, in *c.*19 and 14 BC respectively, and they played contrasting roles in the Julio-Claudian dynasty. Agrippina was Augustus's favourite and would become the mother of an emperor and an empress, and the grandmother of another emperor. Julia's role was minor by comparison and there is reason to think that they had very different characters. They met eerily similar fates, however, demonstrating that no one was safe in a dynasty that severely punished any woman who showed the slightest degree of defiance.

Augustus, meanwhile, was intent on turning the old Roman republic into an empire which his descendants would inherit. He extended its territory substantially, up to the Danube in central Europe, along with northern Spain and Portugal, as well as Egypt and a tract of north Africa. In addition, client kingdoms in the east which had rulers installed or supported by the Romans were converted into provinces and brought under direct rule. Augustus understood that military victories would bring renown and access to wealth, but his plans came to an abrupt halt in AD 9. Roman rulers had always struggled to subdue the ferocious German tribes who lived to the north and three legions were destroyed that year in an ambush in the Teutoburg Forest, leading to the suicide of their commander, Publius Quinctilius Varus. Augustus's response to this rare event suggests that he wasn't quite as certain of the regime's stability as he appeared; he rushed troops onto the streets of Rome, fearing an uprising, and banged his head furiously against the palace doors. 'Give me back my legions, Varus!' he is said to have raged (*Quintili Vare, legiones redde!*).[1] Meanwhile, the city itself was in the process of being transformed by a series of monumental building projects, including a new Forum of Augustus overlooked by a temple of Mars the Avenger (*Mars Ultor*). The emperor boasted about these innovations, exclaiming that he had found a city built of brick and left it clothed in marble (*marmoream se relinquere, quam latericiam accepisset*).²

As a result, Augustus's granddaughters grew up in a city full of building sites. The girls were seven and two when their father died and it's very likely that Augustus took the opportunity to move them into the household he shared with Livia. They were brought up in the same strict conditions he had imposed on their mother, compelled to learn spinning and weaving, but at least they would have had access to his extensive collection of books. Children raised in the same family often have markedly different experiences and that seems to have been the case with the sisters, although we have much less information about Julia. We get a sense of Augustus's fondness for Agrippina from the affectionate letters he wrote to her, although he couldn't resist lecturing her about her writing and speaking style.³ She was allowed to remain unmarried far longer than other girls in the family, but her elder sister was married at thirteen, as though Augustus couldn't wait to get her out of the house.

The husband he chose for her was a half-cousin, Lucius Aemilius Paullus, who was the son of Scribonia's elder daughter, Cornelia. Paullus was at least ten years older than Julia and had been married before, but not much else is known about him. The couple had a daughter in the following year, 5 BC, making Julia a mother as well as a 'married woman' by the age of fourteen. Three years later, when the sisters were seventeen and twelve, scandal engulfed their mother Julia. Whether Augustus gave a moment's thought to the impact on his granddaughters of being denied contact with their surviving parent is unknown, but maternal deprivation would become a tragically common experience for children and teenagers in the dynasty. The scandal didn't prevent Julia's husband, Paullus, becoming consul in AD 1 when their daughter was six. Despite her mother's disgrace, there was no shortage of candidates for marriage to Agrippina, but Augustus was in no hurry, finally marrying her to his great-nephew Germanicus in AD 5. She was nineteen and the marriage could hardly have been more significant, creating a union that was expected to produce children with blood from the Julian and Claudian sides of the family for the first time. Agrippina's union with the dashing young aristocrat, who was the son of Tiberius's late brother Drusus, was a much more glamorous match than Augustus had arranged for Julia. The latter was twenty-four by now and the mother of a nine-year-old daughter, the aforementioned Aemilia Lepida. There is no record of how the sisters got on, if they did, or whether Agrippina's grand marriage drove a wedge between them.

Julia and Paullus led an altogether less public life, although for a time they enjoyed the wealth and privileges of their class. Paullus seems to have fallen out of favour with surprising rapidity because he held no public offices after his consulship. His disappearance from the public record is puzzling, given that he was married to the emperor's granddaughter *and* a brother-in-law of Augustus's designated heir, his wife's brother Gaius. It's not even clear whether the couple had another child, although some authorities believe they had a son about a decade after the birth of their daughter. But it's pretty clear that the storm clouds were gathering: Livia's grandson, the future emperor Claudius, abruptly cancelled his engagement to the couple's daughter, Aemilia. Suetonius blames this event on both parents, claiming they had 'offended' Augustus (*parentes eius Augustum offenderant*) in some way, but he does not specify what they had done.[4] It did at least spare Aemilia the ordeal of marriage to a man who was despised by his closest relatives, but it was an ominous signal that Augustus was angry not just with Julia's husband, Paullus, but with his granddaughter as well. It may be an early indication that Paullus's loyalty to the regime was already suspect, either because he had republican sympathies or he wanted power for himself.

A few years later, Paullus and another man were found guilty of a conspiracy against the regime. We don't know the exact date but AD 6 is likely, when there were rumours that a popular uprising was being planned in Rome. Augustus was unpopular at the time, his standing damaged by a series of natural disasters, destructive fires in Rome and resentment about high taxes. Paullus's name appears with that of someone called Plautius Rufus on a list compiled by Suetonius of individuals who plotted against Augustus; the men are described as ringleaders in one of several conspiracies that were betrayed before they could threaten the regime, but the emperor's rage at the involvement of his granddaughter's husband is not hard to imagine.[5] Paullus would have been exiled at the very least, more likely executed, leaving Julia an attractive young widow in her twenties. She would have been in a similar limbo to that endured by her mother after her separation from Tiberius, but with the added complication of a cloud of suspicion hanging over her head.

Julia's role in all this is difficult to determine. Was she plotting against the grandfather who had exiled two of her closest relatives? The temptation to identify her with her mother has proved irresistible to ancient and modern historians alike, as though she was a grubby but ultimately less intriguing version of the elder Julia. They're much more interested in this Julia's supposed 'immorality', even though she had plenty of reasons to dislike Augustus. Channelling Suetonius, Guy de la Bédoyère suggests that the two women 'seem to have shared a mutual interest' in every form of vice, as though mother and daughter enjoyed the same rather disreputable hobby.[6] 'Chic and flamboyant, she showed alarming signs of taking after her mother in more than name,' is Tom Holland's verdict.[7] These are harsh judgements, especially in light of the losses and abuse she suffered long before her own disgrace: her father's early death, child marriage, teenage motherhood, separation from her own mother, the unexpected deaths of her brothers Gaius and Lucius.

None of this is even considered in the few paragraphs afforded to her by ancient historians, who didn't record as much as a single word she uttered. The few anecdotes that have been preserved are clearly designed to show her in the worst possible light. We're told that Augustus disapproved of her supposed extravagance, once ordering a house she had built to be razed to the ground because he thought it was too ostentatious (a nice piece of hypocrisy from a man whose house on the Palatine boasted *two* libraries and a temple of Apollo).[8] Pliny the Elder, displaying his usual penchant for stories about natural phenomena, claims that Julia owned an unusually small servant, a man called Conopas who was only two feet, five inches tall, something that was evidently the fashion among aristocratic women at the time because Livia had a similarly short freedwoman (former slave) called Andromeda.[9] That's about it, and it's a pretty slender platform on which to base the character assassination Julia has been subjected to by posterity. Guilt by association is powerful, however, allowing Tom Holland to describe her as her mother's namesake, 'notorious for the raciness of her lifestyle and her taste in dwarves'.[10]

Julia is remembered these days as a frivolous airhead – if she is remembered at all, that is. It minimises the absolutely brutal nature of her treatment by her grandfather, which mirrors that of her mother while being even more savage in one respect. In AD 8, Julia was pregnant again. She was twenty-seven, still of child-bearing age and may have given birth to a son a couple of years earlier, so such an event would not have been out of the ordinary. But if it is correct to believe that her husband had been exiled or executed by then, the pregnancy would have been disastrous. The prospect of a leading female member of the Julio-Claudian dynasty giving birth to a child conceived outside marriage enraged her grandfather, challenging one of the most basic rules of Roman patriarchy. (It also, by the way, casts the demolition of Julia's house in a different light, suggesting it might have been done as a punishment rather than out of Augustus's dislike of her extravagance.)

In a previous chapter, we witnessed the degree of control the emperor expected to exert over his daughter's body, and he clearly felt the same about his granddaughter. Augustus would have regarded her swelling stomach as an unforgivable insult to his authority, denting his image of himself as the ruler who restored old-fashioned values in Rome. That much is evident in the contrast between the way he treated her and his remarkably restrained attitude towards the man named by Tacitus as Julia's lover (*nepti Augusti adulter*).[11] He was a senator called Decimus Junius Silanus and the only punishment he suffered was the withdrawal of the emperor's friendship (*amicitia Caesaris prohiberetur*).[12] Silanus correctly interpreted this as a sign that he would be wise to go into exile, but nothing else happened to him (he was allowed to return to Rome and live out the rest of his natural life when Tiberius became emperor).

Why Augustus was so lenient towards him is at first sight a puzzle, unless Silanus decided to confess all and save his own skin. A shabby deal between the two men might explain why he got off so lightly, along with the fact that he doesn't seem to have been involved in Paullus's conspiracy. It was Julia who had committed an unforgivable offence when she allowed a man who was neither her husband nor authorised by her grandfather to have access to her body; the fact that she was almost certainly a widow, and probably desperate to remarry, made no difference, although it may explain why she took the risk of becoming involved with Silanus. Like her mother before her, she had discovered how exposed she was as a patrician Roman woman without a husband, and she may have hoped for protection or even marriage with a man of her own class. Her alarm, when she realised she was going to have another child, is not difficult to imagine; perhaps she tried to hide the pregnancy, avoiding being seen in public and hoping to pass off the infant as belonging to one of her female slaves. But *someone* informed Augustus, bringing down his implacable wrath on her head. She was exiled to yet another island, this one called Tremirus, now part of the mostly uninhabited Isole Tremiti archipelago, off the east coast of Italy.

At this point, Julia's story takes a very strange turn indeed: some commentators have suggested that the sneak was not Silanus but the poet Publius Ovidius Naso, commonly known as Ovid. In what may be nothing more than a strange coincidence, reflecting Augustus's foul mood in AD 8, Ovid was exiled at around the same time as Julia. It's even been suggested that he had an affair with Julia – or, indeed, with her mother – although there is no evidence to support any of it. His sexually explicit poem entitled *Ars Amatoria* (the *Art of Love*) makes very uncomfortable reading today, offering advice on tricking women into bed and recommending force if they put up resistance, but it had been published six years earlier and is unlikely to have been the reason for his expulsion from Rome. The exiled Ovid found himself in rather more comfortable surroundings than Julia in a town on the Black Sea, where he could at least walk round and wince at the inhabitants' execrable Greek, but it didn't stop him complaining. In a series of letters known as the *Tristia* (Sorrows), he makes a cryptic reference to the cause of his exile, suggesting it was 'a poem and a mistake' (*carmen et error*).[13] He hints that he saw something he shouldn't and mentions the myth of a hunter who was punished by being transformed into a stag after he caught sight of the goddess Diana naked.[14]

It's quite a leap from this to the assumption that Ovid glimpsed Julia and Silanus embracing and passed on an irresistible piece of gossip, annoying the emperor so much that he was punished as well. But linking Julia's fate with that of a notoriously explicit poet makes the subliminal suggestion that her behaviour was far worse than a single affair with Silanus, which is evidently what some historians would like to believe. Ovid was never forgiven – and neither was Julia, who suffered one of the worst punishments it's possible to imagine for a young mother expecting another child.

Julia was pregnant when she arrived on Tremirus, and the emperor ordered that her child should be taken from her immediately after the birth and exposed. Suetonius's account of the infanticide is clinical: Augustus 'refused to allow the child born to Julia after her disgrace to be raised or acknowledged by its father' (*ex nepte Iulia post damnationem editum infantem adgnosci alique vetuit*).[15] He ordered the murder of his own great-grandchild, in other words, demolishing Tacitus's claim that Augustus 'never steeled himself to kill any of his relatives' (*ceterum in nullius umquam suorum necem duravit*) – unless, of course, a newborn doesn't count as fully human. We don't even know whether the child was a boy or a girl, although female babies were much more likely to be subjected to this species of infanticide than males. Either way, Julia's mental anguish and physical discomfort, her breasts full of milk and without a friend or relative to comfort her, is dreadful to imagine.

We are not told whether Julia was allowed to have servants living with her or whether she had any contact with other people living on the island; Tremirus is 22 kilometres from the mainland and Julia would very likely have heard about events in Rome when boats arrived with provisions, but she didn't even have her mother's company to sustain her. Around five years into her exile, she might have heard the extraordinary news that Augustus had married her daughter Aemilia to the brother of her ex-lover Silanus, confirming that his family hadn't suffered as a result of the affair. A year later, the death of her grandfather was followed by the elevation of her grim former stepfather to the principate, a development that offered no hope of her sentence being rescinded. On the contrary, news of the murders of her mother and remaining brother, Postumus, would have confirmed the hopelessness of her situation. She survived as long as she did only because her step-grandmother, Livia, supported her with an allowance, similar to the one Augustus made to her mother when she was moved to Reggio di Calabria.[16] The exact year of Julia's death is debated, whether it was AD 28 or 29, but Livia died in the latter year; if Julia was still alive, that was when her allowance would have ceased. She was in her late forties by now and barely remembered in Rome, where she had not set foot for more than twenty years. Tiberius saw an opportunity and allowed his former stepdaughter to starve to death, assuming that no one would care about the murder of the marginal figure she had become. He was correct: Julia's fate was to become one of the most forgotten figures in the Julio-Claudian dynasty.

Forgotten *and* relentlessly mythologised, a process that's still going on 2,000 years later. The official guide to the Ara Pacis, on which she appears as a child, recycles familiar claims about her, describing her as 'famous for her love of luxury, her debauchery and for her being, perhaps, the indirect cause of Ovid's exile'. It also makes the extraordinary suggestion that she died during an escape attempt in AD 28.[17] If only she had: it would be comforting to imagine that Julia's spirit was unbroken and she had sufficient resources left to try it, but twenty years in austere exile makes it highly unlikely. She died a year later, in exactly the same circumstances as her mother, and on the orders of the same man. Tiberius had never forgiven his ex-wife for their failed marriage – and he was already eyeing his next target, Julia's sister Agrippina.

* * *

Unfortunately, She Was a Nymphomaniac

Agrippina's adult life falls into two distinct halves. Her husband was the Roman general known as Germanicus in honour of his father Drusus's military campaigns against the endlessly troublesome German tribes, but his full name is uncertain. He was Livia's grandson, not much older than Agrippina, and theirs was a rare happy marriage in the Julio-Claudian dynasty; Agrippina was an adult at the time of the wedding, probably in AD 5, and she may even have had some say in who she was marrying, given that she was Augustus's favourite granddaughter. Agrippina and Germanicus were the Roman equivalent of a power couple, attracting popular affection in a way the first imperial couple, Livia and Augustus, never had. Agrippina was regarded with admiration and awe as she accompanied her husband to danger spots, effortlessly producing one child after another. Germanicus was modest and good-looking, while Agrippina was attractive and had a marked resemblance to her grandfather. Sculpted heads of the period show a woman with regular features and a long nose, her hair dressed in the more elaborate style that succeeded the *nodus* of earlier decades; she has a centre parting with carefully arranged curls drawn back from her forehead, descending to her shoulders in ringlets.

Her conventionally feminine appearance must have confused patrician men who came up against her steely character, which was already evident in the way she approached her role as a wife and mother. Nine pregnancies did not deter her from accompanying Germanicus on military campaigns in Gaul, Germany and the eastern provinces. Five of their six surviving children were probably born outside Italy, including their youngest daughter, Julia Livilla, who was born on the island of Lesbos as Agrippina and Germanicus toured Greece in AD 18. The couple were enthusiastic sightseers, making side trips to visit sites associated with the history of Rome, including Troy, original home of Aeneas, ancestor of the city's founders, Romulus and Remus; they also stopped off at Actium where their grandfathers, Octavian and Mark Antony, had faced each other in battle.

As well as being keenly aware of the heritage they shared, Agrippina was strong-willed and rash, something that fascinated but also posed a conundrum for Roman historians. She stood up to authority, which they liked, but she challenged their ideas about how women should behave, which they very much did not. Tacitus clearly finds aspects of her character troubling, having to concede that she was 'a little excitable' (*paulo commotior*) for his taste.[18] He describes her as 'greedy for power' (*dominandi avida*) and 'intolerant of equality' (*aequi inpatiens*), suggesting that she cast aside the faults of women in favour of masculine concerns.[19] That may, of course, be a Roman man's take on the fact that Agrippina resented the subordinate position forced on even the most illustrious women in the Julio-Claudian dynasty.

There *was* a precedent for Agrippina in Roman history, but it wasn't one that Roman men recalled with any pleasure. She reminded them of Mark Antony's third wife, Fulvia, who appeared in an earlier chapter of this book when she joined forces with her brother-in-law Lucius Antonius against Octavian. Velleius's sneer that Fulvia was not really a woman shows how poorly she was regarded in ancient Rome, and Agrippina's willingness to intervene directly in military affairs, although on a different scale, caused raised eyebrows half a century later. One incident stands out: in AD 15, when troops commanded by Germanicus believed they were surrounded by the enemy in Germany, they proposed the destruction of a key bridge across the Rhine, but Agrippina would not hear of it. Tacitus has a vivid description of this 'woman of huge spirit' (*femina ingens anima*) confronting the soldiers, preventing the demolition of the bridge and moving among the injured to help dress their wounds.[20]

The anecdote caused excited chatter when it reached Rome, playing well with ordinary people, who loved hearing about the exploits of the city's golden couple, but it made a sinister impression on Tiberius. It was only a year since he became emperor and engineered the death of his ex-wife, but here was her younger daughter interfering in military tactics with the apparent acquiescence of her husband. Tiberius was a dyed-in-the-wool misogynist, who never married again after his divorce from Julia, and Agrippina represented everything he most disliked in a woman. For now, he did little more than mutter darkly about what commanding officers were supposed to do with their time when a woman usurped their role.[21] But it confirmed his suspicions about Agrippina's intentions, which he interpreted as enlisting the loyalty of the legions in case there was one day a struggle between Germanicus and his own biological son, Drusus, for the succession. Augustus had made such a contest inevitable when he forced Tiberius to adopt Germanicus, shortly before the young man's marriage to Agrippina, and now Tiberius complained that she was using her youngest son, Gaius, to court popularity among the rank and file. It is not clear who actually came up with the idea of dressing the boy in a scaled-down soldier's uniform but the troops began calling him by the nickname 'Caligula', derived from the name of the boot (*caliga*) commonly worn by Roman soldiers. But Agrippina's innate sense of theatre would emerge a few years later when she easily won a contest with Tiberius for public sympathy following the death of her husband.

Agrippina's problem, like that of every Julio-Claudian woman who aspired to power, was that she couldn't transcend the limitations imposed by her sex. No matter how ambitious she was, she could exercise power only through a man, and the fact that she appeared to be an equal partner in her marriage – the dominant force, on occasion – obscured her dependence on her husband. Germanicus understood the risk she was running and tried to persuade her to exercise more caution, but it wasn't in Agrippina's character. That much would become clear after his sudden demise in AD 19, which robbed Rome of its most popular general. It was a seismic event, comparable to the deaths of Marcellus and Gaius during the reign of Augustus, but it had absolutely disastrous consequences for Agrippina. As a wife, she was powerful, untouchable even, and widely assumed to be Rome's most likely next empress. As a widow, she was overwhelmed with grief, lonely and unprotected; worse, she was at the mercy of a man whose family connections to her and her children only seemed to intensify his dislike.

Agrippina had every reason to return Tiberius's animosity, given his role in the deaths of her mother and youngest brother, and in AD 19 she would become convinced that the emperor had ordered her husband's murder. The claim that Germanicus's death was a political assassination has never been established beyond doubt, but Tiberius certainly had a motive: the removal of Agrippina's husband cleared the way for his biological son, Drusus, to succeed him as emperor, or so it appeared at the time. What is beyond doubt is the fact that Germanicus's death set in train events that would lead to his wife's destruction by her former father-in-law, initiating what would become one of the most violent and protracted examples of femicide in first-century history.

* * *

In AD 17, two years before his death, Germanicus's career reached new heights when he celebrated a triumph in Rome. He was much more popular than his adoptive brother, Drusus, whose dissolute character was a source of anxiety even to his own father. When Germanicus was given command of the eastern provinces, opinion was divided as to whether it was an honour or a ruse to get him away from Rome, but he arrived full of enthusiasm for his new post. He soon clashed with the newly appointed governor of Syria, a man called Gnaeus Calpurnius Piso, who was believed to be a close friend of Tiberius. The opportunity to have a look at ancient monuments was irresistible, however, and Germanicus seems to have been unaware of Augustus's ruling that senators could not visit Rome's old enemy, Egypt, without permission. (The late emperor was worried that they might succumb to temptation in a wealthy country that had provided a base for Mark Antony during the civil wars.) Early in AD 19, Germanicus annoyed the emperor by embarking on a tour of Egypt from end to end. Word filtered back to Rome that he had been warmly welcomed in Alexandria by people who remembered his grandfather, Mark Antony; Germanicus was careful to rebuke them for greeting himself and Agrippina with titles that applied only to Tiberius and Livia, but the emperor was not placated. To be fair, Germanicus behaved pretty much like a modern tourist during the rest of his trip, travelling to Thebes (Luxor) and marvelling over its antiquities, including the Colossi of Memnon.

On his return to Syria, he settled into quarters outside Antioch (Antakya, now in Turkey) with Agrippina and two of their younger children, Julia Livilla and Caligula. He was furious to discover that all his orders had been revoked by Piso during his absence, and a row broke out. It was at this point, when tensions were running high, that Germanicus suddenly became seriously ill. Agrippina watched anxiously as her husband's condition grew worse, and was hugely relieved when he appeared to recover. Cheering crowds poured onto the streets in Antakya, much to the annoyance of Piso, who ordered them to disperse. It appears that Germanicus ordered him to leave the province and Piso waited at a nearby port to see what would happen. When Germanicus's condition worsened again, he was convinced that Piso and his wife, Plancina, who was said to be friends with a notorious poisoner, were behind it. Germanicus died in October, with Agrippina at his bedside. He was thirty-three. When Piso heard his enemy was dead, he couldn't resist celebrating the news, going to temples and making sacrifices, while his wife was even more delighted.[22]

The cause of Germanicus's death is still debated. His symptoms included dark spots (*livores*), which appeared all over his body, and foaming at the mouth (*spumas quae per os fluebant*).[23] The fact that no one in his entourage had any of these symptoms would appear to rule out an infectious disease, although the course of his illness might indicate malaria or even rabies (there is no record of Germanicus being bitten, however). In a bizarre turn of events, a sickening stench in the dying man's bedroom prompted a search, revealing signs of what the superstitious Romans recognised as witchcraft. In a scene reminiscent of a horror film, the searchers discovered, behind the walls and under the floor, disinterred body parts (*erutae humanorum corporum reliquiae*), curses, ashes mixed with blood, and lead tablets engraved with Germanicus's name.[24]

It is the best indication we have of premeditation, because this gruesome collection of artefacts must have been planted *before* he moved into the room. Someone clearly wished Germanicus ill, but this crude attempt at witchcraft seems designed to frighten rather than kill him; it isn't even clear whether Piso had any connection with it, although the idea that there were two separate plots seems far-fetched. Germanicus certainly shared Agrippina's conviction that he had been poisoned, pleading with friends as he lay dying to use his wife to stir up public feeling against Piso and Plancina.[25] It was a risky course in relation to Agrippina, and Germanicus evidently knew it because he advised her to control her temper and avoid provoking powerful people when she returned to Rome.[26] He was more specific in private, presciently warning her about 'danger from Tiberius' (*metum ex Tiberio*).

Agrippina's next move, following her husband's death, was to display his corpse in the public square in Antakya. She was copying the example of Fulvia, who had put the body of her first husband, Clodius Pulcher, on show in Rome following his murder by a rival gang boss seventy years earlier; Fulvia's motive in staging this ghastly demonstration was a desire for revenge, and Agrippina's actions were likewise a warning that she wasn't going to remain quiet about what she believed to be her husband's murder. Rumours reached fever pitch when it was reported that Germanicus's heart was found intact following his cremation, supposedly a sign that it was steeped in poison.[27]

The grieving widow collected his ashes and began the long journey back to Rome, staging what has become one of the great theatrical scenes of first-century history. It was late in the year to embark on a sea crossing – Germanicus died on October 10 – and Agrippina paused for a few days at Corcyra (Corfu), struggling to contain her grief, before disembarking at Brundisium (Brindisi) in southern Italy, where she was met by huge crowds.[28] Local people climbed onto walls and roofs to catch a glimpse of her, and even waded into the shallows to meet her ship. Tiberius's son, Drusus, who was Germanicus's brother by adoption, travelled to meet the sorrowful procession, accompanied by the dead man's actual brother, the future emperor Claudius, and the couple's four other children. (Germanicus's sister Livilla, who was married to Drusus, was unable to join them because she had recently given birth to twin sons in Rome.) Tacitus claims that virtually the only people who didn't take part in this outpouring of grief were Tiberius and Livia, who remained out of sight because everyone knew the emperor was struggling to hide his pleasure at the death of his adopted son, and they feared looking like hypocrites.[29] Conspiracy theories flourished, and the words 'Give us back Germanicus!' (*Redde Germanicum!*) appeared on walls in Rome and were shouted aloud in the streets at night.[30] Perhaps it was at this point that the emperor realised what a formidable opponent he had in Germanicus's widow, setting in train a deadly conflict that would last for a decade.

Agrippina's public performance of grief and rage was so effective that Tiberius had little choice but to allow Piso to be put on trial for mutiny and murder; his wife saved herself by appealing to Livia, who interceded on her behalf, but Piso's trial went ahead amid hostile demonstrations outside the Senate. The evidence against him was inconclusive, but feelings were running high and few senators believed that Germanicus had died naturally. When Piso realised that Tiberius wasn't going to intervene on his behalf, he went home and was found the next morning with his throat cut and a sword lying beside him on the floor. Rumours circulated to the effect that his death was not a suicide but a murder, carried out before he could produce evidence of Tiberius's complicity in Germanicus's death. Tacitus says he knew elderly men who claimed to have seen a document (*libellum*) in Piso's hands on more than one occasion, which supposedly contained the emperor's instructions in relation to Germanicus, but no such orders were ever produced.[31]

Whatever the cause of Germanicus's death, it changed Agrippina's status overnight. It would have been hard enough for her to adapt to these new circumstances, after years of travelling with her husband and receiving the adulation of crowds, but she had lost her protection from a man she now regarded as her husband's murderer. The fact that she was able to hold her head up and challenge her former father-in-law, as she did repeatedly over the next few years, is astonishing. The horrors she had endured might have dealt a crippling blow to a less determined woman, especially now she found herself and her children marginalised, but Agrippina didn't lack courage. She would need every ounce of strength she possessed because Tiberius's son Drusus was his presumed successor, while her own sons were out of the picture. She wasn't even allowed the consolation of having them live with her; following the custom of boys being brought up in the household of their nearest male relative, her eldest sons were sent to live with their uncle, Drusus. For the moment, Agrippina *was* allowed to look after the three girls and the youngest boy, Caligula, all of whom were considered negligible in dynastic terms. (It was a judgement that could hardly have proved more wrong, but that was way in the future.) For now, the pendulum had swung in favour of the Claudian side of the family, temporarily minimising the importance of Augustus's bloodline. Agrippina was profoundly unhappy, but the situation did at least appear stable – or as stable as it could be with a hostile and unpredictable man like Tiberius in control of her destiny.

Suddenly, in AD 23, the bad luck of the Julio-Claudian men struck again. Drusus died suddenly – almost certainly of natural causes, as we shall see in the next chapter – not long after the death of one of his twin sons with Livilla. These deaths meant that Tiberius's plan for the succession, which had looked secure only four years earlier, was in tatters. With two of his preferred heirs dead, and the third only four years old, he had little choice but to turn back to Agrippina's teenage sons. Nero and Drusus were seventeen and fifteen, an age when they were considered old enough to begin taking on the responsibilities of young men destined for the highest office. Tiberius seems to have been resigned to the situation, adopting both boys and telling the Senate they were his 'only consolation in these times of trial' (*unica praesentium malorum levamenta*).[32] But he soon began to resent the boys' popularity, especially when he witnessed the Roman crowd's affection for Nero, who was said to bear a remarkable resemblance to his father. Whether or not Tiberius had had a hand in Germanicus's death, it must have felt as though the wildly popular general had returned to haunt him.

Tiberius's natural tendency towards suspicion was encouraged by Lucius Aelius Sejanus, the increasingly powerful and widely feared prefect of the Praetorian Guard (the Praetorians were the emperor's bodyguard). Tiberius had few blood relations and his refusal to marry again after his divorce from Julia meant he did not have the valuable family connections that would have come with a wife from another patrician family. He was susceptible to men who knew how to manage him, playing on his insecurities and telling him what he wanted to hear. Sejanus was far from patrician but he made himself indispensable to Tiberius, even hoping he would eventually be able, like Agrippa half a century earlier, to marry into the imperial family. Drusus's death made his widow, Livilla, the perfect candidate, but Sejanus knew that Tiberius would need time to come round to the idea of marriage to his own niece. In the meantime, Agrippina and her sons stood in his way, with every new honour confirming that her eldest boy, Nero, and not Livilla's surviving son, Gemellus, was Tiberius's heir. Sejanus encouraged the emperor's hostility towards Agrippina, surrounding her and her sons with informers. Her star appeared to have risen again, but she was in grave danger – and much worse was to come.

* * *

The full details of Agrippina's persecution by Tiberius were struck from the official record by a deliberate act of destruction. When her youngest son, Caligula, became emperor in AD 37, he staged a bonfire in the forum of official documents recording his mother's and brothers' trials on a variety of trumped-up charges. He insisted that he hadn't read them beforehand, implying that he wasn't going to pursue any of the men named as informers, no doubt prompting sighs of relief among senators who had played a less than honourable role during Tiberius's vendetta against his former daughter-in-law. Nothing Caligula said could be taken at face value, however, and it was not long before he produced what he said were the originals, accusing the men named in them of causing the destruction of his family.[33] What happened to the records after that, always assuming that Caligula was telling the truth this time rather than having memorised names before the bonfire, is anyone's guess. But histories of Tiberius's reign reveal an escalating campaign against Agrippina between AD 23 and 29, when she was finally put on trial. She was in her late thirties by now, approaching middle age in Roman terms, but there is no doubt that any number of patrician men would have jumped at the chance of marrying Germanicus's widow.

A new marriage was certainly not on Tiberius's agenda, however, and he set about isolating Agrippina by arresting her friends and sending a powerful warning to anyone who might otherwise have supported her. The emperor began picking off her confidantes in AD 24, when he ordered the arrest of her close friend, Sosia Galla, and her husband, a general called Gaius Silius. The latter committed suicide, while Sosia had her property confiscated and was sent into exile, where her eventual fate is unknown. It was only a year since Tiberius had recognised Agrippina's sons as his heirs, but he couldn't hide his irritation towards the boys, taking every opportunity to insult them and their mother. He reprimanded the priests who included prayers for the safety of Nero and Drusus beside his own, demanding to know whether they had been put up to it by Agrippina, and warned the Senate that the 'young men's impressionable minds' (*mobiles adulescentium animos*) should not be encouraged by receiving premature honours.³⁴

In AD 26, two years after Sosia's exile, Tiberius's persecution of Germanicus's family stepped up a gear; according to Tacitus, 'the chain of events leading to Agrippina's destruction' (*series futuri in Agrippinam exitii*) was initiated by the trial of her friend and second cousin, Claudia Pulchra.³⁵ (This Claudia is not to be confused with Augustus's first wife of the same name. She was the widow of the Roman general Varus, who killed himself after his defeat at the battle of the Teutoburg Forest.) The charges against her were lurid: a wearily familiar accusation of adultery was accompanied by accusations of witchcraft and involvement in a plot to poison Tiberius. Always impetuous, Agrippina was furious when she heard about Claudia's arrest, bursting in on Tiberius while he was making a sacrifice to a statue of Augustus, who had been declared a god after his death. She did not hold back, accusing him of hypocrisy for appearing to worship the late emperor while persecuting his descendants. She reminded him that she was a blood relation of Augustus, something Tiberius could not claim, and accused him of targeting her friends as a means of undermining her. Tacitus presents her words in reported speech:

> [Her grandfather's] divine spirit had not been transferred into mute statues. She, his true image, the product of his sacred blood, understood the danger she was in and had begun to dress herself in mourning. It was pointless to prosecute Pulchra, whose destruction was caused solely by her choice of Agrippina as a friend, forgetting that Sosia Galla had suffered for the same offence.³⁶

Instead of listening to her complaints, Tiberius mocked Agrippina in Greek, seizing her arm and telling her she shouldn't blame him for the fact she wasn't empress.[37] It was an unusual outburst on the emperor's part, exposing his loathing of Agrippina. She could not save Claudia, who was convicted and died in exile.

It is clear that Agrippina was fragile at this point in her life, her every move controlled by a man who exercised as much power over her as any abusive spouse. In the same year, Tiberius paid a visit to her before he left Rome for good and went to live on Capri, a confrontation she clearly dreaded. Tacitus found an account of the meeting in the memoirs of her daughter, the empress Agrippina, who heard about it from her own mother. The elder Agrippina was physically ill (*morbo corporis inplicata*) at the thought of another meeting with the emperor, and too distressed to speak for several minutes. After 'weeping for a long time in silence' (*profusis diu ac silentium lacrimis*), she pulled herself together and spoke, pouring out reproaches and pleas:

> He must relieve her loneliness and give her a husband. She was still young enough and there was no comfort for virtuous women except in marriage. There were men in Rome who would be happy to accept the wife of Germanicus and his children.[38]

Tiberius was too cowardly to reply. Agrippina could not marry anyone outside her own class and he was all too well aware of the status that would be conferred on a senator who married Augustus's granddaughter. Even though Agrippina was around forty by then, and presumably at the end of her child-bearing days, Tiberius was not going to take any risks with a woman renowned throughout the Roman world for her fertility. He simply ignored her, unmoved by her distress, and left her in the same invidious position as her mother and sister before her.

Agrippina was genuinely frightened of Tiberius by now, and with good reason. When Sejanus manipulated her through her remaining friends, telling them to warn her about a non-existent plot by the emperor to poison her, she believed every word. Why wouldn't she, when she was convinced that her husband had been poisoned on his orders? It led to an excruciating scene when Agrippina was placed next to Tiberius at a dinner party but was too terrified to eat. She sat through the evening, silent and touching nothing, until the emperor offered her an apple. She took it but handed it uneaten to a slave. It was a test: Tiberius turned to his mother and suggested it would hardly be surprising if he took extreme measures against a woman who had falsely accused him of trying to poison her (*a qua veneficii insimularetur*).[39] The incident encouraged speculation that the emperor wanted to get rid of Agrippina but didn't dare do it openly, looking instead for a means to do it on the quiet.

We would know a great deal more about the sequence of events that followed had it not been for the destruction of crucial documents by the emperor Caligula. In AD 27, Agrippina and her eldest son, Nero, were most likely put under some form of house arrest, where they were spied on by informers employed by Sejanus. Nero was kept in Rome, but at some point Agrippina was confined in a 'very beautiful villa' she owned near Herculaneum (it held such bad memories that Caligula had it demolished when he became emperor).⁴⁰ Her daughters, the future empress Agrippina and her sisters, Julia Drusilla and Julia Livilla, were sent to live with their great-grandmother, Livia.

Their brother Nero was twenty-one at the time of these events. He was impulsive, like his mother, and Sejanus encouraged bad blood between him and his younger brother Drusus, who resented Agrippina's obvious preference for the elder boy and his own position as second in line to the throne. The two young men were very different in character, with Drusus said to have a 'savage temper' (*atrox . . . ingenium*), but they were also being set up.⁴¹ In the autumn of AD 29, Tiberius sent a shocking letter to the Senate from Capri, accusing Agrippina of planning to start a rebellion. According to Suetonius, the emperor claimed she was preparing to seek sanctuary beside a statue of her grandfather – the image seems to have offered some degree of protection against legal proceedings – or throw herself on the mercy of the legions.⁴² Tacitus frames the emperor's attack in much more personal terms; he has Tiberius complaining about her 'haughty language and defiant spirit' (*adrogantiam oris et contumacem animum*), confirming that he regarded Agrippina as a woman who had not submitted to his patriarchal authority. He is also said to have chickened out when it came to Nero, accusing him of having sex with men (*amores iuvenum*) rather than treason.⁴³

The letter caused shock waves in Rome and angry crowds converged on the Senate, carrying effigies of Agrippina and Nero. Scared by the uproar, the senators hesitated, except for one brave soul who suggested that the emperor might one day regret the elimination of Germanicus's family. Tiberius reacted furiously when he heard about the Senate's delay, writing another letter in which he renewed his attacks on Agrippina and Nero. This time, the Senate backed down. Agrippina and Nero were tried, convicted and exiled to separate islands in the Pontine archipelago. They were treated like common criminals, moved around the country in chains (*catenatos*) and in closed litters, guarded by soldiers to prevent passers-by from catching sight of them.⁴⁴

Agrippina was sent to Pandateria, which must have had dreadful connotations as the place where her mother had spent five lonely years. Nero was confined on a larger island, Pontia (Ponza), until AD 31, when he was confronted by an executioner who claimed to have been sent by the Senate. The man showed him a noose and hook used for dragging corpses (*laqueos et uncos*), and the message was clear.⁴⁵ Whether Nero was murdered or anticipated his fate by committing suicide is unknown, but he was the first of Agrippina's children to meet a violent end. His brother Drusus lasted two more years, languishing in the deepest confines of the imperial palace in Rome, where he had been locked up after being accused of treason. In AD 33, after three years' imprisonment, he was starved to death, a process so horrific that Drusus tried to eat the stuffing of his mattress.⁴⁶

The boys' mother had been in exile on Pandateria for four years by then. Tiberius took a close interest in the conditions of her imprisonment, surrounding her with spies who reported that she continued to rail against him, complaining bitterly about how she had been treated. He responded with customary venom, ordering her to be savagely beaten by a centurion, as though her exile was not punishment enough. The assault was so brutal that she lost an eye (*oculum per centurionem verberibus excussit*), a nightmarish injury to endure on an island without access to Roman doctors.⁴⁷ Even that didn't satisfy the emperor, however. When Agrippina stopped eating, presumably the only method of suicide open to her, Tiberius was reluctant to let her escape his clutches. He gave orders that she should be force-fed, telling her guards to prise open her jaws and stuff her mouth with food (*per vim ore diductor infulcri cibum iussit*).⁴⁸ Amazingly, Agrippina defied him to the end, finally succeeding in starving herself to death in AD 33. News of the death of her son Drusus a few days earlier may not have arrived by the time her exhausted body gave out. She was forty-six and hardly recognisable as the imperial princess she had been in her youth.

Tiberius responded to the news of Agrippina's death by launching a tirade. Like other men who have tormented and murdered female relatives, he flung outlandish accusations against her, trying to sully her memory. He had not dared accuse her of sexual impropriety while she was alive, given that her devotion to Germanicus was so widely known, but now he let rip. He accused her of adultery with Asinius Gallus, widower of his first wife, Vipsania, an allegation made even more preposterous by the fact that he had kept Gallus in prison for years before starving him to death. No one in Rome was brave enough to say so, however. Tiberius persuaded the Senate to decree Agrippina's birthday a day of ill omen and even took credit for the manner of her death, pointing out that he could have had her strangled and thrown down the Gemonian steps in Rome.[49] The Senate, pliant as ever, passed a decree praising Tiberius for this supposed show of mercy. Sixty years after Augustus created a system of one-man rule, Rome's most eminent men were thoroughly cowed, thinking only about how to save their own skins.

Augustus's daughter and now both his granddaughters were dead, their reputations trashed without a single voice raised in their defence. His granddaughters could hardly have led more different lives – one more or less private, the other with a commanding role on the public stage – yet the outcome was the same. They died within four years of each other, exiled and alone, unable to protect their children. They had four daughters between them, still living in Rome, and the femicide that had claimed their own lives would continue for two more generations.

5

The Woman Who'd Had Enough

Livilla (13 BC–*c*.AD 31): sister of the emperor Claudius, daughter-in-law of the emperor Tiberius, aunt of the emperor Caligula. **Starved to death**, aged 42 or 43

Antonia (36 BC–AD 37): niece of the emperor Augustus, mother of Germanicus, Livilla and Claudius, grandmother of the emperor Caligula. **Poisoned or forced into suicide**, aged 72

From the outset, the Julio-Claudian emperors lived in fear of a coup or an assassination. The Romans had got rid of their kings centuries earlier and the dynasty lacked legitimacy in what Augustus and his successors like to pretend was still a republic. The first emperor and his descendants responded without mercy to threats to the regime, but one of the most troubling risks came from family members. Creating a dynasty propelled women to the forefront, but they had every reason to feel aggrieved, handed over to one man after another, even if the cause of their resentment was personal rather than political. Germanicus's sister, Claudia Livia Julia – always known as Livilla, or 'little Livia', to differentiate her from her grandmother – was married twice to men who were heir to the empire, but that is not why she is remembered.

We met her first in Chapter 1, in an entirely fictitious scene in *I, Claudius* in which she accuses Postumus of rape; Livilla was the perfect candidate for Graves's calumny because her reputation had been destroyed by the Senate and Roman historians. She was the first of the Julio-Claudian women to suffer *damnatio memoriae*, an official declaration that she was a non-person, leading to the wholesale destruction of statues and inscriptions in the wake of her death.[1] It turned her into one of the most vilified women in first-century history – erased from official records, yet such a significant figure in the dynasty that it's possible to piece together her story even though the most important source, Tacitus, is so thoroughly biased against her.

Livilla is the youngest victim of child marriage in this book. She was married at twelve, widowed at sixteen and remarried a few months later. Her parents were Augustus's niece Antonia and Livia's son Drusus, making her Julio-Claudian royalty. She rebelled against this fate, quietly but disastrously, and would become the first female member of the dynasty to be killed in Rome rather than on a distant island. The most extraordinary thing about her, however, is the allegation that her own mother was complicit in her death, making it a very early example of what's now known as an 'honour' killing. In the modern world, it's more often mothers-in-law who take part in such murders, punishing a young woman (and occasionally a young man) for choosing a partner not sanctioned by the family. But Antonia's loyalty to the Julio-Claudian dynasty was unsurpassed, making her a detached and sometimes cruel parent.

Her only daughter was a gawky child who grew up to be a very beautiful woman, according to Tacitus,[2] but the Senate's *damnatio* was so effective that very few images of her have survived. A poignant cameo in the Altes Museum in Berlin shows her in profile as the goddess Ceres, in honour of her fertility, and the presence of her twin sons at the bottom suggests it was made not long after their birth in AD 19. Livilla would have been in her early thirties at the time and her simple *nodus* hairstyle gives her a youthful appearance, even though the artist has given her a surprisingly heavy chin. Images of her mother are plentiful, by contrast, reflecting her status as one of the few universally admired women

in the dynasty. An even more striking indication of the esteem in which Antonia was held is provided by a priceless cameo showing her as the goddess Juno, wearing a gold crown studded with rubies, in the Museo Archeologico Nazionale in Florence.

Antonia was pretty much the Romans' ideal woman, always putting the family's interests ahead of those of her children, and her willingness to do the family's dirty work won her plaudits in the ancient world. She was even used as a human shield by Tiberius following the death of her son Germanicus, staying (or being kept) behind closed doors during the extravagant scenes of mourning in Rome to make the emperor's absence less noticeable.[3] There is no record of her trying to intercede with Tiberius during his persecution of her daughter-in-law, Agrippina, and her eldest grandsons, Nero and Drusus – unsurprisingly, perhaps, because her impact on the lives of her surviving children, Livilla and the future emperor Claudius, was nothing short of disastrous. Her role in the dynasty always came first, putting her on course to be the family's second matriarch after the death of her mother-in-law, Livia.

Antonia was the younger daughter of Augustus's sister, Octavia, and Mark Antony. She was born in Athens in 36 BC and never knew her father, being raised by her mother and uncle after Antony abandoned Octavia for Cleopatra. She was taken back to Rome as a baby and grew up in an unusually populous household, which included one full sister, also called Antonia; three half-siblings from her mother's first marriage; Antony's son, Iullus Antonius; and three of Cleopatra's children with Antony. (Perhaps that's why she was so willing, after her own children married and moved into their own households, to provide a home for the offspring of family members who had been exiled or executed.) Antonia was six when her father killed himself and she inherited estates in Italy, Greece and Egypt, making her a wealthy woman in her own right.

Her assets, and the fact that she was the emperor's niece, made her a catch, but she married unusually late by the standards of Julio-Claudian women, becoming Drusus's wife (and Tiberius's sister-in-law)

when she was twenty. They had three children, but the marriage was cut short after only seven years by Drusus's fatal accident in Germany. Antonia was not even thirty at the time and she would have been expected to marry again. She managed to avoid it, presumably because of the esteem in which she was held by her uncle, Augustus, who found her a great deal easier to deal with than his own daughter. Antonia benefited greatly from her status as what the Romans called *univira*, a woman who had only one husband; at a time when such women were rare, they were regarded as shining examples of wifely devotion.

We don't know how much say Antonia had about Livilla's marriage to Augustus's adopted son and heir, Gaius, as soon as she reached the minimum age of twelve in 1 BC. It's unlikely that Livilla had even begun to have periods at the time, and it's hard to see the marriage of a female child to a nineteen-year-old man as anything other than legalised rape. But Antonia's loyalty to the dynasty would more than likely have eclipsed concern for the welfare of her daughter, who was now on course to become Rome's second empress. Fortunately for Livilla, Gaius was sent overseas on a military campaign not long after the wedding and spent much of their marriage away from Rome before his death in AD 4. Unsurprisingly, the union was childless.

Livilla's second marriage, to Tiberius's son Drusus, took place within months of her becoming a widow, confirming that her childhood was long over. Her younger brother, Claudius, did not marry for the first time until he was eighteen, allowing him to spend more time at home with his mother, but that was not something to be thankful for. Claudius was disabled; unlike his athletic older brother Germanicus, he had weak legs that tended to buckle when he walked. He embarrassed his mother by bursting into spasms of uncontrollable laughter and drooling; he had a stammer and suffered from a nervous tic that led to frequent shaking of the head.[4] Modern authors have speculated about the cause, with cerebral palsy or Tourette's syndrome being the favoured diagnoses, but ancient attitudes to disability were harsh. Antonia didn't bother to disguise her contempt for her youngest child, making scathing comments about him to anyone who would listen, and her behaviour would now be considered a form of abuse. She frequently described him as a 'monster of a man' (*portentum eum hominis dictitabat*), claiming that he had emerged from the womb unfinished. She mocked his mental capacities, dismissing anyone she wanted to insult as a 'bigger fool than her son Claudius' (*stultiorem aiebat filio suo Claudio*).[5] Claudius would have had a difficult enough childhood as a disabled boy and young man at a time when doctors had no understanding of his condition, but his mother's scorn and contempt had lasting effects. Despite Robert Graves's sympathetic portrait of the future emperor in *I, Claudius*, he grew up to be a sex-obsessed glutton who often drank himself senseless.[6]

Livilla's relationship with her younger brother has been used as another stick to beat her with, even though he was only nine when she married for the first time and left the family home. Tom Holland accuses her of being 'notably spiteful' as a child, claiming that she mocked Claudius's disabilities, but the adjectives he uses about her as an adult – 'fractious, flighty, and bitterly resentful' – recall Anthony Blond's similarly disdainful dismissal of Augustus's daughter Julia.[7] It suggests that a stereotype of the Julio-Claudian women is in play here and it's important to bear in mind that accounts of Livilla's character are heavily influenced by her much later affair with the Praetorian prefect Sejanus, a sinister man who was loathed in Rome. By the time ancient historians came to write about her, Livilla had been 'convicted' in the court of public opinion of conspiring with Sejanus to murder her second husband – a 'murder' which probably never happened, as we shall see later in this chapter.

Some of the stories about Livilla are not even credible, such as the exclamation she's supposed to have made when someone suggested that Claudius might one day become emperor: she is said to have prayed loudly that the Roman people might be spared such 'a dreadful and undeserved fate' (*tam iniquam et tam indignam sortem*).[8] Yet she died in AD 31, a decade before her younger brother became emperor, and at a time when no one seriously imagined that this widely mocked junior member of the family might one day reach such an elevated position. It's hard to see why anyone would have raised such an unlikely eventuality in front of Livilla, something that suggests her supposed reaction was an invention made with the benefit of hindsight. Then there's the anecdote about Livilla's daughter, Julia Livia, who was married to her cousin Nero, Germanicus and Agrippina's eldest son; the girl is said to have spied on her husband, repeating to her mother everything he said and telling her how long he lay awake at night, information that Livilla reported to her lover Sejanus.[9] Whether either woman's intention was malicious is unclear – the marriage was unhappy and perhaps Julia Livia found a more sympathetic listener in her mother than Livilla had in Antonia – but few ancient or modern authorities are prepared to give them the benefit of the doubt.

Antonia was approaching her mid-sixties when her mother-in-law, the former empress Livia, died, and she took over care of her grandchildren, Germanicus's daughters Julia Drusilla and

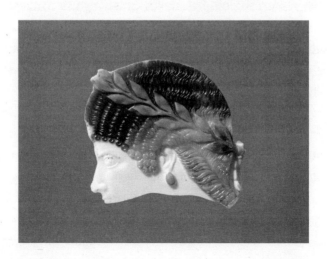

Julia Livilla, who were thirteen and eleven at the time, and his seventeen-year-old son Caligula. (The eldest daughter, Agrippina, was married by now and living with her husband.) Antonia's subsequent failure to supervise her grandchildren exposed at least one of the girls to childhood sexual abuse, something their grandmother only found out about when she discovered Caligula having sex with Drusilla (*in concubitu*) in her house.[10]

Suetonius is clear that the sex was non-consensual, claiming that Caligula 'is believed to have violated the girl Drusilla before he had even reached adulthood' (*Drusillam vitiasse virginem pratetexatus adhuc creditur*). The verb *vitiare* means 'to spoil' or 'to corrupt', and the authority on Latin sexual vocabulary, J. N. Adams, confirms that it can sometimes refer to a violent act 'even if it is not regarded as such by its perpetrator (or even victim)'.[11] It clearly suggests that Caligula was *forcing* Drusilla to have sex with him, and we know that any intervention Antonia tried to make was ineffectual; the rapes continued after Drusilla's marriage to a former consul, Lucius Cassius Longinus, and Suetonius even claims that Caligula took his sister from Cassius and 'openly treated her as his lawful wife' (*in modum iustae uxoris propalam habuit*).[12] When Caligula became emperor in AD 37, he forced Drusilla to divorce Cassius and married her to his friend, Marcus Aemilius Lepidus, presumably expecting that the latter would not oppose his claims on his sister (Caligula was rumoured to have had a sexual relationship with Lepidus himself). Dio says starkly that Caligula treated Drusilla 'as a concubine'. The future emperor would eventually be accused of 'ravishing' all three of his sisters.[13]

Modern historians have rushed to discredit these claims. Anthony A. Barrett argues that 'one should be highly sceptical' about the allegations of incest against Caligula, while Annelise Freisenbruch writes flippantly about Caligula 'bed-hopping with his sisters' and advises readers to take the 'rumours' with a grain of salt.[14] In her TV documentary about the emperor, Mary Beard casually dismisses the anecdote about Antonia discovering Caligula having sex with

Drusilla as 'granny finding them in bed'.[15] Guy de la Bédoyère is an honourable exception, arguing that there are reasons 'for considering at least a significant basis for believing the stories about incest'.[16]

It's striking, though, that so many modern commentators brush off the allegations in trivialising language. Not only is it another example of how readily they acquit the Julio-Claudian men of some of the most serious accusations against them, but it also reflects a persistent failure to recognise the scale and impact of brother–sister incest more generally. There has long been a tendency to portray it as little more than harmless sexual experimentation between siblings, even though what we know now paints a very different picture. Sensational anecdotes about Caligula's behaviour as emperor, scandalising Rome with his larger-than-life extravagance and practical jokes, have obscured the fact that he grew up in exactly the type of family where incestuous relationships were likely to happen. One modern study suggests that the absence of a father plays a key role in many instances of brother–sister incest, and we've already seen that Agrippina's children were deprived of their father in traumatic circumstances.[17] We also know that children who grow up in fractured families, clinging to each other because they cannot get sufficient affection and attention from their parents, are at greater risk of incestuous relationships. Indeed, a traumatic family history *creates* the conditions in which unhealthy and coercive sibling relationships may occur – and that exactly describes the situation in which the children of Germanicus and Agrippina found themselves. Brother–sister incest is up to three times as common as sexual abuse of a child by a parent or step-parent and almost always occurs in the context of an older boy and a younger girl who doesn't have the confidence and physical strength to resist him.[18] (Caligula was four years older than Drusilla, boys are bigger and stronger than girls, and he would have occupied a much more powerful position in the family than his sisters.) It has very harmful effects on the girls involved, producing intense feelings of guilt, low self-esteem and an inability to trust future relationships.

Had it already begun when the children were living with their great-grandmother Livia? In such a patriarchal set-up, who could Drusilla turn to when her brother began using her for sex? Even before her exile, her mother Agrippina had been distracted by grief and the conflict with Tiberius described in the last chapter. Her youngest children were shifted from pillar to post, ending up in households headed by widows who lacked the authority to restrain a headstrong teenage boy like Caligula. Antonia clearly struggled to control him, failing to put a stop to his rape of his sister, and it is not difficult to imagine the emotional scenes that followed her discovery of what was going on. Caligula's vindictive behaviour towards his grandmother when he became emperor sounds very much like that of a petulant young man, recalling ancient grievances and keen to get his own back. He would no doubt have been relieved when a summons arrived from Capri in AD 31, when he was nineteen, ordering him to go and live with his great-uncle Tiberius.

If Antonia failed as a grandmother, her shortcomings on that score were more than matched by her treatment of her own daughter. Livilla married her cousin Drusus in AD 4, reviving her hopes (more likely her mother's) of one day becoming empress; Tiberius's adoption by Augustus that year meant that his son's young wife was now one of the most prominent women in Rome. If Livilla's first marriage had been short and childless, however, her second was a disaster.

The Woman Who'd Had Enough

Drusus was around a year older than Livilla but he was widely agreed to be one of the most unpleasant young men in Rome. He was the son of Tiberius and his first wife, Vipsania, and his childhood was characterised by separations from both parents at different times. He was three when his parents divorced and it seems likely that he was taken from his mother to live with Tiberius and his stepmother, the elder Julia. When the marriage broke down and his father disappeared to Rhodes, the eight-year-old Drusus was left behind in Rome, presumably in the care of his mother. Tiberius's attitude to his son was at best ambivalent, perhaps because of the doubts raised about the boy's paternity by Vipsania's second husband, Asinius Gallus. He nevertheless encouraged Drusus's military career, at one point asking Germanicus to step aside and allow his cousin to take over an important campaign in Germany.[19]

But Tiberius also had doubts about his son's character and history tells us they were well founded. Drusus was volatile, cruel and untrustworthy. On one occasion, he went back on a deal with the leaders of a mutiny, putting them to death after sending a delegation to Rome, supposedly to ask for instructions about how to respond to the soldiers' demands.[20] Even his father was dismayed by his son's bloodthirsty temperament, reprimanding him after he organised a gladiatorial contest in Rome and 'took much pleasure in the spilling of blood, no matter how worthless' (*vili sanguine nimis gaudens*).[21] The emperor evidently thought that urban life had too many temptations for someone of Drusus's inclinations, sending him on a military campaign in the Balkans to prevent him from 'revelling in the excesses of city life' (*urbano luxu lascivientem*).[22] Dio describes Drusus as 'most licentious and cruel', claiming his reputation was so bad that the sharpest swords were nicknamed 'Drusian' after him.[23] He says Drusus regularly got into fights and was such a heavy drinker that he once turned up drunk to help the Praetorian Guard put out a house fire; when the desperate residents begged for water, Drusus mocked them by calling out that it should be served hot.[24]

Ominously for Livilla, Drusus felt intense rivalry towards the Praetorian prefect Sejanus, whose influence over his father infuriated him. The two men once came to blows when Drusus lost his temper and raised his fist to Sejanus, who retaliated by hitting him in the face.[25] Suetonius confirms this picture, describing Drusus as leading a 'loose and dissolute life' (*fluxioris remissiorisque vitae erat*).[26]

All of this suggests that the marriage was a nightmare for Livilla. Men who display a short fuse in public are rarely more restrained at home, and it is unlikely that she was spared the consequences of her husband's foul moods. One of the hints that they did not get on is evident in the history of the marriage, which is unusual, to say the least: their daughter Julia Livia was born in AD 7, but no further pregnancies are mentioned until 19, when Livilla gave birth to twins, Tiberius and Germanicus Gemellus ('gemellus' means twin in Latin).

The gap may be accounted for in part by Drusus's absence on military campaigns, but a twelve-year interval between children is unusual. Tiberius was so thrilled at the time that he boasted to the Senate that twins had never previously been born to such an important Roman.[27] Drusus was equally delighted, boasting that he missed his 'dearest wife and their many children' (*uxore carissima et tot communium liberorum*) whenever he was absent from Rome, as though they had half a dozen rather than three.[28] But it seems that Tiberius came to be unsure about the twins' paternity and suspected that their father was Sejanus, who was rumoured to have begun an affair with Livilla even before her husband's death in AD 23. (If Drusus had heard the rumours, it would explain why he was rash enough to get into a fight with the Praetorian prefect.)

Drusus's son Tiberius Gemellus was coming up to his fourth birthday when his father died. (His brother, Germanicus Gemellus, had died earlier in the year.) Drusus was almost thirty-six and his death caused shock waves in Rome, throwing the succession into doubt once again. But it's important to bear in mind that it raised no suspicions at the time, being blamed on a constitution weakened by Drusus's dissolute habits (*cum morbo et intemperantia perisse existimaret*).[29] His illness lasted for weeks but was not initially expected to be fatal, something confirmed by the fact that his father continued to turn up for meetings of the Senate.[30] Disease was rife in first-century Rome, but once again an infectious agent can be ruled out because there is no record of anyone else displaying similar symptoms. There are plenty of other conditions that could account for his death, however, and it was not the first time Livilla had lost a husband to an unidentified illness.

Tacitus makes a point of saying that no one suspected poison at the time, which is all the more remarkable given how many premature deaths in the dynasty had given rise to accusations of murder. Not a breath of suspicion attached to Livilla, or indeed Sejanus, who would both find themselves sensationally accused of murder eight years later; it was only at this point, when details of the so-called plot were revealed in the most melodramatic fashion imaginable, that a death from natural causes suddenly became accepted as foul play. This crucial sequence of events is obscured by Tacitus's year-by-year method of narration in the *Annals*, where he inserts allegations not even hinted at until AD 31 into his account of the year 23, treating them as though they were known and uncontested at the time of Drusus's death. He claims that Livilla was 'seduced into crime' (*corrupta ad scelus*) by Sejanus, who went on to recruit a eunuch called Lygdus who had a valued position in Drusus's household.[31] Tacitus admits that what he then describes, a slow-acting poison being given to Drusus with the help of Lygdus without arousing a single suspicion, only became 'known' eight years later (*octo post annos cognitum est*).³² He also acknowledges that Sejanus was so widely hated by the time of his disgrace and death in AD 31 that even the most absurd stories (*quamvis fabulosa et immania*) were believed about him.³³ That Livilla's involvement in her husband's 'murder' might be one of these fabrications does not seem to have been considered by ancient historians, although Tiberius's biographer Barbara Levick considers the accusation 'implausible'.³⁴

Livilla's involvement with Sejanus requires explanation, but will come as no surprise to anyone who has studied the behaviour of women who have been habituated to domestic abuse. He was a spectacularly poor choice of prospective husband, assuming that the sources are correct and she was keen to marry him after Drusus's death. But she was thirty-five when her husband died, and she had spent her entire adult life married to men she had not chosen. After almost twenty years with a man as unpleasant as Drusus, she would have been easy prey for someone who presented himself as her husband's polar opposite – and the evidence suggests that Sejanus was a skilled manipulator. Even Velleius, who was a friend of the prefect, portrays him as self-effacing when it suited, describing him as a man 'who demands nothing for himself and so acquires everything' (*nihil sibi vindicantem eoque adsequentem omnia*).³⁵ Velleius also praises Sejanus's virtues, describing him as vigorous in body and mind, and endowed with an 'old-fashioned cheerfulness' (*hilaritatis priscae*), a perplexing phrase given that the heroes of the Roman republic appear somewhat solemn to the modern eye. If it implies a light-hearted approach to life, however, it must have been a welcome change for Livilla after Drusus's volatile temper.

If Sejanus conspired with Livilla to kill Drusus and marry her, however, his subsequent behaviour is puzzling. He seems to have divorced his wife, Apicata, while Drusus was still alive but he was in no hurry to find a new wife; he waited until Livilla had been a widow for two years before writing to the emperor, seeking permission to marry her – and then it was because Livilla was demanding the marriage he had evidently promised her (*promissum matrimonium*), not the other way round.[36] Sejanus's letter to Tiberius, as quoted by Tacitus, sounds like an exercise in dissimulation, asking only to be considered as a candidate if the emperor happened to be looking for a husband for his daughter-in-law. Tiberius responded at length, still showing no suspicions about his son's death but reluctant to give a clear answer. The episode shows the emperor at his most controlling, replying that he could have given the easy answer (*promptum rescriptu*) that Livilla could make up her own mind or seek the advice of her mother and grandmother. But Tiberius, as usual, blamed somebody else, claiming to be anxious about how Agrippina would react and mentioning rivalry between the two women (*aemulationem feminarum*). It is true that Agrippina would have been angry if the emperor's other widowed daughter-in-law was allowed to choose a new husband when she was not, but Tiberius had private reasons for opposing the marriage – namely the prospect of the couple having a child together, creating a conflict with the interests of Drusus's surviving son, Tiberius Gemellus. The emperor cited the class difference between the couple but took care to avoid giving a definitive no, hinting that he would not always oppose 'what you and Livilla decide' (*neque tuis neque Liviae destinatis adversabor*).[37] The prefect evidently decided not to push his luck and dropped the subject, for the time being at least. A crucial section of the *Annals* is missing shortly after this point but there doesn't seem to be any record of his raising the subject with Tiberius again, which seems curious if he and Livilla had been prepared to go as far as killing her husband to make it happen.

By the beginning of AD 31, Livilla had been a widow for seven years. Tiberius was becoming worried about how much power Sejanus had accumulated since he left Rome and took up permanent residence on Capri. He suspected the prefect of plotting a coup and decided to take decisive action, allaying Sejanus's suspicions while making plans to destroy him. He offered Sejanus fresh honours, including a consulship, and held out the hope that he might finally be allowed to marry Livilla (*spe affinitatis*), who was now in her forties.[38] The Jewish historian Flavius Josephus claims that Tiberius's decision to bring down Sejanus was prompted by an explosive letter from Antonia, who had somehow discovered the prefect's designs and warned Tiberius against him.[39] It's a curious story, because even a mother as detached from her offspring as Antonia would surely have been aware of the risk that Livilla would not escape unscathed from her lover's downfall; it would be even odder if she denounced the prefect while having suspicions of his and her daughter's involvement in a plot getting on for eight years earlier to murder her son-in-law.

With or without his sister-in-law's intervention, Tiberius decided to proceed cautiously, unsure how much support Sejanus had in Rome. In October that year, he wrote to the Senate in terms that began with praise for the prefect, who was present and listened with anticipation as Tiberius's letter was read aloud, believing he was about to be given a formal share of power with the emperor.[40] But the letter gradually changed in tone and became more critical, ending with a request that two of the prefect's supporters in the Senate should be punished and Sejanus himself detained. Events then moved with great speed: Sejanus was arrested and imprisoned, while the Senate convened another meeting later the same day and condemned him to death. He was executed and his body thrown down the Gemonian steps, where it was left for three days, kicked and spat upon by passers-by before being dragged away and thrown into the Tiber. In the uproar that followed, senators who had been friends or clients of the prefect desperately tried to distance themselves, but dozens were arrested, forced into suicide or executed. Livilla's reaction to her lover's violent death is not recorded, but she would soon be dragged into the purge of Sejanus's supporters with horrific consequences.

One of the people most affected by this sequence of events was Sejanus's former wife, Apicata. It is impossible not to feel sorry for this woman, who believed she had been rejected for the emperor's daughter-in-law, but the revenge she took now was terrible. Apicata had two sons with Sejanus, Strabo and Capito Aelianus, and a daughter called Junilla. In a mark of the esteem Sejanus had enjoyed during his ascendancy, Junilla had been betrothed in infancy to the son of Livilla's brother Claudius and his first wife, Plautia Urgulanilla. The engagement ended with the boy's early death after choking on a pear,[41] but it must have been a bitter pill for Apicata to see her daughter lined up to marry her rival's nephew. Now her elder son was arrested and suffered the same fate as his father, his corpse desecrated on the Gemonian steps. Dio says Apicata saw the bodies of all three children, which must be a mistake because the younger children were murdered later, but it is entirely possible that she saw the savagely beaten remains of her ex-husband and elder son. Apicata was distraught, a circumstance which requires that what she did next should be interpreted with extreme caution. According to Dio, 'she withdrew and composed a statement about the death of Drusus, directed against Livilla, his wife, who had been the cause of a quarrel between herself and her husband, resulting in their separation'. She sent the statement to Tiberius and then killed herself.[42] Apicata's intention was clear: her final action was to seek the destruction of the woman whom she blamed for breaking up her family and causing the deaths of her ex-husband and son.

This document – a missive composed *in extremis* by a woman who had just witnessed unimaginable horrors – is how the alleged 'poison' plot against Drusus came to light. Suddenly the cause of his death eight years earlier was no longer years of heavy drinking and unhealthy habits, as everyone believed at the time, but poison administered by an unfaithful wife and her lover. It's hard to think of a version of events more likely to appeal to Roman misogyny, which regarded an adulteress as capable of anything, including murder. In his version of previously unsuspicious events, Tacitus launches into one of his most splenetic outbursts:

> Assuming the role of a passionate lover, [Sejanus] drove [Livilla] into committing adultery, and after the first disgrace had been achieved – for a woman who has lost her honour will refuse nothing – pressed her towards the hope of marriage, a partnership in power and the murder of her husband. And she – the great-niece of Augustus, daughter-in-law of Tiberius, and mother of Drusus's children – shamed herself, her ancestors and her descendants with a provincial adulterer, in order to exchange her present honourable status for a shameful and uncertain future.[43]

Tacitus is so obsessed with Livilla's 'lost honour' (*amissa pudicitia*) and her offence against the Roman class system that he hasn't stopped to think about the improbability of Apicata's accusations. In effect, he is asking us to believe Livilla would risk everything she already had in her grasp – the prospect of becoming empress on Tiberius's death and seeing her son, Tiberius Gemellus, recognised as her husband's successor – for what he himself admits was a highly uncertain outcome. Nor is it clear, given how ambitious the Julio-Claudian women were on behalf of their sons, why she would risk incurring the emperor's disapproval when Tiberius had another possible successor, his great-nephew Caligula, as an option. There had by now been plenty of warnings about what happened to women who incurred the wrath of the emperor, and none of them had been accused of anything as serious as murder.

Tiberius threw himself into an 'investigation' conducted from Capri, becoming so obsessed with finding evidence that he ordered the torture of an old friend from Rhodes, mistaking him for an important 'witness' in the case; when his error emerged, Tiberius had the man killed in an attempt to keep the story quiet.[44] He does not seem to have asked himself obvious questions: how did Apicata know about the 'plot' and why did she keep quiet for so long? The prime movers in the so-called conspiracy were members of Drusus's household, not Sejanus's, and it's not clear how she would have gained access to its most confidential secrets. Men do not usually make a habit of confiding dangerous secrets to angry ex-wives, which was certainly the category Apicata fell into. Are we supposed to believe that the eunuch Lygdus was careless enough to gossip about what he had done? That the admission reached Sejanus's ex-wife, but no one else in a city as gossipy as Rome?

Unsurprisingly, the only 'evidence' Tiberius could obtain came from Lygdus and Livilla's friend and doctor Eudemus, even though the latter seems to have been dragged into the affair only because he visited Drusus during his illness. Both 'confessed' to their part in the plot under torture. Testimony secured under torture is notoriously unreliable, but Tiberius had what he wanted: two 'accomplices' implicating his former daughter-in-law. It did not save Lygdus or Eudemus, who were sentenced to death. So was Livilla. The two men were executed but her punishment was delayed, although it's not clear whether this was due to hesitation on Tiberius's part or a consequence of the method chosen to dispatch her. Livilla's execution took place during the missing section of the *Annals*, which picks up again with her condemnation by the Senate, leaving Dio to supply the only account we have: 'I have, indeed, heard that [Tiberius] spared Livilla out of regard for her mother Antonia, and that Antonia herself of her own accord killed her daughter by starving her.'[45]

It's a horrifying story, although in keeping with Antonia's track record of always putting the interests of the dynasty before those of her own children. What happened next is extraordinary: Livilla was turned into a hate figure on a scale without precedent for a woman in ancient Rome. No fewer than forty-four speeches denouncing her were made in the Senate, with senators competing to condemn and insult her. Even Tacitus sounds taken aback, recording that the jeers and insults continued into the following year as though her crimes (*flagitiis*) had only just been exposed. 'Savage measures' (*atroces sententiae*) were decreed against her images and the very memory of her existence (*effigies quoque ac memoriam eius*) – a reference to the *damnatio memoriae*.[46]

It's hard not to believe some of this outrage was confected by senators currying favour with the emperor following the purge of Sejanus's supporters, although Livilla's alleged crime – being an accessory to the murder of the emperor's only son – no doubt caused shock waves. But it also suggests an unconscious attempt to justify Livilla's dreadful and protracted death: if Antonia was believed to have starved her own daughter, it followed that she must have been very wicked indeed to deserve it, and senators spent several months trying to convince themselves of exactly that. It feels like an overblown exercise in victim-blaming, but it also seems to have worked, because Antonia's reputation was not damaged. Indeed, the contrast between history's treatment of her and Scribonia, who had put loyalty to her daughter above everything else a generation earlier, is telling. And so is the fact that it was Antonia, not Scribonia, who was held up as a model in antiquity for other Roman women.

There is a coda to these terrible events. Antonia outlived her only daughter by five and a half years. Of her three children, only her despised son, Claudius, was still alive. Her grandson Caligula looked increasingly likely to succeed Tiberius, but he was living with his great-uncle on Capri, 270 kilometres from Rome. Caligula was seven years older than Antonia's other grandson, Tiberius Gemellus, and the revelation of his mother's affair with Sejanus had left a question mark over the boy's paternity. Tiberius couldn't decide which of the two young men to designate as his heir and hedged his bets, naming both of them in a will he wrote two years before his death in AD 37.[47]

At the beginning of that year, he embarked on a rare visit to Rome, but changed his mind within sight of the city, frightened by the death of a pet snake which he took to be a bad omen. He became ill on his way back to Capri, stopping at Misenum (Miseno) on the bay of Naples, where he ate and drank late into the night. He waved his guests off, but his return to the island was delayed by bad weather, and he died in March after a reign of almost twenty-three years. When it became known that he had died, rumours began to fly, including one that he had been given a slow, wasting poison by Caligula or denied food as he recovered from a fever (an ironic turn of events, bearing in mind how many of his enemies had been starved to death during his reign). The accounts of ancient authors are confusing and Seneca, who was alive at the time and no fan of Caligula, dismissed claims of an assassination. According to Suetonius, who had read Seneca's account, the emperor realised he was dying and tried to summon his servants; when no one came, he got out bed, collapsed and died. But Suetonius also says it was widely believed that Tiberius had been smothered with a pillow, either by Caligula or someone acting on his behalf.[48] Tacitus identifies the supposed culprit, claiming that that an order to suffocate the elderly emperor was given by Quintus Naevius Cordus Sutorius Macro, Sejanus's replacement as Praetorian prefect;[49] Dio says it was Caligula who wrapped Tiberius in thick clothes, pretending he needed to be kept warm, while Macro helped smother him.[50] Tiberius was seventy-seven and so loathed that when the news reached Rome, people ran through the streets calling for his body to be thrown down the Gemonian steps and into the Tiber, like that of a common criminal. But Caligula organised a show of mourning, accompanying the funeral procession that carried Tiberius's remains to Rome, where his ashes were installed in the Mausoleum of Augustus. Tiberius Gemellus was seventeen by now – Tacitus describes him as 'closer in blood and dearer' (*genitus sanguine et caritate proprior*) to the late emperor – but he could not compete with the glamour attaching to Caligula as the son of the greatly loved Germanicus.[51]

The Senate had declared Caligula emperor before his arrival in Rome and Antonia now found herself the new ruler's grandmother. They had not met for years, but Caligula showered her with honours, giving her all the titles bestowed on Livia during her lifetime, including that of 'Augusta'. Behind the scenes, however, his behaviour was very different. When Antonia asked to speak to him in private, he humiliated her by refusing to see her except in the presence of the Praetorian prefect, Macro. There were to be no confidential conversations with his grandmother and Caligula added an ominous warning: 'Remember I can do anything I like to anyone I like' (*Memento . . . omnia mihi et in omnis licere*).[52] Suetonius says Antonia's exclusion from the circle of her grandson's trusted advisors was one in a series of deliberate 'slights and irritations' (*indignitates et taedia*) that she found unbearable.

When Antonia died just six weeks into Caligula's reign, the timing was so suspicious that it produced all sorts of rumours, including one that he had poisoned her.[53] Antonia was seventy-two by now and her health may have been failing, but Dio has a different version of events, also identifying Caligula as the culprit; he claims the young emperor was furious when Antonia dared to tell him off about something and forced her to kill herself.[54] Caligula did not even pretend to be in mourning, watching his grandmother's funeral pyre calmly from his dining room.[55] Antonia's efforts on behalf of the Julio-Claudian dynasty, which she had made her life's work, appeared for the moment to have produced the most bitter of results – and all that was left in the way of consolation for the family's most loyal matriarch was a place for her ashes in the family mausoleum.

6

The Misogynist's Apprentice

Junia Claudilla (birthdate unknown–AD 34–37): first wife of the emperor Caligula. **Died in childbirth**, age unknown

Ennia Thrasylla or **Ennia Naeva** (*c.*AD 15–38): wife of the Prateorian prefect Macro, lover of the emperor Caligula, **forced to commit suicide**, aged around 23

Livia Orestilla (dates uncertain): second wife of the emperor Caligula. **Exiled**, cause of death and age unknown

Lollia Paulina (*c.*AD. 15–49), third wife of the emperor Caligula. **Forced to commit suicide or murdered**, aged around 34

Milonia Caesonia (birthdate unknown–AD 41): fourth wife of the emperor Caligula. **Assassinated**, age unknown

Julia Drusilla (AD 16–38): sister of the emperor Caligula. **Died of infection**, aged 21

The young man who arrived in Rome as emperor in AD 37 had none of the experience previous heirs to the principate had gained while they were preparing for the role. He was twenty-four and had never been sent to command Roman legions, surrounded by former consuls and generals who could advise him about strategy. He had no knowledge of or interest in how the constitution worked, instilling a contempt for the Senate that led to frequent conflicts. He was pretty much an unknown quantity, greeted by cheering crowds in Rome who remembered his father, the 'lost' emperor Germanicus. Caligula made much of his distinguished heritage, travelling to the Pontine islands in stormy weather to retrieve the remains of his mother, Agrippina, and his brother Nero. The urns containing their ashes were carried to the Mausoleum of Augustus at midday, when the streets of Rome were crowded, and he appointed an annual day of games and ceremonies in honour of his mother, at which her image would be paraded in a covered carriage.[1] He seems to have felt some guilt over his failure to protest about the murders of Agrippina and his brothers, boasting that he once crept into Tiberius's bedroom carrying a dagger, intent on revenge, but could not bring himself to harm the old man. (As well as showing Caligula in a good light, the story appears designed to cast doubt on the rumours about his involvement in a later assassination.)[2]

At the beginning of his reign he was idealised, displayed to the Roman people and empire in images that emphasised his youth, good looks and agility. A statue of a naked young man on a prancing horse, now in the British Museum's Great Court, has been tentatively identified as Caligula and it is certainly the kind of propaganda piece that he favoured; it's a celebration of youthful athleticism, the rider utterly unselfconscious about his nakedness and easily controlling a skittish steed. But Caligula's iconography was as much about vanity as visibility; he once commissioned a life-sized gold statue of himself (*aureum iconicum*) for a temple he built in Rome, where it was dressed each day in clothes identical to those he was wearing.³ The purpose of these grandiose gestures was to impress

the citizenry, but perhaps also himself, because Suetonius's account of his appearance tells a very different story.

Far from displaying the well-proportioned torso of the young man in the British Museum, Suetonius describes Caligula as 'very tall, with an exceedingly pale complexion and an unshapely body' (*statura fuit eminenti, colore expallido, corpore enormi*). He says the emperor had a spindly neck and legs, hollow eyes and a forbidding forehead. Most dramatically, Suetonius claims that Caligula was completely bald on the crown of his head, something that caused him great embarrassment and sat oddly with his very hairy body, which resembled a goatskin. He is said to have been so self-conscious about his appearance that he announced it was a capital offence for anyone to look down on his bald patch or even mention the word 'goat'.⁴

His insecurity was made worse by the fact that he was physically and mentally ill. As a child he suffered from seizures, like his ancestor Julius Caesar, which Suetonius attributes to the 'falling sickness' (*comitiali morbo*), or epilepsy.⁵ His unpredictable behaviour and random outbursts of cruelty suggest he had inherited the mental instability that emerged in the behaviour of his uncle Gaius after he was wounded in the ambush in Armenia more than three decades earlier. He soon displayed his ruthlessness, ordering the murder of his aunt Livilla's son, Tiberius Gemellus, even though the Senate had readily agreed to set aside Tiberius's will in which the boy was named co-heir.[6] Caligula had argued that the late emperor was not of sound mind when he made his final testament, pointing out that his grandson was too young to be a member of the Senate, let alone joint ruler of Rome. At the same time, Caligula courted popularity by honouring the legacies specified in the will, including a substantial bequest to the Roman people, along with cash gifts to troops stationed in the city. It secured him a reputation for generosity, for the moment at least, but he did not trouble to hide his pleasure in imposing pain;[7] the young emperor ordered the manager of his gladiatorial and wild-beast shows to be whipped with chains in his presence over several days, only allowing the man to be killed when the smell from his suppurating wounds became unbearable.[8] And he forced men to witness the murders of their sons, once inviting a father to dinner immediately after his son's execution, where he tried to force him to join in laughter and ribaldry as though nothing had happened.[9]

Caligula's volatile mental state was not helped by chronic insomnia, which meant that he seldom slept for more than three hours a night.[10] He had three senators woken up and brought to the imperial palace, where they expected to be sentenced to death, only to see the emperor burst onto a stage, dressed in a shawl and an ankle-length robe, and perform a song-and-dance routine before disappearing just as suddenly.[11] Such behaviour could be interpreted as an elaborate practical joke, designed to enliven a boring night, but it's clear that Caligula had a spiteful sense of humour.

He lavished titles on himself and behaved as though he was on intimate terms with the gods, appearing to hold whispered conversations with a statue of Jupiter on the Capitol.[12] It's unclear whether this was consciously performative behaviour or a symptom of mental illness, but it certainly reveals a perverse pleasure in unsettling everyone around him. When his death was announced in AD 41, people were so scared that they refused to believe it, fearing that Caligula had spread the rumour as a ruse to find out what they really thought about him.[13]

Of course the 'mad' emperor has had a bit of a makeover in recent years, just like his nephew, Nero, leading modern historians to challenge some of the most famous anecdotes about him. According to their interpretation, Caligula was an inexperienced young ruler who attracted malicious gossip, which was passed on as fact by authors hostile to the Julio-Claudian dynasty. 'Was Gaius [Caligula] really as monstrous as he has consistently been painted?' ponders Mary Beard, going on to characterise anecdotes about him as 'an inextricable mixture of fact, exaggeration, wilful misrepresentation and outright invention'.[14] Tom Holland hedges his bets when he mentions the famous story about Caligula threatening to make his horse a consul, suggesting it was one of his 'corrosive jokes' at the expense of senators who opposed him, as though they were no more worthy of the highest office than a quadruped.[15] (Holland admits that the satire, if that is what it was, 'was so cruel . . . that it seemed to the aristocracy almost a form of madness'.)[16] Another hostile story has the emperor lining up an army on the beach in Gaul, ready for an invasion of Britain, and then ordering them to collect seashells in their helmets instead.[17] (Both Augustus and Caligula considered sending forces to the islands, but it wasn't until the reign of Claudius that it actually happened.) This has been reinterpreted by modern historians either as an act of mercy on Caligula's part or another of the emperor's savage 'jokes', intended to mock soldiers who had mutinied and refused to obey orders, instead of imposing a condign punishment such as decimation (killing one in every ten). And so it goes on, humanising Caligula by endowing him with a mordant sense of humour and challenging the accusation of mental illness made by ancient authors – and by the emperor himself, according to Suetonius. He says that Caligula 'recognised his own mental infirmity' (*mentis valitudinem et ipse senserat*) and sometimes thought about withdrawing from Rome to clear his head.[18]

But it's striking that the aspect of his behaviour that really sticks in modern throats is his extensively documented abuse of women. The charges are described in detail in the ancient sources: incest with one or all of his sisters; forced marriages to women he very quickly dumped and exiled in at least one case; and his habit of inviting married women to dinner where he decided which one to rape in a nearby bedroom. A similar accusation was made on at least one occasion against his great-grandfather Augustus, as recounted in Chapter 2, although Caligula added a cruel twist of his own: when he brought his chosen victim back to the dining room, he deliberately humiliated her by praising or disparaging her sexual performance in front of her husband and the other guests.[19] Of course it is possible that the story has been recycled to damage Caligula's reputation, but it is of a piece with the rest of his behaviour, which includes many documented examples of extreme domestic abuse. What he's accused of is far worse than anything his grandmother Julia is supposed to have done. Yet it is *her* memory that's been smeared on the basis of 'evidence' from the very same ancient authors whose accounts of Caligula's reign are sneeringly dismissed as overheated or outright fabrications. It's almost as though allegations about a male member of the dynasty indulging in repeated bouts of non-consensual sex are easier to dismiss than the idea of a prominent woman becoming such a slave to lust that she slept with half the men in Rome.

Caligula's abuse of women was so obvious to ancient historians that Dio actually remarks on it, suggesting that the emperor would have turned on his fourth wife, Milonia Caesonia, if they had both lived long enough. (Dio's observation also refers to Caligula's second marriage, to a woman called Livia Orestilla, whom he abducted and raped at her wedding to someone else.) He writes:

> Though [Caligula] had proved himself the most libidinous of men, had seized one woman at the very moment of her marriage, and had dragged others from their husbands, he afterwards came to hate them all save one; and he would certainly have detested her, had he lived longer.[20]

It is rare to see Roman misogyny so frankly identified in the ancient world. It raises two questions: where did Caligula's misogyny come from and why are modern commentators so keen to downplay it?

The answer to the first question lies in the Villa Iovis, the vast palace that now lies in ruins on a headland on Capri. The jagged walls stand on cliffs overlooking precipitous drops to the sea, surrounded by startlingly blue water and offering spectacular views in all directions. Even now, it's an impressive sight and the vast cisterns that provided the inhabitants with fresh water hint at the sheer effort required to make the place habitable. It doesn't attract many visitors these days, allowing the goats that gave the island its name (*capra* is the Latin word for a she-goat) to crop the grass contentedly in what were once outer rooms of the palace. On the approach to the ruins, there is a reminder of a darker history in the form of a signpost bearing the words *Salto di Tiberio*, marking the spot from which the irascible emperor allegedly had his enemies thrown to their deaths.

Most of the stories told of Capri by ancient historians, however, are about sex, voyeurism and heavy drinking. Tiberius was nearing seventy when he arrived on the island in AD 26 and one of the first things he did was construct a kind of den (*sellaria,* literally a room with seats but also a play on the word for 'toilets'), whose interior is said by Suetonius to have included erotic wall paintings and statues displaying sexual positions, supposedly to encourage his flagging performance.[21] It also housed the emperor's porn collection, which included texts by a woman called Elephantis, a Greek poet whose sex manual, now lost, was well known in the ancient world. Pride of place in his bedroom was given to a painting by the celebrated Greek artist Parrhasius, which showed the mythical hero Meleager being fellated by the huntress Atalanta (*in qua Meleagro Atalanta ore morigeratur*).[22] Erotic frescoes are familiar to us from Pompeii, where wall paintings depicting sexual acts were acceptable forms of interior decoration and certainly not confined to taverns and brothels. But the most serious accusations against Tiberius go way beyond enthusiastic enjoyment of consensual sex, characterising him as a voyeur, rapist and paedophile. He is said to have collected boys and girls 'adept in unnatural sexual practices' (*monstrosique concubitus repertores*), who were brought to the island and required to perform threesomes in front of him. He had boys dressed up as the semi-human god Pan, who had horns and goats' legs, and posted them in stands of trees and caves alongside girls dressed as nymphs.[23] Gossip along these lines got back to Rome where it prompted ribald jokes and led to the island acquiring a nickname, Caprineum, which was a play on the word *caprinus*, meaning 'goatish'.

Tacitus offers fewer details of depravity on Capri but he refers to 'hidden lusts' (*obtectis libidinibus*) that the emperor concealed until his mother's death allowed him to 'burst into both crime and vice' (*in scelera simul ac dedecora prorupit*).[24] Tiberius rarely left the island, but Tacitus describes a journey he made to the outskirts of Rome in AD 32, three years after Livia died. He couldn't make up his mind whether to enter the city, and eventually cut short the trip so he could hurry back to the Villa Iovis:

After frequently stopping in neighbouring locations, and visiting gardens by the Tiber, he returned to the rocks and solitude of the sea, shamed by the crimes and lusts whose uncontrollable urges so inflamed him that he corrupted the offspring of freeborn parents with his vices in the manner of a king. It wasn't just beauty and attractive bodies that incited his lust but youthful modesty in some and honourable ancestry in others.[25]

Such stories have exercised a morbid fascination for centuries, dividing historians as to their veracity. John Jackson, whose translation of the *Annals* was published in 1937, summed up both sides of the dispute in a pithy passage: 'It remains impossible that all can be true and incredible that all can be false.'[26] What they also have done, however, is divert attention from the things we can say about Tiberius with some certainty. The first is the fact that his hypervigilant, distrustful character, formed when he was on the run in Italy and Greece with his parents, was already evident in childhood; one of his tutors, Theodorus of Gadara, memorably described him as 'mud, kneaded with blood' (*lutum a sanguine maceratum*).[27] Second, his adult life was characterised by an inability to form and sustain relationships with people of either sex, with the sole exception of his first wife, Vipsania. Even if he felt genuine affection for her, it didn't stop him displaying pathological jealousy of her second husband and plotting his revenge for decades. Disloyalty and abrupt withdrawals of friendship were among his most pronounced character traits, so that men who believed themselves to be longstanding friends would find themselves facing trumped-up charges, exile or enforced suicide, especially during the later years of his reign when his paranoia unleashed wave upon wave of purges.

Most striking of all, however, is his contempt for women. After his divorce from Julia in 2 BC, Tiberius would have been expected to marry again; he was thirty-nine or forty and had only one son, Drusus, at a time when more than one child was regarded as an essential defence against the hazard of premature death. After his return to Rome from Rhodes in AD 4, when he was named Augustus's heir, he was one of the most eligible men in the empire. Even if women were put off by his forbidding character, his mother and adoptive father could have found him a new wife, but Tiberius chose to remained unmarried for the rest of his life. He could not even get on with his mother Livia, who not only promoted his career at every turn but had elevated dealing diplomatically with thin-skinned men into an art. Whether or not the allegations about his sexual interest in children and teenagers have any basis in fact, the record shows he was an unrepentant misogynist who abused women long before he hid himself away on Capri.

Hatred and fear of women do not preclude a keen appetite for sex. For some men, obsessively seeking out new sexual partners is a way of 'proving' their masculinity and obscuring their deep-seated antipathy towards the opposite sex. In what appears to be a reference to oral rape, Suetonius claims that Tiberius performed humiliating sexual acts on the mouths of women from even the most illustrious families (*capitibus . . . solitus sit inludere*).[28] Dio suggests that the risk he posed towards girls and women was well known in Rome, so much so that his erstwhile friend Sextus Marius hid his own daughter 'to prevent her being outraged' by the emperor.[29] Other acquaintances were more accommodating: when Tiberius was invited to dinner in Rome by a 'lecherous and extravagant old man' (*libidinoso ac prodigo seni*) called Cestius Gallus, he agreed on condition that he would be waited on by naked girls (*nudis puellis*).[30] His decision to move to Capri removed him from the scrutiny of his mother, who was still alive at the time, and allowed him to surround himself with the pornographic images and staged performances he preferred to relationships with flesh-and-blood women.

Such was the household Caligula found waiting for him when he arrived at the Villa Iovis at the age of nineteen. His rejection of boundaries was already evident in his use of his middle sister, Drusilla, for sexual purposes, but the defining event in his life was his lengthy stay with Tiberius. The future emperor spent the next six years living in an atmosphere that was both sinister and depraved, destroying any notion he might have had about what was and wasn't acceptable. He also learned to dissimulate, treating his great-uncle with such extreme servility that he didn't even object to the murders of his mother and brothers; he arrived in the year his exiled brother Nero was murdered or forced to kill himself on the orders of Tiberius but Caligula uttered not a word of protest. It was the same two years later, when his mother and surviving brother Drusus were killed in circumstances that amounted to torture. His silence did not go unnoticed: in a memorable phrase, Tacitus says that 'neither the condemnation of his mother nor the destruction of his brother caused his voice to speak out' (*non damnatione matris, non exitio fratrum rupta voce*).[31] Suetonius says much the same, reporting that every attempt by his companions to lead Caligula into criticising the emperor met with failure, even after the 'slaughter of his relatives' (*obliterato suorum*).[32]

Apologists sometimes describe Caligula as a hostage during his time on the island, but his behaviour recalls an observation by Suetonius, who describes him as having two contradictory faults, 'extreme self-confidence and extreme timidity' (*summam confidentiam et contra nimium metum*).[33] It's a combination often found in bullies and Caligula evidently made a conscious attempt to conceal his 'monstrous character' (*immanem animam*) from his great-uncle. He carried the deception to such a degree that he waited to see what mood Tiberius was in each day and copied it, even using words and phrases similar to those employed by the emperor. His behaviour was so contemptible that one of his friends, if anyone can be accurately described in such terms, once observed that 'there

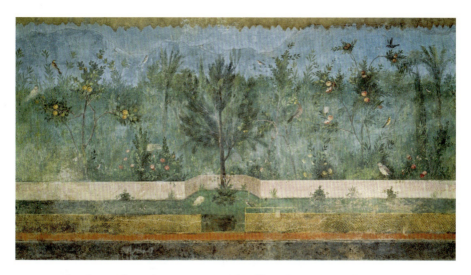

Garden fresco from the empress Livia's villa at Prima Porta, 1st century BC
(Palazzo Massimo alle Terme, Rome)

Marble head of Livia as a young
women; an AD 4 copy of an
original from 27–23 BC
(Ny Carlsberg Glyptotek, Copenhagen)

Marble head of Julia the Elder, 12–11 BC
(Musée Saint-Raymond, Toulouse)

Cameo of Tiberius as emperor with his mother Livia, AD 14–29
(Museo Archeologico Nazionale, Florence)

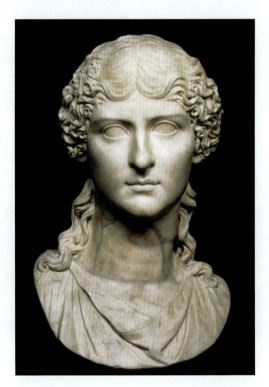

Marble head of Agrippina the Elder
(Musei Capitolini, Rome)

White chalcedony head of Antonia dressed as a priestess of Augustus, AD 41–54
(Getty Museum, Los Angeles)

Rare cameo of Livilla as Ceres with her twin sons
(Altes Museum, Berlin)

Opposite:
Marble statue of Messalina holding Britannicus,
inspired by an earlier Greek statue, *c.* AD 45
(Louvre, Paris)

Messalina returning from the brothel, Aubrey Beardsley, 1896
(V&A, London)

Marble relief of Agrippina the Younger crowning Nero, AD 54–58
(Archaeogical Museum, Aphrodisias, Turkey)

Double cameo of an imperial couple, possibly Nero and Octavia, mid-1st century AD (Museum of Fine Arts, Boston)

Marble statue, possibly of Poppaea Sabina, AD 62–65 (Archaeological Museum of Olympia, Pelopponese, Greece)

had never been a better slave or a worse master' (*neque meliorem umquam servum neque deteriorem dominum fuisse*).[34]

Tiberius was not deceived, recognising his great-nephew's 'savage and abusive temperament' (*naturam tamen saevam atque probosam*), and suggesting that in Caligula he was nurturing a viper (*natricem*) for the Roman people. Yet he allowed Caligula to throw himself wholeheartedly into 'gluttony and adultery' (*ganeas atque adulteria*), teaching him that he could take what he wanted without consequences.[35] Sex was in the air, day and night, and it is clear that the future emperor's stay on Capri confirmed all his worst traits: extravagance, exhibitionism, narcissism. But what the two men really had in common, and Tiberius no doubt encouraged, was a profound contempt for women and girls; an environment in which they had no function other than as slaves and prostitutes turned into nothing short of an apprenticeship in misogyny. No doubt the emperor would have been pleased to discover that Caligula was a chip off the old block, watching him adapt to the vile habits of the Villa Iovis without difficulty. Perhaps Tiberius enjoyed showing his young charge the famous painting in his bedroom, the one of Atalanta giving a blow job, and the excitable young man could hardly have missed his great-uncle's collection of pornography. What is clear is that when Caligula returned to Rome as emperor, he was a fully fledged sexual predator who took all his sinister predilections with him.

If Suetonius's physical description of Caligula is accurate, it is very likely that he knew himself to be unattractive to women. It is not uncommon for men who are insecure about their appearance to torment wives and sexual partners, taking pleasure in humiliating them. Caligula's sneering remark comparing his great-grandmother Livia to Ulysses shows how little he valued intelligence in women; he even added to the sensational stories circulating about his grandmother Julia, claiming she slept with her own father, Augustus,[36] who was the real father of his own mother, Agrippina (his actual grandfather, Agrippa, wasn't posh enough for Caligula). The young emperor revelled in scaring women, making a habit of kissing the throat of his current wife or lover while whispering that 'this beautiful neck will be severed as soon as I give the order' (*tam bona cervix simul ac iussero demetur*).[37] It is hard to imagine a creepier remark, given that Roman emperors really did have the power of life or death over everyone, including wives, lovers and siblings.

Indeed, there is little difference between Caligula's behaviour towards other men's wives and his own – who, remarkably, were often one and the same person: two of his spouses were actually married to other men when he forced them into marriage. He went through women at speed, even for a Roman patriarch, marrying his first wife, Junia Claudilla, while he lived on Capri. She was the daughter of a distinguished senator, Marcus Junius Silanus, who brought her from Rome to Antium (Anzio), a coastal town about 50 kilometres south of Rome, for the wedding, no doubt thrilled by the honour that was being conferred on his family.[38] Tiberius left the island to attend the ceremony, suggesting it was a grand affair, and the two men returned to Capri with Caligula's bride when the festivities were complete. Claudilla thus found herself far from her family and friends in Rome, living in a libidinous atmosphere with her husband and his great-uncle and with very few women who could become friends or support her. Presumably she had attendants, slaves owned by the family who accompanied her from Rome, but her only purpose in being on the island was to produce an heir. Suetonius records that Claudilla died in childbirth before the death of Tiberius but her significance to the Julio-Claudian dynasty was so slight that we don't know the precise date, leading to speculation that it must have happened at some point between AD 34 and 37.

Caligula was far from grief-stricken. By the time he became emperor, he was having an affair with a young woman called Ennia Thrasylla, who was the wife of the Praetorian prefect, Macro. She was also the grand-daughter of Tiberius's astrologer, Tiberius Claudius Thrasyllus, whose family were Greeks who had settled in Egypt. Not much is known about Ennia, who is called Ennia Naeva in some texts, but the discrepancy in age between her and Macro is striking; she was sixteen at the most when she was married to the prefect, who was around fifty at the time of the marriage. Caligula had effectively been an exile from Rome since AD 31, so the affair must have started when the couple visited the island. Suetonius asserts that Caligula targeted Ennia after the death of his wife, Claudilla, flattering her with his attentions until he was able to seduce her (*Enniam Naevam, Macronis uxorem . . . sollicitavit ad stuprum*). Suetonius claims that Caligula even promised to marry Ennia if he became emperor and hints that her husband was not averse to the affair, which brought him closer to the power he craved.[39] Tacitus makes a more sinister suggestion, arguing that the prefect deliberately encouraged his wife 'to seduce the young man by pretending to be in love with him' (*imitando amorem iuvenem inlicere*), hoping that the affair would further his own career.[40] Either way, Ennia was being used by one or both men and the plan, if that was what it was, backfired; on his return to Rome, Caligula used Macro to deliver Tiberius's will to the Senate, but he soon decided that the prefect had become too powerful – or knew too much about the late emperor's death.[41] He appointed Macro governor of Egypt, possibly to get him out of the way, but changed his mind and forced the couple to kill themselves.[42] Caligula had had enough of Ennia, who had served her purpose, and Suetonius records that both she and her husband were rewarded for their intimate knowledge of the emperor with a 'gory death' (*cruenta mors*).[43] Caligula had other interests to pursue, including finding a wife to replace the equally unlamented Claudilla. He showed his contempt for his connection with the dead girl's family by accusing his father-in-law, Silanus, of disloyalty and forcing him to cut his own throat.

Caligula's second marriage began at a wedding, although it was not his own. The emperor had been invited to the marriage of a woman called Livia Orestilla to Gaius Calpurnius Piso, a tall, good-looking senator who was widely liked in Rome. Piso was the grandson of the governor of Syria who had been accused of poisoning Caligula's father, Germanicus, and the emperor took great pleasure in publicly humiliating him. During the wedding feast, Caligula claimed to have taken a fancy to the bride. 'Stop hugging my wife!' (*noli uxorem meam premere*) he called out to Piso, as though he himself were the bride-groom; he then leapt up from the couch, dragged Orestilla from the room and took her home.[44] The very next day Caligula issued an announcement that he had acquired a wife 'following the example of Romulus and Augustus' (*exemplo Romuli et Augusti*) – that is, by seizing her from her husband. It's a startling admission from within the dynasty that Augustus's marriage to Livia was non-consensual, but Caligula despised his great-grandmother and wouldn't have cared. He soon tired of Orestilla, who presumably resented being transferred from one man to another like a parcel, and divorced her (within days, according to Suetonius, or after two months in Dio's version). A couple of years later, Caligula banished Orestilla for the heinous offence of returning to Piso, a rare instance of a woman being punished for 'adultery' with her own husband. Piso was exiled as well, only returning to Rome in AD 41 after Caligula's assassination. There is no record of what happened to Orestilla.

His third marriage, to an heiress called Lollia Paulina, followed a similar pattern to his second. Paulina was married to a former consul, Publius Memmius Regulus, who happened to be governor of Achaea, a province that included large sections of Greece. She was with him in the province when Caligula heard a rumour that her grandmother had been a remarkably beautiful woman, although stories about Paulina's fabulous wealth – she owned a very desirable set of gardens on the Esquiline Hill, close to what is now Termini railway station – may have been an additional attraction. He impulsively summoned Paulina to Rome, ordered her to divorce Memmius and married her. Once again, Caligula quickly turned against his new wife, claiming she was infertile, and divorced her. Abusive men can't bear to give up control, even over a woman they no longer want, and Caligula issued a spiteful order that Paulina was forbidden to have sex with anyone else for the rest of her life. It suggests she had not turned out to be the compliant wife Caligula had hoped for, perhaps because she was unusually wealthy and used to being treated with respect. (She was certainly good at putting on a show, attending a wedding in Rome wearing priceless emeralds and pearls during her brief spell as empress.)[45] Paulina is the only one of the emperor's wives we can say for certain outlived him, and she didn't have any intention of obeying her former husband's ridiculous order of lifelong celibacy, as we shall see in a later chapter.

Caligula's final wife, Milonia Caesonia, is said by the sources to have been neither young nor beautiful, but they were prejudiced against any woman who became involved with the emperor. Suetonius accuses her of 'reckless extravagance and promiscuity', but she had managed to give birth to three daughters, which would have been an attraction for the childless Caligula.[46] He seems to have been obsessed with her, dressing her in military costume and taking her with him to review the army, and she was one of the few women who seems to have had feelings for him. Roman authors found their relationship so hard to fathom that the satirist Juvenal accuses Caesonia of giving Caligula an aphrodisiac that drove him mad, but that's just another instance of ancient misogyny.[47] Even Caesonia was not spared his abusive habits, however, which included parading her naked to his friends, and Caligula refused to marry her until she was about to or had actually given birth to their daughter in AD 39 or 40.[48] Caligula named the child Julia Drusilla, after the sister he had begun raping as a teenager, and declared with pleasure that the infant's spiteful tantrums proved he was her father.

It could hardly be clearer that Caligula cared nothing for women, using and discarding them at will. He was exactly the kind of sexual predator who would have regarded his sisters as fair game as adults, yet most modern commentators baulk at the claim, as though even Caligula would not break that particular taboo. The young emperor showed no such inhibitions, once boasting about having sex with at least one of his sisters to a former consul called Gaius Sallustius Passienus Crispus. In a private conversation while they were travelling together, Caligula asked Passienus whether he had, like himself, ever slept with his own sister. 'Not yet' (*nondum*), Passienus replied, anxious to avoid upsetting the emperor by expressing shock or disapproval.[49]

Passienus appears to have told this story himself, and he was in a better position to check the truth of Caligula's boast than anyone else in Rome, having become the second husband of the emperor's eldest sister, Agrippina, after the death of her first. Tom Holland suggests they are merely a repetition of slurs used to discredit famous men in republican Rome, although he acknowledges that the earliest source, Josephus, *was* well informed about Caligula's reign.[50] Mary Beard includes the allegations in a list of tales she considers 'simply implausible', largely based on the fact that there are no contemporaneous accounts of incest.[51]

That is true, but it is also the case that key texts that might have been the source are missing. The senator and historian Cluvius Rufus not only knew Caligula but was involved in one of the conspiracies to assassinate him, yet his entire work is lost, as are the memoirs of the emperor's sister Agrippina. Tacitus *was* able to draw on Cluvius's history when he was writing the *Annals* and had clearly read Agrippina's autobiography, but his account of Caligula's reign is missing in its entirety. We can't know what these texts might have contained but Seneca, who knew Caligula and narrowly escaped execution during his reign, makes a telling observation about the emperor's character; he suggests that nature created Caligula to demonstrate what the greatest vice (*summa vitia*) is capable of when combined with unrestrained power.⁵² Seneca doesn't specify the 'vice' he has in mind, but what he is saying, in modern language, is that Caligula had no boundaries – and that is one of the characteristics of serial sexual predators.

Several later texts *do* mention incest, suggesting that it was recorded in either an oral tradition, lost manuscripts or both. Josephus asserts that Caligula committed incest with one sister: a reference to Drusilla, although she is not named. He provides the most detailed extant account of Caligula's assassination, possibly basing it on Cluvius's history, and he claims that the emperor's sexual relationship with his sister was so notorious that it turned the Roman people against him.⁵³ Suetonius writes about incest with all three sisters and says Caligula made no attempt to hide it, placing each of them in turn in the seat normally reserved for his wife at banquets.⁵⁴ The Latin contains a sexual innuendo – *infra se*, literally 'beneath him' – which was no doubt a sly reference to the rumours.

One of the things we know about sex offenders is that they flourish on impunity – and who has ever enjoyed a greater sense of impunity than a Roman emperor? To begin with, Caligula threw up a smokescreen, showering his sisters with honours and putting their heads on Roman coins. In what must have been an ironic gesture, given

the rumours flying around, he awarded them all the privileges enjoyed by the Vestal Virgins – priestesses of the goddess Vesta, who had to remain celibate on pain of death. Agrippina, Drusilla and Julia Livilla were allowed to sit alongside him in the imperial seats at the Circus Maximus, the stadium where chariot races and gladiatorial contests were staged, while magistrates and priests were instructed to offer prayers for their welfare. In reality, he seems to have cared little for two of his sisters while being mesmerised by Drusilla. When he became seriously ill during the first year of his reign, he named her the heir to his property *and* the empire, making her the first Roman woman to receive such an honour.

Caligula recovered but Drusilla fell ill the following year, during one of the fevers that periodically swept through Rome. She died at the age of twenty-one and Caligula was distraught, declaring a period of mourning so strict that it was a capital offence to laugh, go to the baths or dine with family members. Drusilla's funeral was a public affair, with the Praetorian Guard marching round the pyre, and she was declared a goddess under the Greek name Panthea ('All the Gods'). Caligula became a victim of his own credulity, paying a huge reward to a senator who claimed to have seen Drusilla ascend to heaven, and he ordered that a golden effigy of his sister should be installed in the Senate House. He also instructed that a statue should be set up in the temple of Venus in the forum, choosing the home of the goddess of love in what sounds like another nod to their relationship.[55]

It was extraordinary behaviour for a man who usually dumped wives and lovers without a second thought, and Caligula did not care what these extravagant gestures revealed about his relationship with Drusilla. What they do not tell us, of course, is anything about Drusilla's feelings towards him. She had been treated by her brother since adolescence as little more than a sex toy, married to two men chosen for her by male relatives, and endured a lack of agency in her own life for which no amount of titles and statues would have compensated. There is no reason to assume that she was content with the situation she found herself in, any more than her surviving sisters.

Siblings who grew up in a family with so much experience of grief and loss might be expected to have formed enduring bonds, but Agrippina and Julia Livilla hated their brother enough to join a coup against him in AD 39. The plot of 'three swords' or 'three daggers' was named after the weapons Caligula put on display in the temple of Mars the Avenger, with a placard claiming they were going to be used by his sisters to kill him. It was an extraordinary gesture, admitting that his own siblings were so desperate to get rid of him that they were prepared to risk their lives to overthrow him. It could only be the consequence of extreme abuse at his hands, which is exactly what Suetonius suggests; he claims that as well as having sex with his surviving sisters himself, Caligula 'often prostituted them to his horrible mates' (*saepe exolitis suis prostraverit*).[56]

Even more extraordinarily, the man accused of conspiring with Agrippina and Julia Livilla was their late sister's widower, Marcus Aemilius Lepidus, who was supposedly intended to become emperor in their brother's place. Lepidus's parentage is unclear but if he was the son of the younger Julia, as some authorities suggest, he would have been a great grandson of the emperor Augustus and might have felt he had a claim to the principate. A trial was hastily arranged before the Senate and the proceedings were sensational, involving the production of letters implicating both sisters in the plot *and* in affairs with Lepidus. Accusations of adultery were a common feature of treason trials but it sounds as though the two women were tricked into implicating themselves, with Suetonius claiming that the incriminating letters were obtained 'by deception and debauchery' (*fraude ac stupro*).[57] Lepidus, who seems to have been visiting Agrippina on her estate near Perugia when the plot was exposed, was sentenced to death and had his throat cut. In a cruel parody of her mother's journey from Syria twenty years earlier with her father's ashes, Agrippina was ordered to carry an urn containing Lepidus's bones back to Rome.

Caligula made history repeat itself again by exiling his sisters to the Pontine islands, from which he had made such a show of retrieving their mother's remains only two years earlier. Her awful fate must have weighed heavily on both women's minds as they were banished to separate islands in the archipelago, Julia Livilla to Pandateria and Agrippina to Ponza. Agrippina was forced to leave her infant son, the future emperor Nero, behind in Rome, ensuring that another child in the dynasty suffered maternal deprivation at a crucial point in his childhood. Caligula revelled in his sisters' punishment, packing them off with the threatening message that he 'had swords as well as islands' (*non solum insulas habere se sed etiam gladios*).[58] Always short of money, due to his wild extravagance, the emperor made a profit out of his sisters' exile by auctioning off their property. He had squandered the entire fortune of twenty-seven million gold pieces left by Tiberius and he sold his sisters' jewellery, furniture, slaves and even their freedmen at inflated prices, impoverishing them and making a tidy sum for himself.[59]

If the sisters feared they were doomed to die in the Pontine islands like their mother and eldest brother, they did not have to wait long for a reprieve. Caligula was so loathed by now that it was only a matter of time before he was assassinated, and one of several plots succeeded less than two years later, in January AD 41. Ironically, given Caligula's omnivorous sexual tastes, the conspiracy was led by a tribune of the Praetorian Guard, Cassius Chaerea, who could no longer stand being taunted on a daily basis as 'soft and effeminate' (*mollem et effeminatum*) by the emperor.[60] He struck the first blow in a passageway on the Palatine hill as Caligula, who had a hangover after overindulging the previous evening, returned to the imperial palace from watching the rehearsal of a play. Chaerea's first blow landed between Caligula's neck and shoulder but did not kill him, leading him to writhe on the ground and cry out that he was still alive. He was then hacked to pieces, and the fact that some of the sword thrusts were deliberately aimed 'at his genitals' (*per obscaena*) shows that his sexual misconduct was at the forefront of his assassins' minds. The attack was so ferocious that he received as many as thirty wounds.[61]

Caligula was twenty-eight at the time of his assassination and had been emperor for less than four years. He had done a great deal of damage in his short life, not least to the women closest to him. By the time of his death, two of his three sisters were in exile, where their lives hung by a thread. His fourth and final wife, Caesonia, survived him only by minutes. She was discovered shortly after his murder, lying beside her husband's body, distraught and covered in his blood. Making no attempt to escape, she stretched out her neck and was dispatched with a sword. One of the assassins then picked up her eighteen-month-old daughter, Julia Drusilla, and dashed the child's brains out against a wall.[62] It was a brutal end to a brutal reign, making Caesonia the first Julio-Claudian empress to be murdered, but she certainly wasn't the last.

Her husband would gradually metamorphose into something resembling a pantomime villain, a reminder that it is easy to laugh at dictators when you are not personally threatened by them. The Senate declared *damnatio memoriae* on the late emperor but it was the Roman people, who had grown to hate him, who dragged his statues from their pedestals and threw his images into the Tiber.[63] Some busts were altered to resemble later emperors, but so many statues of Caligula existed throughout the empire that the *damnatio* was not entirely effective.

A much more successful obliteration of images was waiting in the wings for a teenage girl called Messalina, who had been married for a couple of years by now to Caligula's uncle Claudius. She was about to become the next empress *and* one of the most reviled figures in Roman and, indeed, western history, demonstrating that it is always women who are impossible to forgive.

7

Unfortunately, She Was a Nymphomaniac: Part II

Valeria Messalina (birthdate uncertain–AD 48): Roman empress, third wife of the emperor Claudius, mother of the empress Octavia. **Stabbed to death**, mid- to late 20s

Julia Livilla (*c*.AD 18–*c*.AD 41): sister of the emperor Caligula. **Executed**, aged 22 or 23

Julia Livia (AD 7–*c*.AD 43): daughter of the younger Drusus and Livilla. **Executed**, aged around 37

Messalina was a peripheral figure in the Julio-Claudian dynasty when the Praetorian Guard discovered her husband hiding on a balcony in the imperial palace, following the assassination of his nephew. The Senate was dithering, unable to decide whether to choose a new emperor from its own ranks or declare the restoration of the republic, so the soldiers took matters into their own hands. They dragged Claudius out and proclaimed him emperor, making his young wife empress just three weeks before she gave birth to their second child. She would have spent the early days of her new role preparing for and recovering from the birth of her son, Tiberius Claudius Germanicus, which made her the mother of the presumptive next emperor as well as the wife of the latest incumbent.

The image of Messalina as a mother, cradling her infant son, is about as far as it is possible to imagine from the 'nymphomaniac' who has come down to us through Roman and later literature. But that is how she appears in a statue in the Louvre, one of only a handful of known portraits to survive the official order to obliterate her memory. It is a modest image, showing her as a young Roman matron with her robe pulled up to cover her hair, which is arranged in formal curls over her forehead. The boy, now aged two or three and known as Britannicus in honour of his father's conquest of Britain, is balanced on her left hip, suggesting that the sculpture is intended to represent Messalina a couple of years into her husband's reign.

The survival of the statue is remarkable and suggests that it might have been kept hidden for a time after her death. It is a poignant reminder that two children, Britannicus and his elder sister Claudia Octavia, lost their mother when Messalina was murdered. It is also in stark contrast to the popular image of the empress, who is still being presented in the twenty-first century as a sex fiend who emasculated her besotted husband: 'Messalina was notorious for her wantonness and ascendancy over her husband', according to an entry describing the statue in the catalogue of the library of the Massachusetts Institute of Technology.[1] So how did the young mother come to be transformed into the Messalina we know today, whose name has become shorthand for any woman who cannot contain her sexual urges?

Much of the damage can be traced back to Juvenal, who wrote about her in his Sixth Satire around the year AD 115, almost seven decades after her murder. Even now, it is hard to disentangle the real woman from the nightmare version created by Juvenal's poison pen. The poem consists of a lengthy diatribe against Roman women and marriage, and its most famous set piece presents Claudius as the hapless victim of his evil spouse:

A soon as [Claudius's] wife believed him to be asleep, this prostitute-empress (*meretrix augusta*) dared to put on a travelling hood and set out with no more than a single maid, preferring a mattress to her bedroom in the palace. Hiding her black hair with a blonde wig, she entered the brothel, which had a foul smell of stale blankets, and headed to her own empty cubicle; there, standing naked and for sale with her gilded nipples on display, and using the working name Lycisca [she-wolf], she exposed the womb you came from, noble Britannicus. She greeted new arrivals with flattery and asked them for money. Too soon for her liking, when her pimp sent away his girls, she left the brothel reluctantly, closing her cubicle at the very last moment, still burning with the lust of her stiff clitoris (*adhuc ardens rigidae tentigine vulvae*). She left exhausted by her clients but nothing like satisfied, a filthy creature with cheeks dirty and blackened by smoke from the lamp, taking the disgusting stench of the brothel back to the cushioned couch of the palace.[2]

It hardly needs saying that this is a complete fabrication. It is nothing more than a pornographic fantasy, seething with prurient excitement and disgust (the blonde wig is a telling detail, blonde hair being associated with foreign women and prostitutes). Yet its influence has been incalculable, fixing Messalina in the popular imagination as the empress to whom nothing mattered but sex. Juvenal knew exactly what he was doing when he wrote about Messalina in this way: *meretrix augusta* is one of the most lethal phrases ever applied to a Julio-Claudian woman, chosen to remind Roman readers of a similar insult – *meretrix regina*, or 'prostitute-queen' – hurled at Cleopatra by the poet Propertius more than a century earlier. The satirist's choice of words links Messalina to a foreign monarch who posed a serious military threat to Rome (more accurately, to Octavian's plan to found a dynasty) and Roman ideas about masculinity. It also serves as a reminder that Messalina's great-grandfather Mark Antony abandoned his chaste Roman wife, Augustus's sister Octavia, for an Egyptian 'whore'.

We have already seen that the label 'prostitute' was applied liberally in the ancient world, meaning little more than a woman who had sex with someone other than her husband, so it comes as a shock to find Juvenal interpreting the 'prostitute' part of the phrase literally – and an even greater shock that so many people have accepted it as fact. As recently as 2004, the zoologist and popular author Desmond Morris repeated Juvenal's slur and embroidered it in one of his books, talking about 'the wild nymphomaniac Messalina' and the 'nymphomaniac wife of the long-suffering Claudius'. Morris seems to think Juvenal was reporting real events, claiming in his book that the empress was so excited by brutal sex with strangers that she would sneak out at night wearing 'a whore's wig' and prowl the streets, sometimes engaging in such violent 'lovemaking' that she knocked off her wig.[3] It is not just ancient authors who enjoy fantasising about Messalina.

She is not, of course, the first woman from the imperial family to be accused of selling her body. Juvenal's fictional account of the empress's shifts in the brothel recalls Seneca's claim about the supposed forays into prostitution of Augustus's daughter Julia in the forum half a century earlier. Where Julia was portrayed as an amateur, however, Messalina is evidently more enterprising, finding herself a job and a pimp. The common factor is that both women are accused of doing it not for money, which neither of them needed, but because they could not get enough sex through affairs. We might spare a thought for the men of the Julio-Claudian dynasty at this point – was it something in the genes that drove their wives and daughters to behave as recklessly as this?

The calumnies heaped on Messalina suggest a rather different explanation, which is that as the role of women in the dynasty became more prominent, the misogyny of Roman authors was becoming ever more extreme. No doubt conditions in ancient brothels were unpleasant, not least because the women were at risk of disease and violence, but the smells and sights in Juvenal's fantasy are designed to trigger revulsion. He's so keen to disgust his readers that he doesn't even attempt to explain how the sweaty, smelly subject of his fantasy got back into the imperial palace, one of the most closely guarded establishments in Rome, without raising suspicions. Suetonius tells us that Messalina and Claudius were still sharing a bedroom two years into his reign, which raises the question of why he never woke up to find her missing and ask where she was.[4] Did anybody in the ancient world ever ask *any* questions at all – or were they too busy enjoying a vivid piece of porn?

Juvenal's use of language exposes the conflicting emotions felt by Roman men when they contemplated a woman who deviated from the narrow maternal ideal required to maintain the bloodline. The giveaway is the Latin noun *tentigo*, which was typically used of a *male* erection, to describe the state of Messalina's clitoris at the end of a long night in the brothel.[5] Even Mark Antony's wife Fulvia, who was such an alarming figure for Roman men during the civil wars, was allowed to keep her woman's body, but Messalina's lust turns her into a woman with something more like a male sex organ. It is impossible to avoid wondering at this point whether Juvenal had ever actually seen a clitoris, most of which is located inside the female body, but that is not the point. Her state of insatiable arousal is a reminder of her voracious sexual appetite, which threatens to wear out and emasculate a constant stream of lovers, her 'erection' long outlasting theirs.

Juvenal's masturbatory fantasy was probably inspired by a gross anecdote in Pliny the Elder's *Natural History*, a curious work that mixes scientific observations with literally incredible claims. The book was published in AD 77, not quite thirty years after Messalina's murder, and includes a scholarly treatise on the sexual habits of various animals, with one startling exception. Pliny observes that while most animals come on heat at specific times of the year, men are able to have sex at any time and are never satisfied, but the only example he offers is a woman, Messalina. He claims that the empress was so proud of her sexual stamina that she once set up a contest with a 'notorious' professional prostitute to see which of them could get through the greatest number of lovers in a single session; according to Pliny, Messalina won easily, having sex with one man after another until she had exhausted twenty-five partners.⁶ If you ask any woman about this anecdote, she will look horrified, imagining the bruises, abrasions and vaginal tears that a sexual marathon of this kind would inflict on the female body; it is something more likely to be imposed on women against their will, as the Japanese military did to captured Korean women during the Second World War, than to be embarked on voluntarily. But a modern website exaggerates even further, claiming that Messalina slept with 150 men in a single night.⁷

Such stories were a gift for generations of artists and authors. In the seventeenth century, a play entitled *The Tragedy of Messalina, the Roman Empress*, was performed in London, where it presented her as suffering from a 'pleurisy of lust'.⁸ Around the same time, the Dutch artist Nicolaes Knüpfer painted a bare-breasted Messalina romping on a four-poster bed with one of her lovers; the Rijksmuseum in Amsterdam, which owns the painting, tells us that its subject is the 'promiscuous' empress whose 'frenzied greed ultimately led to her downfall'. A late eighteenth-century painting by a Danish artist, Nicolai Abildgaard, is nominally a portrait of the dying Messalina and her mother, but the empress looks more like a woman exhausted by an enthusiastic bout of sex.

We are clearly in the realm of high-class pornography here, providing male artists with an excuse to paint bare breasts, like an early version of the *Sun* newspaper's notorious Page 3. But the artist who was most faithful to Roman writers' misogynist vision was the Victorian author and illustrator Aubrey Beardsley, who produced two portraits of the empress in 1895 and 1896 for a privately printed edition of Juvenal's Sixth Satire. They are cruel caricatures, the first showing her setting out for the brothel with a servant, blonde wig askew and huge breasts billowing over the top of her corset, a garment not invented until long after the Roman empire collapsed. In the second, she is returning to the palace after a busy night servicing clients, dragging herself up a flight of stairs with a grumpy expression, presumably because of that throbbing clitoris. The V&A, which owns the latter drawing, helpfully explains that it shows Messalina 'angry that her lusts remain unsatisfied'. In both illustrations, Beardsley has portrayed her as a distinctly flabby middle-aged woman, even though Messalina was not even thirty at the time of her murder.

It's easy to forget there was a real woman behind these hostile representations, a girl rather than a woman in fact, and that she was forced into a sexual relationship with a dissolute man more than thirty years older than her. The *damnatio memoriae* declared by the Senate following her murder did its job all too well, turning Messalina into a blank screen onto which generations of men projected their fantasies. Piecing together the facts of her life is difficult, given her erasure from the official record, and key historical texts have been lost. The manuscript of Tacitus's *Annals* for the early part of Claudius's reign is missing, picking up again only in the year before Messalina's murder, while Suetonius sticks very much to the official line. He denounces her 'shameful deeds and crimes' (*flagitia atque dedecora*), although he does at least acknowledge that it was Claudius, who affected to know nothing about it, who condemned her to death.[9] Dio writes about her at length, but he doesn't even try to conceal his bias against her.

Valeria Messalina was empress from AD 41 to 48 but we don't even know her age with any certainty. It's usually assumed she was in her late teens when she married Claudius in AD 38 or 39, but some modern commentators believe she may have been as young as fifteen.[10] Patrician girls were usually married in their early teens and Messalina was one of the most eligible young women in Rome; it's not obvious from her name, which is the feminine version of her father's, Marcus Valerius Messalla Barbatus, but she was Julio-Claudian royalty to the core. As well as being descended from Augustus's sister Octavia, she was a cousin of the future emperor Nero, and had connections to the Claudian family as the niece of the Claudia Pulchra banished by Tiberius. Her mother was a woman called Domitia Lepida, but we don't know the date of her marriage to Messalla. (Domitia Lepida and her elder sister, also called Domitia, were granddaughters of Mark Antony. The exact dates of their births are not known but the elder girl may have been considerably older than her sister. Messalina's mother is usually known as Lepida to avoid confusion between the two women.) Messalina's immaturity and impulsiveness during her period as empress certainly favour the idea that she was in her mid-teens at the time of her marriage to Claudius. But there is no doubt about the age gap between bride and groom, given that the future emperor was approaching fifty when Messalina was handed over to him. He was actually a contemporary and a cousin of her father, and had already dumped two previous wives, one of them in a singularly unpleasant fashion.

We know very little about the early years of their marriage, when Claudius would have been preoccupied with his research (he wrote histories of Rome, the Etruscans and the Carthaginians, none of which survive) and Messalina was pregnant with their children. But his new role following Caligula's assassination meant that he had weightier matters on his mind. Claudius knew the history of his family and realised that one way to consolidate his unexpected position as *princeps* was to follow the example of his great-uncle Augustus and expand the empire. His reign saw a dramatic expansion of Roman territory to include the province of Judaea, along with parts of modern-day Turkey, Bulgaria, Greece, Austria, Slovenia, and a swathe of north Africa. But his most ambitious plan was to extend the empire's northern boundary.

No Roman ruler had attempted an invasion of Britain since Julius Caesar's incursions in 55 and 54 BC, almost a century earlier, but Claudius's mind turned to the islands within two years of becoming emperor. The Roman legions, led by a general called Aulus Plautius, quickly dealt with any local resistance although attempts to assert wider control would continue for many years. Claudius travelled to Britain to celebrate their victory in AD 43, narrowly avoiding being shipwrecked en route. The emperor was away from Rome for six months in all and Suetonius is scathing about the shameless way he took credit for the successful campaign; he points out that Claudius neither took part in any battle nor shed any blood (*sine ullo proelio aut sanguine*) but awarded himself an extravagant triumph (*triumphavitque maximo apparatu*) on his return to Rome.[11] His young wife followed his chariot through the streets in a covered carriage, although she is fully visible in a fantastical cameo now in the Cabinet des Medailles in Paris, portraying the imperial couple in a chariot drawn by serpents.

The emperor's absence on his British adventure may well have come as a relief to Messalina, who would later take advantage of another of his trips from Rome to go through a bigamous wedding with her lover. Four or five years into her marriage to Claudius, the empress had had plenty of time to become familiar with her husband's disgusting personal habits; Claudius was gluttonous, a heavy drinker, and believed it was bad for the health to hold back farts, even during dinner. Here is Suetonius's description of his behaviour at meals:

> He was greedy for food and wine whenever and wherever he happened to be . . . He never left a dining room until he was bloated with food and soaked with wine (*distentus ac madens*), and as soon as he was lying on his back with his mouth open, a feather was inserted to relieve his stomach.[12]

Once he had woken up and vomited, no doubt he would have wanted sex; if anyone in this book could fairly be described as sexually insatiable, the fourth Julio-Claudian emperor is the perfect candidate, although I've never seen him accused of satyriasis, which is the male equivalent of 'nymphomania'. Suetonius talks about his 'huge appetite for women' (*libidinis in feminas profusissimae*), while Tacitus supplies the names, Calpurnia and Cleopatra, of the two 'concubines' – prostituted women, most likely – with whom he had sex most frequently.[13] He certainly wasted no time in impregnating his young wife: their daughter Octavia was born towards the end of AD 39 or the beginning of 40, followed by Britannicus in February 41.

In the light of Messalina's reputation, it's striking that Claudius had no doubts about the paternity of either of the children they had together. He had previously divorced his first wife, Plautia Urgulanilla, with whom he already had a son, while she was pregnant for a second time because he suspected she had been unfaithful with a freed slave called Boter; he publicly repudiated the daughter she gave birth to less than five months after the divorce, having the child placed naked outside the door of Urgulanilla's house in a deliberate act of humiliation.[14] After two pregnancies in such a short space of time, Messalina had no more children, despite her youth and the emperor's 'passionate love' (*amorem flagrantissimum*) for her.[15] It was not reciprocated, confirmed by the fact that she tried to divert his attention elsewhere by providing him with 'housemaids' with whom he could have sex.[16] The women were probably slaves and not in a position to refuse, which hardly reflects well on Messalina, but it's a sign of the sexual disgust she felt towards her farting, snoring, vomiting husband. It's also evidence of his promiscuity, raising the possibility that he infected his wife with a sexually transmitted disease that made her infertile.

But the fact that the young empress did not get pregnant at all after the birth of Britannicus is not easy to explain, if – and it is a big if – she had as many lovers as ancient authors claim. The list is so long, and based on so little evidence, that it seems she had only to smile at a man or do him a favour to have it assumed that they were lovers. Take a soldier called Sabinus, for instance, whom Dio describes as the former prefect of Caligula's German bodyguard. The officers chosen by the late emperor included a number of Thracian gladiators and it may be that this Sabinus was one of them (and thus not to be confused with the Cornelius Sabinus who was a tribune in the Praetorians and one of Caligula's principal assassins). Claudius loved watching men fight to the death and he took great pleasure in ordering Sabinus to take part in a fight with a professional gladiator, which Sabinus was supposed to lose. When he unexpectedly won the match and was about to be killed on the orders of the emperor, Messalina stepped in to save his life, leading people to jump to the conclusion that they had had an affair.[17] A diametrically opposite story is told about Polybius, one of Claudius's former slaves, who was supposedly executed after the empress made false accusations against him, even though they had been lovers.[18]

It should be evident by now that Messalina could not win, that any interaction with a man was interpreted as evidence that they had slept together, even when other explanations were equally if not more plausible. Her friendship with a well-known doctor, a knight called Vettius Valens, is said to have been sexual, even though a fertile young woman who did not want to get pregnant again might well have sought out a doctor for medical advice. The empress's avoidance of further pregnancies was sufficiently striking to be a matter of speculation in Rome, but no one seems to have imagined that she might have consulted a doctor; they preferred to see it as 'evidence' that she had either been a prostitute herself or knew women who were, because they were believed to have superior knowledge about how to prevent conception. The notion that Messalina moved in such circles, and sought advice from women who worked in brothels, was irresistible to ancient misogyny. But it is remarkable how often women accused by Roman historians of having an unbridled appetite for sex did not get pregnant as a result.

What we can say with certainty is that Claudius's elevation to the principate brought about an equally dramatic change in the fortunes of his wife. Messalina was transformed overnight from leading an uneventful (and probably miserable) life as the spouse of a man widely considered a buffoon to being the most prominent woman in Rome. A vista of unlimited flattery, wealth and influence opened before her and it would have turned the head of many girls, especially one with as little experience of life as the new empress. Seventeen-year-old girls are not even regarded as adults according to most modern conventions and it is hard to think of anyone less qualified for the position Messalina now found herself in, without even a useful role model to guide her conduct.

Augustus's carefully orchestrated invention of the principate, less than a century earlier, had provided a handful of women in the imperial family with unparalleled visibility and influence. But Livia was older and a great deal more mature than Messalina when she became Rome's first empress, and the position remained vacant during Tiberius's period as emperor. Caligula's first two marriages after he became emperor were too brief and chaotic for his wives to make a mark, and while his final spouse, Caesonia, was technically empress, she hadn't held the position for long when she was assassinated alongside him. Messalina might well have been nervous about stepping into Caesonia's shoes but there is no evidence that she was – or that she understood she was at risk of becoming the perfect scapegoat for her husband's cruel and authoritarian rule.

Claudius's portrayal as a scholar-emperor, more interested in history and academic research than political intrigue, obscures the fact that his reign was as brutal as those of his predecessors. It was certainly comparable in terms of treason trials and death sentences: thirty-five senators and 300 knights were executed while Claudius was in charge, according to Suetonius, who had access to official records.[19] As the first emperor whose predecessor had been assassinated, Claudius lived in perpetual fear of meeting the same fate, made worse by his awareness that he was not the Senate's choice. He saw threats in every quarter and targeted men he regarded as rivals, by virtue of their wealth or standing, with mostly trumped-up charges. Members of his own family weren't spared, but these executions didn't sit well with his image of himself as an unworldly and, indeed, reluctant monarch, prompting some truly remarkable memory lapses.

It is worth bearing in mind, at this point, that Claudius was by his own admission a talented actor who had used his physical disabilities as cover during his nephew Caligula's reign, freely acknowledging that he employed a pretence of 'stupidity' (*stultitiam*) to stay alive.[20] As emperor, he repeatedly threw up his hands and denied all knowledge of death sentences he had himself ordered, laying claim to a degree of absent-mindedness that simply defies belief. The pretence served him well, allowing him to portray himself as so forgetful that he could not remember orders he had given in the previous twenty-four hours; he sometimes sent for men to give him advice or play dice, appearing to work himself up into a temper when they failed to appear, and had to be 'reminded' that he had sentenced them to death just days earlier. His amnesia supposedly extended even to Messalina, whose absence at dinner he queried shortly after her murder.[21] The anecdote is literally incredible, designed to absolve him of responsibility for ordering the execution of the mother of two of his children. But Claudius's 'forgetfulness' has been taken largely at face value, allowing him to disclaim knowledge of executions and forced suicides that suited him down to the ground.

Some of these sentences were obtained in highly irregular circumstances, in a room in the imperial palace rather than at a formal trial before the Senate, and the obvious inference is that they were staged in this way to allow Messalina to be present. History loves a Lady Macbeth figure and the young empress's attendance at scenes that led to someone's condemnation appears at first sight to lend credence to the notion that she was pulling the strings. What emerges from a closer reading of the sources, however, is a portrait of an impressionable young woman who was easily manipulated by older, utterly cynical men; not just her husband but a trio of freed slaves, Pallas, Narcissus and Callistus, who had been granted positions of unprecedented power and influence at Claudius's court.

Some freedmen were highly educated and of Greek origin, and their origins were not necessarily obscure. At least one of the three, Pallas, had longstanding links with the imperial household; he had originally been owned by Claudius's mother, Antonia, who was said by some sources to have trusted him so much that she used him to carry her letter denouncing Sejanus to Tiberius on Capri. Slaves could not be manumitted (freed) until they were at least thirty, and Claudius's freedmen had had time to reach high office at the imperial court, suggesting they were closer in age to the emperor than his wife. They were in effect ministers or secretaries of state, wielding so much power that Suetonius sneers that Claudius 'played the part of a servant, not an emperor' (*non principem sed ministrum egit*).[22] This spiteful remark is also a jibe against Messalina, but it is a misreading of her relationship with her husband's ministers, who were adept at working through other people to get what they wanted.[23] The idea that the empress, in her late teens or early twenties, was able to manipulate a cabal of men in their forties or fifties who knew some of the dynasty's closely kept secrets is implausible. But she was useful to them and her husband, allowing political motives for getting rid of prominent people to be obscured by allegations that they were a consequence of her jealousy of other women or her vindictiveness when a man refused to sleep with her.

Claudius was not reticent when it came to killing members of the imperial family, including two of his nieces. Suetonius is clear that it was the emperor who ordered their executions, but Roman historians were more than happy to pin the blame on Messalina. Caligula's youngest sister, Julia Livilla, was targeted early in the new emperor's reign, probably during the first year, when Claudius was feeling far from secure. The emperor had recalled both her and her sister Agrippina from the Pontine islands, where they had been sent by Caligula following the exposure of the 'three daggers' plot, but Julia Livilla was soon in trouble again. She was a beautiful young woman, and she seems to have been accused of adultery with Seneca, whose political career had brought him into the highest echelons of Roman society. He had been elected as a public official (*quaestor*) during the reign of Caligula, entitling him to a seat in the Senate, but his skill as an orator infuriated the emperor. He sentenced Seneca to death but on being told that the philosopher was gravely ill and unlikely to survive, he didn't insist that it should be carried out.[24] If the accession of Claudius felt like a reprieve, however, Seneca's relief didn't last long. Dio says the charge of adultery with Julia Livilla was an excuse for the emperor to get rid of his niece, but Seneca would spend the next eight years in exile on Corsica.[25] (If Seneca was wrongly accused of sexual misconduct with Julia Livilla, it didn't give him pause for thought when he came to write about her grandmother, the elder Julia, fifteen or so years later.) Julia Livilla's real offence was most likely her marriage in AD 33 to a senator called Marcus Vinicius, who had been considered as a possible next emperor by the Senate in the hours after Caligula's assassination. The combination of his popularity and his wife's bloodline made them a formidable couple, and Julia Livilla soon found herself heading back to the Pontine islands. Messalina would have been recovering from the birth of her son at the time, with two children under the age of three to occupy her, but Dio blames the entire affair on her jealousy. She was supposedly worried about her husband's affection for his niece, a puzzling claim since the emperor wasn't sufficiently fond of Julia Livilla to spare her life; within months of her return to Pandateria, she was starved to death, becoming the fifth Julio-Claudian woman to be murdered in this horrible way.[26]

Not long afterwards, Claudius ordered the execution of her confusingly named cousin, Julia Livia, once again with an obvious political motive; she was well connected in Julio-Claudian terms, being a granddaughter of Tiberius, and had a son by her second marriage who was a possible rival to Britannicus. Julia Livia was put to death by the sword even though she had not faced formal charges (*quamvis crimine nullo*) and was given no chance to defend herself.[27] Dio can't resist blaming this murder on Messalina as well, claiming she was jealous of Julia Livia 'just as she had been jealous of the other Julia'.[28] He even claims that she murdered Julia Livilla's widower, Vinicius, three years later, because he refused to sleep with her.²⁹ Vinicius was in his fifties by then and there is no evidence that he died of anything but natural causes, but ancient historians love the idea that so many powerful men died because they refused the petulant empress's advances.

A hostile stereotype, the sexually and emotionally incontinent woman who can't bear rejection, is very much in play here; Dio even claims that Messalina tried to sleep with her stepfather Appius Silanus, a former governor of Spain, who was exactly the kind of influential figure who would have made the emperor anxious.³⁰ Dio and Suetonius both accuse the empress of conspiring with one of the imperial freedmen, Narcissus, to incriminate Silanus by exclaiming they had had the same dream, in which he attacked the emperor.³¹ But neither historian considers the possibility that Claudius was in on it, using his wife and his minister to get rid of an over-powerful rival. Messalina's role in the trap suggests she was both easily manipulated and singularly lacking in emotional intelligence, for she doesn't seem to have considered the impact of Silanus's execution on his widow, her mother Lepida. It prompted a breach which was not mended until hours before the empress's murder five years later, removing a confidante who might have advised her against the foolhardy behaviour that led to her destruction.³²

But Messalina's involvement in the 'trial' of another leading figure, the former consul Decimus Valerius Asiaticus, adds to the impression that she colluded with her husband – and offers a revealing glimpse of the highly charged emotional atmosphere in which the couple operated. Claudius distrusted Asiaticus, who was originally from Gaul where he could command the loyalty of local tribes. Asiaticus was also fabulously wealthy and believed by many to have been involved in the assassination of Caligula, although he never admitted it. (According to Josephus, when Asiaticus was publicly accused, he replied simply by expressing regret, saying 'I wish I had been'.)³³ It was hardly an anecdote that would have reassured Claudius, yet Messalina was blamed for instigating the prosecution against Asiaticus, supposedly because she was jealous of his mistress, a well-connected woman called Poppaea Sabina.[34] Claudius presided over the proceedings, which were held in a bedroom of the imperial palace, a highly irregular procedure that allowed Messalina to observe. The trial was a farce, with the prosecutors trading insults with Asiaticus as they accused him, confusingly, of adultery with Poppaea Sabina *and* effeminacy. Asiaticus's defence greatly moved several of those present, including Claudius, while Messalina was reduced to tears. It sounds more like an episode of *The Jeremy Kyle Show* than a formal hearing, and Asiaticus was so disgusted by all the histrionics that he went home and killed himself. So did his lover, Poppaea, supposedly after she was threatened with imprisonment. Messalina was rewarded for her part in the affair with the famously beautiful Gardens of Lucullus, which Asiaticus had been renovating on the hill where the Borghese Gardens now stand.

These events are not to the empress's credit, but they suggest she was an accomplice in plots that originated with Claudius and his ministers, rather than the prime mover. If she *was* being used by these cunning older men, rather than the other way round, we would expect her to survive only as long as she was useful to them – and that is exactly what happened. Nothing could illustrate the power imbalance more than the circumstances of her murder, which was orchestrated by the very men who were supposed to be her closest allies. And it is telling that they decided to destroy her at the moment when she provided irrefutable evidence that she had moved not just beyond her usefulness, but beyond their control.

In AD 48, Messalina took the biggest risk of her life, going through a bigamous marriage with a senator called Gaius Silius during her husband's temporary absence from Rome. The question of why she did it, and how she could possibly have expected to get away with it, has exercised the minds of historians ever since. What they have rarely, if ever, taken into account is the impact on the character of a teenage girl of being forced into a premature sexual relationship with a physically repellent and flagrantly unfaithful older man.

Adult men have always wanted to have sex with much younger women. That taste is catered for in the twenty-first century by a proliferation of 'sugar daddy' websites that bring together men with ample financial resources and women in their teens or twenties who are short of cash. The relationship is essentially mercantile, trading 'gifts' for sex, even though the websites go out of their way to present it as a fair exchange rather than a disguised form of prostitution. The exploitative nature of the transaction is more obvious when it involves the phenomenon known as 'grooming', where girls from impoverished backgrounds are lured into sexual relationships by older men who work in the night-time economy. Gangs of sexual predators have been exposed in a series of English towns and cities where girls as young as twelve were drawn into illegal relationships with men in their forties and fifties through gifts and attention, sometimes becoming pregnant as a result. Some perpetrators have been prosecuted and received long prison sentences for rape and sexual assault, but it emerged during a series of inquiries that police officers and social workers routinely indulged in victim-blaming, accusing the girls of being 'promiscuous' or 'slags who knew what they were getting themselves into'.[35]

Such assumptions ignore the fact that this kind of sexual exploitation is very damaging, teaching girls that relationships are transactional rather than based on mutual affection and respect. Messalina would have learned as much early in her marriage to Claudius, yet it is striking how often assumptions about culpability and free will are misapplied to girls in previous centuries. Cultural acceptance of coerced marriage in ancient Rome did not mitigate the damage – rather the opposite, in fact, because children and teenagers married to elderly husbands had no escape route.

Messalina may have regarded the attention she received when she became empress as compensation for being forced to have sex with a man more than thirty years older than herself. But that doesn't alter the fact that what influence she had derived from a toxic relationship in which she was very much the junior partner.

Some recent biographers have suggested that Messalina regarded sex as a route to power. Guy de la Bédoyère argues that 'her use of sex is perhaps best seen as an expression of power in its own right, rather than the pursuit of carnal pleasure',[36] but that doesn't explain a series of infatuations with personable men who were decades younger than her husband. She had nothing to gain from her affair with a popular actor and dancer called Mnester, who evidently entranced a number of prominent women. The relationship did her a great deal of damage, making her the subject of malicious gossip, while Tacitus describes patrician outrage at the thought of 'an actor prancing in the emperor's bedroom' (*histrio cubiculum principis insultaverit*).[37] Dio's version of the affair makes it sound like an adolescent crush, claiming that Messalina could not bear to be parted from Mnester and made him miss performances, infuriating audiences who had paid to see him and knew perfectly well what was going on.[38]

It evidently suited Claudius and his freedmen to play along with Messalina, allowing her to believe she was more in control of events than she actually was; perhaps she had by now come to regard the emperor as an indulgent father figure, especially if she had succeeded in providing him with substitutes to avoid having sex with him herself. But it is very likely that the men's skilful manipulation of the naive young empress led her to make a catastrophic error about what she could get away with. The fact that she had in effect been groomed from a very young age, denying her the opportunity to mature emotionally and learn how to make sensible decisions, is the key here.

Messalina's infatuations had always been risky, but after a decade of marriage she fell in love with the persuasive Silius and listened to him when he held out the prospect of an entirely different future. Silius was twenty-five years younger than Claudius, reputed to be the best-looking man in Rome, and his career was on the rise; he was due to be consul the following year, having restored his family's fortunes after the disgrace of his father who had killed himself during the reign of Tiberius.[39] Silius worked on Messalina's fears and desires, telling her he was prepared to adopt Britannicus and suggesting that a marriage would leave her power and status undiminished, while waiting for Claudius's death was fraught with risks. The emperor was approaching sixty, but his health had improved dramatically since he rose to power, and he might easily live for another ten or fifteen years.

Messalina was anxious about the situation she found herself in, worrying that Silius was using her and might discard her once her husband was out of the way. At the same time, her behaviour suggests she was genuinely in love and desperately wanted to believe that a different life was possible. Tacitus says as much, observing that she gave in to Silius's entreaties because she 'longed for the name of wife' (*nomen . . . matrimonii concupivit*), implying that she had never really felt married to Claudius.[40] Indeed, the fact that she agreed to 'marry' Silius, despite her doubts, shows something that has rarely been acknowledged about Messalina: far from being a scheming femme fatale, she was accustomed to pleasing male authority figures. Like other young women who have been manipulated by older men since childhood, she was used to doing what *they* wanted. Her judgement, which had been clouded by the hothouse emotional atmosphere of her husband's court, let her down badly – and the consequences were catastrophic.

This is very much the version of events proposed by one of the earliest texts to mention Messalina's bigamous marriage. A play called the *Octavia*, written not more than thirty years after Messalina's death, has already been mentioned in the introduction to this book. The identity of the author is unknown, but it was written by someone who was an insider at the imperial court, although the traditional attribution to Seneca is now thought to be unlikely; he's hardly noted for his sympathy to the Julio-Claudian women, and, in any case, the play refers to events after his suicide in AD 65. The main character is Messalina's daughter, Octavia, and it's set in the year 62, when she was divorced and exiled by her husband, the emperor Nero. It is remarkable first and foremost for its sympathetic account of Octavia's ordeal at Nero's hands, providing one of the earliest descriptions we have of the impact of deliberate and sustained domestic abuse. But it is also notable for its treatment of her mother, which represents a radical departure from the victim-blaming familiar from later Roman texts.

The play predates the histories written by Suetonius and Tacitus by around half a century, suggesting the existence of a very different tradition in relation to the empress which has been all but buried by hostile interpretations. It presents Messalina as unable to resist her passion for Silius, driven to desperate measures by Venus, the goddess of love; Octavia herself refers to 'the cruel madness of my poor mother' (*furore miserae dura genetricis meae*) and blames her death on Claudius, holding her father responsible for an 'abominable murder' (*caedem . . . nefandam*). She recognises that the marriage to Silius was doomed, conjuring up a nightmare vision of the couple's wedding where one of the Furies appears, her hair scorched and snakes writhing about her body; she steals the torches from the marriage chamber and quenches them with blood, plunging the lovers into darkness. There is no mention in the play of Messalina having any lovers apart from Silius, nor of the sexual incontinence attributed to her by later authors. When Octavia starts to work herself up, remembering the terrible consequences on herself of her mother's folly, her elderly nurse intervenes, telling her not to disturb Messalina's ghost. 'She has paid a heavy price for her madness' (*graves furoris . . . sui poenas dedit*), the nurse reminds her.[41] It is a sentiment rarely, if ever, expressed in later sources – and it suggests that much of what has been alleged about Messalina by Roman authors is a post-mortem addition.

By the year 48, the empress was in her prime. Her husband had already divorced two previous wives, but he showed no sign of wanting to get rid of her, and the idea of a Roman empress initiating a divorce was unthinkable. Messalina was stuck in a miserable marriage, with no obvious way out until the mad idea of marrying Silius came along. Naturally, ancient historians don't see it like that, making ludicrous claims about her motivation: Tacitus accuses the empress of growing bored with adultery and being in search of 'new thrills' (*incognitas libidines*), while Dio makes the implausible claim that she was embarking on an experiment in polygamy.[42] There is, of course, a much simpler explanation, which is that the young empress was acting out a romantic fantasy – and, like many people in the grip of a fantasy, she refused to acknowledge the likely outcome.

This interpretation is confirmed by the fact that she made no plans for the aftermath of the 'wedding', which took place in the autumn of that year when Claudius left Rome to visit the harbour he was constructing at Ostia, around 30 kilometres south-west of the city. Even for someone travelling in a litter, as Claudius usually did, it was only a matter of hours from Rome, but it seems to have been a case of out of sight, out of mind, as far as Messalina was concerned. She behaved as though her husband did not exist, which was wishful thinking on a grand scale, but Silius's failure to think ahead is perplexing. Did he assume that marrying the empress would automatically make him emperor – or that his own status, as a senator and consul-elect, would be enough to facilitate a transfer of power? He would have been wrong on both counts, but the couple paid more attention to the wedding and the party that followed than the political earthquake they had unleashed.

In contrast to the horror-movie scenario described in the *Octavia*, the wedding was a joyous affair with all the trappings of a legal marriage: the empress wore a *flammeum*, the flame-coloured Roman wedding veil, sacrificed to the gods and held a celebratory dinner. The happy couple then spent the night together 'as husband and wife' (*noctem denique actam licentia coniugali*), blissfully unaware of the alarm ripping through Claudius's ministers.[43] To begin with at least, Pallas, Narcissus and Callistus appear to have believed they were witnessing a coup, so much so that 'the imperial household trembled' (*domus principis inhorruerat*).[44] It was only seven years since the assassination of Claudius's predecessor, Caligula, and the imperial freedmen were terrified by the prospect of chaos or, even worse, regime change. Like the empress, they overestimated Silius's intelligence and strength of mind, which would soon turn out to be an illusion, but they decided she had to be eliminated.

There is something repellent about the spectacle of these powerful men, supposedly Messalina's closest allies, coldly discussing how best to save themselves; they condemned her out of hand, deciding she should not be allowed a chance to defend herself, and that meant avoiding a trial at all costs. What they were proposing was, in effect, a coup against the empress. Two of the freedmen started to have second thoughts at this point, perhaps recalling the fate of their colleague Polybius, whose execution had been blamed on Messalina. Their alternative suggestion was to threaten her into leaving Silius while keeping the wedding quiet. They decided, however, that such a course of action would effectively make them accomplices and was too risky for themselves, leaving an opening for Narcissus. He insisted on reverting to a version of the original plan, which was that the empress must be condemned without advance warning. And the way they would do it was to present her as flagrantly unfaithful, hurling names of her supposed lovers at the emperor until he felt thoroughly humiliated.

Whether Messalina and Silius seriously intended to seize power is doubtful, and it is clear that the target of the conspiracy being planned in Rome was not the emperor but his wife. Claudius's extended stay at Ostia, where no one had yet dared tell him about the marriage, worked in the freedmen's favour; as the lovers partied, blithely assuming they were safe while the emperor was out of the city, his ministers moved fast to secure their destruction. One of their main concerns was how to deliver the bad news to Claudius without themselves becoming a target of the emperor's rage. In a vivid example of Roman double standards, Narcissus decided to use the emperor's concubines, the women with whom he regularly committed adultery, to reveal his wife's adultery with Silius. Calpurnia and Cleopatra jumped at the chance, rushing to Ostia and blurting out that Messalina had 'married' Silius. Narcissus, who had hung back while this was going on, launched into a cunning speech, couched in terms of concern for the emperor's welfare while offering a list of the empress's alleged lovers. He concluded with a killer line, asking Claudius if he was even aware he had been divorced.[45] He hadn't, of course, but the emperor was shaken to the core. He summoned his friends and advisers, including the prefect of the Praetorian Guard, Lusius Geta, who confirmed the awful news of the 'marriage'. When they urged Claudius to act, he revealed his cowardly nature, asking plaintively whether he was still emperor (*an ipse imperii potens*).[46]

The 'newlyweds', meanwhile, were oblivious to all this. It is hard to fathom what they were thinking: Messalina behaved like a bride who could not get enough of her new husband, while he simply went along with the charade. They amused themselves by staging a pretend grape harvest in the grounds of Messalina's house, surrounded by vats overflowing with wine, while her female attendants wore animal skins in imitation of followers of the Greek god Dionysus. If it sounds like a *Bacchae*-themed party, the revellers would have been well-advised to remember that Euripides's play ends with the young king of Thebes being torn apart by women who've been driven mad by the god. The empress's hair was dishevelled and she appeared to be in a state of post-coital bliss, prompting Tacitus to denounce her as 'never more given over to voluptuousness' (*non alias solutior luxu*).[47] It's a puzzling observation if Messalina had really had as many lovers, and was as jaded by sex, as ancient authors suggest; if it's accurate, perhaps it's another indication that the stories about her promiscuity have been wildly exaggerated. Silius was just as relaxed, wearing an ivy wreath and the platform-soled boots favoured by actors on the Athenian stage, while a noisy chorus whirled around him.

These details confirm what should be evident by now: this was a staged event, with everyone – bride, groom and attendants – celebrating the couple's nuptials as though it was all just one long jamboree. Indeed, the empress's friends seem to have regarded the whole thing as a huge joke, evidenced by a remark of her supposed lover, the doctor Vettius Valens, who climbed a tall tree in the garden as a prank. Asked what he could see, he called down cheerfully, 'a fierce storm heading from Ostia!' (*tempestatem ab Ostia atrocem*).[48] It is highly unlikely that he would have made such a joke if anyone in Messalina's entourage seriously expected to be put to death within hours.

When word arrived that Claudius was on his way back to Rome from Ostia, furious and intent on revenge, the mood changed. The enormity of what they had done finally seems to have dawned on the couple, although neither of them had any way of knowing that their enemies were scheming to bring about their deaths. Messalina and Silius said hurried farewells and went their separate ways, not knowing if they would ever see each other again. If anything, Silius seems to have been even more detached from reality than his 'bride', making his way to the forum as though nothing untoward had happened – either that, or he was resigned to his fate.

The empress showed more spirit, leaving the detritus of the wedding party and going to the Gardens of Lucullus, where she began trying to work out the best line of defence. She decided her best shot was to throw herself on her husband's mercy with their children in tow. She sent word that the children should set out to meet their father on the road from Ostia while she asked for a meeting with Vibidia, the most senior of the Vestal Virgins. As she pleaded with Vibidia to intervene with the emperor on her behalf, the empress was abandoned by all but three attendants, according to Tacitus, who is keen to portray her as shamed and isolated. He claims she had to walk from one side of the city to the other, and the only vehicle she could find on the road to Ostia was a cart used for removing garden waste (*vehiculo quo purgamenta hortorum excipiuntur*), a detail that may be accurate but seems designed to associate her with death and decay.[49]

Messalina's instincts were sound, however. The army had remained loyal to Claudius, there had been no attempt at an assassination and there was no evidence that she had planned a coup; perhaps she hoped to persuade her husband that he was dealing with exceptionally foolish behaviour rather than a serious attempt at regime change. Narcissus had taken too many risks to change his plan, however, and he made sure to get a place in the litter that was to take the emperor back to Rome, dripping poison into his ear throughout the journey. Indecisive as ever, Claudius seems to have been wavering, at one moment bemoaning his wife's 'shameful conduct' (*flagitia uxoris*) and at the next giving the impression he was prepared to forgive her, recalling 'episodes from their marriage and their children's infancy' (*memoriam coniugii et infantiam liberorum*).[50]

Soon Messalina came into view, presumably getting down from the rubbish cart in time to make herself presentable. The two parties met in the road, where the empress wept and begged Claudius to listen to the mother of Octavia and Britannicus. In another of the highly charged scenes that characterised Claudius's reign, Narcissus began shouting over her, producing a document prepared in advance that listed her supposed infidelities. What happened next contradicts portrayals of the empress as an isolated and despised figure; it was not just the children who joined her in the road but Vibidia, who spoke 'indignantly' (*multa cum invidia*) on Messalina's behalf, insisting that a wife should not be executed without being permitted a defence.[51] This woman, who was in every sense the antithesis of the empress – the Vestals were required to remain virgins on pain of death – took an enormous risk when she spoke up for Messalina.

Narcissus was furious and ordered the children to be taken away, but there was not much he could do about Vibidia; he knew it would be sacrilege for him to give instructions to as august a person as the chief Vestal, and he was forced into a climb-down. He assured her that Claudius would give Messalina a hearing and suggested that Vibidia should now return to Rome and attend to her religious duties. The Vestal's intervention had an effect because Messalina was not arrested, in spite of the accusations against her, and she was allowed to return to the Gardens of Lucullus, where she began preparing her defence for the following day. She was evidently recovering her spirits because Tacitus describes her as 'not without hope and with occasional flashes of anger' (*nonnulla spe et aliquando ira*).[52] Messalina knew she had been reckless and pushed the emperor too far, but she also knew that she was not guilty of involvement in a serious conspiracy.

Narcissus feared events were getting away from him and he insisted on taking the emperor's party direct to Silius's house in Rome, where he pointed out heirlooms from the imperial family which had been given to him as gifts by the empress. The ploy was successful: Claudius worked himself up into a fury, even though he still had not been presented with evidence of a coup. He allowed Narcissus to escort him to the Praetorians' camp, but he was so overcome by shame that he could barely speak coherently. Silius was brought onto the platform for some sort of trial, where he did not even attempt to mount a defence, merely asking that he should be allowed a quick death.[53]

Messalina's friends, including some who had taken part in the festivities that followed the 'wedding', had also been rounded up. There is a parallel here with the arrests that followed the exile of Augustus's daughter Julia, when fun-loving young men who may have been no more than close friends were punished for sleeping with her. The doctor, Vettius, 'confessed' but we don't know to what.[54] At least ten men were executed as 'accomplices' in the so-called plot but it's unclear what the charges were; the defence offered by some of the accused suggests they were charged with sleeping with the empress rather than trying to effect regime change. The actor Mnester protested that he had sex with Messalina only after being told to obey her wishes by the emperor himself, and pointed out that taking part in a coup would have been against his interests, putting him at the mercy of Silius if he became emperor.

Claudius appeared to be on the verge of forgiving Mnester, but the freedmen protested, claiming that when his offence was so serious it didn't matter whether it was voluntary or coerced (*sponte an coactus*).⁵⁵ It seems they were suggesting that adultery with the empress was as deserving of the death penalty as treason, and that was certainly true in the case of a good-looking young man called Sextus Traulus Montanus, who was accused of nothing more than being summoned by Messalina to spend a single night with her. She was not present to challenge any of these claims, and the proceedings appear to have been as much about Narcissus's scheme to portray her as sexually insatiable as proving the existence of a plot to overthrow her husband. As with Julia before her, the accusations stuck, allowing her 'depravity' to be fixed in the minds of Roman men, and setting the scene for her later portrayal as a 'nymphomaniac'.

What happened next sounds as much a charade as the behaviour of the wedding party. Having been beside himself with rage and humiliation, the emperor returned to the imperial palace, where he apparently had a sudden change of heart. Claudius, remember, was a skilled actor and he sat down to eat as though nothing had happened, his temper rapidly 'soothed by a timely feast' (*tempestivis epulis delenitus*) and generous quantities of wine. He talked about Messalina in forgiving terms, issuing an order that someone should go and tell 'the poor woman' (*miserae*) to appear before him the next day and insisting that he was prepared to hear her defence. Tacitus takes all this at face value, complaining that Claudius's 'anger was beginning to cool, while his love was returning' (*languescere ira, redire amor*).⁵⁶ Whether or not the emperor had genuinely changed his mind, Narcissus was taking no chances. He left the room, telling the centurions and a tribune of the Praetorian Guard who were on duty that evening to hurry to the Gardens of Lucullus and kill Messalina (*exequi caedem*) on Claudius's orders. He even sent a loyal freedman, Evodus, in advance to make sure she would not realise the danger she was in and try to escape. It is of course likely that Claudius, who was perpetually reluctant to take responsibility for murders he had ordered, knew perfectly well that Narcissus had left the dinner table to pass on instructions he had previously been given in private.

In the gardens, Messalina had taken refuge indoors, probably in the old villa that was one of their most charming features. It does not seem to have been lavishly furnished, because she was lying on the floor, exhausted by the events of the day. Even now she was not alone: her mother, Lepida, had rushed to her side in these desperate moments, despite their long estrangement. If Messalina was as despised as Roman historians claim, it is surprising that two eminent women, Lepida and the chief Vestal, Vibidia, were willing to risk the emperor's wrath to support her, while a cabal of male ministers, led by Narcissus, plotted her destruction. Lepida believed the situation was hopeless and urged her daughter to kill herself, but Messalina was still convinced she could win round her husband.

What happened next is about as horrible as it is possible to imagine: the soldiers, acting on Narcissus's orders, broke down the door and Evodus loomed over her, shouting out a stream of 'insults in the language habitually used by slaves' (*servilibus probris*).[57] Messalina finally realised the situation was hopeless, grabbed a dagger and lifted it to her throat and chest, but her hand faltered. At this point, one of the soldiers plunged his sword through her body (*ictu tribuni transigitur*).[58] The little group of assassins then left the empress's corpse with her mother and returned to the palace, where Claudius was still finishing his dinner. He was informed that his wife was dead but not how she had died, whether by her own hand or in an extrajudicial murder. He did not ask a single question, but called for another glass of wine and went on stuffing himself as usual (*nec ille quaesivit, poposcitque poculum et solita convivio celebravit*).[59]

Claudius was the first emperor to order the murder of his current wife, an act of femicide unparalleled in Roman history. In the days that followed, he showed no emotion, despite the great passion he was supposed to have felt for her. He must have known that the girl he had married was more to be pitied than despised, but his wounded pride could not be assuaged by the thought of merely divorcing her. He displayed neither grief nor sadness even when his children, aged around nine and seven, were distressed and in mourning for their mother. The Senate obediently agreed to obliterate Messalina's memory, allowing Roman historians and other authors to tarnish her reputation with increasingly lurid fantasies. Tacitus couldn't even provide an account of her pitiful death, in her middle or late twenties, without sexualising her. 'There was no decency in that spirit corrupted by lust' (*animo per libidines corrupto nihil honestum inerat*), he wrote as he visualised Messalina lying on the floor, weeping and moaning, moments before her murder.[60] In a testament to the irresistibility of victim-blaming, a reckless young woman was thus transformed into a sexual spectre who would haunt the male imagination for centuries.

8

The Last Woman Standing

Agrippina (*c.*AD 15–59): Roman empress, sister of the emperor Caligula, fourth wife of the emperor Claudius, mother of the emperor Nero. **Beaten and stabbed to death**, aged around 43

Domitia Lepida (*c.*5 BC–AD 54): mother of the empress Messalina, sister-in-law of the empress Agrippina. **Executed**, aged *c.*58

It did not take Claudius long to start thinking about another wife. His initial reaction to Messalina's bigamous marriage had been to swear off wives altogether, telling the Praetorian Guard he had decided to remain celibate in future.[1] No one believed him for a moment and he was soon trying to decide between three women who competed with each other to become his fourth spouse. The candidates in what resembled a beauty contest were Lollia Paulina, who had briefly been empress during her marriage to Caligula; Claudius's ex-wife Aelia Paetina, with whom he had a daughter called Claudia Antonia; and his sole surviving niece, Agrippina, who was very much a surprise entrant on the list.

Marriage between an uncle and niece was prohibited by law

and, more to the point, Agrippina knew that Claudius was responsible not just for the murder of his most recent wife but those of her own sister, Julia Livilla, and her cousin, Julia Livia. A shrewder man than Claudius might have wondered why Agrippina was willing to overlook these obstacles, especially since she seemed to have undergone a very abrupt change of character. She had spent the last few years keeping a low profile, something that allowed her to survive the turbulent politics of her uncle's reign, but now she put her habitual reserve to one side. She began to visit Claudius frequently, using their family relationship as an excuse, and took every opportunity to kiss and embrace him; she had spotted a route to power and she was determined to take it, even if it required her to overcome her natural distaste for her gluttonous, drunken uncle.

The outcome of the contest was by no means certain, however, and the emperor kept changing his mind. His ministers, scarred by their recent experience with Messalina, realised his choice of a new wife was important and lined up behind different candidates. Claudius convened a meeting and asked them to state the case for each woman; Pallas shrewdly backed Agrippina, Callistus argued for Paulina and Narcissus made the schoolboy error of urging Claudius to remarry Paetina, whom he had divorced almost twenty years earlier for what Suetonius describes as 'trivial offences' (*ex levibus offensis*).[2] Paetina was always the least likely candidate and Agrippina's campaign, however disingenuous, began to work, so much so that ancient historians claim she was soon sleeping with Claudius.[3]

Once the emperor had made up his mind, all that remained was to persuade the Senate to change the law to permit the marriage. Claudius enlisted one of the most senior magistrates in Rome, Lucius Vitellius, to speak on his behalf and the man made a stirring speech; he praised Agrippina's fertility, despite the fact that she had only ever had one child, and described her character in glowing terms.[4] What's striking about this speech is that it's a rare instance of a Roman man having a good word to say about Agrippina; the Senate got the message and the ceremony took place on new year's day in 49, just a few months after Messalina's murder.

The marriage propelled Agrippina to a position of prominence and power never enjoyed by any other Roman woman. She had suffered immeasurably to get there, but she also displayed an unparalleled ability to see opportunities in situations that would have driven other women to despair. Agrippina's self-control was remarkable, and never more so than when she became Claudius's wife, which was her only route to the role not just of empress but co-ruler of Rome. Tacitus can barely contain his horror:

> From that moment, the state was utterly changed. Everything was done in obedience to a woman, but not one like Messalina, who treated affairs of state as a toy to satisfy her appetites. It was a tightly controlled and almost masculine tyranny; in public Agrippina appeared austere and often arrogant, while at home she was never immodest except in the pursuit of power.[5]

It's the same charge that had been made against Fulvia; Roman men couldn't contemplate a powerful woman without seeing her as not really a woman at all. It's also, of course, an accusation that Agrippina used sex as a route to power, concealing her true character under an appearance of modesty. Rather than being a 'nymphomaniac' like some of her predecessors, she was doing something that alarmed Roman men much more: pretending to feel sexual attraction to get what she wanted.

They didn't know what to make of her. A few chapters after commenting on Agrippina's austere public image and modest behaviour even in private, Tacitus completely contradicts himself. Comparing her to her former sister-in-law, Messalina's mother Lepida, he condemns both women as 'immoral, notorious and fierce' (*utraque inpudica, infamis, violenta*).[6] Dio charges her with doing the most outrageous thing he can imagine in a woman, which is aiming for absolute power herself. He claims that having the same power as Claudius was not enough for her and she 'desired to have his title outright'.[7] It's not a charge supported by her actions, which suggest that she understood the limitations imposed on her by Roman law and culture – chiefly the fact that she needed to exercise power through a husband or a son. But it confirms that what was regarded as acceptable behaviour in men was intolerable in a woman – and that is the context in which the most sensational accusations against Agrippina should be viewed.

Unlike previous women in the Julio-Claudian dynasty, whose rebellions were largely an attempt to escape the suffocating control of their male relatives, Agrippina's aims were political. It was a different order of challenge to the Roman system and the accusations against her – dissimulation, ambition, ruthlessness and a willingness to resort to murder – were ramped up accordingly. Tacitus ends his earlier diatribe by throwing in an accusation that she had an insatiable greed for gold (*cupido auri immensa*), adding avarice to all the other vices laid at her door.[8] It goes some way towards explaining why her name has come to stand for the immorality of the Julio-Claudian dynasty in spite of the terrible behaviour of the men, who were guilty of much worse offences. But it also obscures the fact that Agrippina's survival to become empress was remarkable, given that she herself was the victim of some of the dynasty's worst excesses.

The attrition rate in Agrippina's immediate family is extraordinary. By the age of thirty-four or thirty-five, when she married Claudius, she was literally the last woman standing. Her five siblings were dead, only one of them from natural causes, leaving Agrippina as the sole surviving great-granddaughter of both Augustus and Livia. She was lucky to be alive and she knew it; the slaughter of her relatives was so relentless that she could easily have been mistaken for someone who had survived a protracted civil war. The damage stretched back to her grandmother Julia, who had been starved to death shortly before she was born. Her mother Agrippina, with whom she shared a name, had been beaten, blinded in one eye and died in the same horrible manner. So had her aunts, Julia and Livilla, and her sister Julia Livilla, while her cousin Julia Livia had been executed by a blow from a sword. (So many women with similar or identical names says something about the way family took precedence over individuals in Roman society.) The story was similar among Agrippina's male relatives: her uncle Agrippa Postumus and her two eldest brothers, Nero and Drusus, had been murdered or forced to kill themselves, and her youngest brother Caligula assassinated. Even her father, Germanicus, had died in suspicious circumstances.

As a child, Agrippina's inheritance was grief and fear, and she learned about the total control exercised by her male relatives when she was handed over to a man at least twice her age just after her thirteenth birthday in AD 28. It was a dynastic marriage, arranged by the emperor Tiberius, who chose a grandson of Augustus's sister,

Octavia, as her new husband. It was a disastrous choice: there is disagreement about the exact age of Gnaeus Domitius Ahenobarbus when he married Agrippina but he was one of the most unpleasant individuals in Rome, described by Suetonius as 'hateful' (*detestabilem*). (Guy de la Bédoyère agrees, calling Domitius a 'brutal and unpleasant man'.)[9] He is said to have got away with murder on two occasions, killing a servant for disobeying an order to drink as much as himself and deliberately speeding up his chariot to run over a boy who was playing on the Appian Way. Like his great-uncle Augustus, he was personally violent, once gouging out the eye of a man who criticised him in the forum. He was notorious for failing to pay his debts, refusing to pay for items he had bought or to distribute prize money to the winners of chariot races he presided over as a magistrate.[10]

The marriage forced Agrippina into a physical relationship before her periods had even started and Domitius was singularly ill-equipped to comfort her as she experienced a series of devastating losses; her mother and two eldest brothers were arrested the year after her wedding and all three would be dead before her eighteenth birthday, a level of bereavement rarely experienced in peacetime. It's not even as though Domitius was faithful to his young wife: in AD 37, when Agrippina was around twenty-one, her husband was embroiled in a scandal that starkly exposed his extra-marital activities. A woman called Albucilla, who bears the brunt of Tacitus's misogyny – he describes her as notorious for her many lovers (*multorum amoribus famosa*) – was charged with disloyalty (*inpietatis*) towards Tiberius. Domitius was one of three prominent men accused of complicity with Albucilla and of having sex with her. The timing, as the emperor was nearing the end of his life, suggests an attempt to clear out anyone who might pose a threat to the accession of Caligula, as does the fact that the future emperor's ally, Macro, took charge of examining witnesses and the torture of slaves. In the event, the death of Tiberius put an end to the business, although not before one of the accused men, Lucius Arruntius, had killed himself. (Albucilla, who had also tried to commit suicide, was thrown in prison.)[11] How Agrippina felt about her husband's affair becoming the subject of gossip is not known, but it must have been a mortifying experience for Germanicus's daughter.

A less resilient woman might have buckled under such a weight of humiliation and heartbreak, but Agrippina's subsequent history suggests she learned instead to cauterise her feelings. She would have needed to, because a remark by Domitius following the birth of their son in December that year – he said that nothing good could come of a child with himself and Agrippina as parents – adds weight to the assumption that the marriage was unhappy.[12] His churlish reaction is another indication of his character, given that the birth was breech and mother and child were lucky to survive; Agrippina recorded the fact in her lost autobiography, and while it is impossible to know whether she sustained permanent damage during the delivery, it's striking that she did not have children with either of her two subsequent husbands. The boy was called Lucius Domitius Ahenobarbus after his grandfather, and he would be known as Lucius until his adoption by his stepfather Claudius at the age of twelve. He is better known to us as the emperor Nero.

A few months before the birth, Agrippina's brother Caligula had become emperor and returned to Rome. Lucius was only around eighteen months old when his mother was convicted of involvement in the 'three daggers' plot and exiled, leaving the boy in the care of his father's family. Domitius died of dropsy (oedema) when Lucius was three, during Agrippina's absence from Rome, and his elder sister, Lepida, turned out to be a poor foster-parent.[13] She was wealthy but notoriously mean and Lucius was brought up in conditions 'close to penury' (*paene inops*), while his aunt chose a dancer and a barber as his tutors, presumably because they were cheap.[14] Their influence on the boy was nevertheless profound, instilling a lifelong obsession with performance and the adulation of crowds. When Agrippina was recalled to Rome, following her uncle Claudius's accession, she didn't like what she found, prompting an enmity with her former sister-in-law that lasted for years. Her return was accompanied by a significant change in her fortunes, however, because Claudius returned the property left to Lucius in his father's will and appropriated by Caligula.

Agrippina was now a widow in her twenties. For the first time in her adult life she was not trapped in a miserable marriage, but she knew from her mother's and grandmother's experience that patrician women on their own were vulnerable, subject to gossip and false accusations. She didn't wait for suitable candidates for a second marriage to present themselves, showing that she was already thinking about how best to protect herself and promote the interests of her son. She approached Claudius and asked him to find her a husband, suggesting that the future emperor Servius Sulpicius Galba was a promising candidate. Galba was seventeen years older than Agrippina and more interested in men than women, according to Suetonius, but he came from a distinguished family and had held a number of important positions.[15] He was governor of Upper Germany at the time, commanding the legions that once served under Germanicus, and it sounds as though power and influence were more important to Agrippina than personal qualities. She may already have been thinking about Lucius's career, aware that support of the army was essential for a future emperor, but it was a rare misstep on her part; Galba already had a wife and Agrippina's proposal annoyed his mother-in-law so much that she gave her a very public slap in the face.[16]

Agrippina's next suggestion was that Claudius should approach the highly regarded former consul Gaius Sallustius Passienus Crispus on her behalf. (Passienus has already appeared in this book, deftly sidestepping the emperor Caligula's question about whether he had slept with his sister.) It was an extraordinarily bold move because Passienus was married to none other than Agrippina's former sister-in-law,

Domitia, and the two women already regarded each other with acrimony. But Passienus did not have any illusions about his wife's character, once making an acerbic observation about a legal dispute between Domitia and her brother Domitius over family property; neither of them was short of the very thing they were fighting over, Passienus pointed out, confirming the siblings' reputation for greed.[17] It may not have been a burden to him to end the marriage and he was, in any case, as keen to preserve good relations with Claudius as he had been with Caligula. He divorced Domitia and married Agrippina, exacerbating the feud between the two women.

Passienus had been consul in AD 27, suggesting he was in his mid-fifties by now, but he was a canny choice on Agrippina's part. He was wealthy, witty and slightly eccentric, and the marriage clearly suited them both; Passienus's career prospered, including a spell as governor of Asia when Agrippina very likely accompanied him to the province. He had a second consulship, in AD 44, but died at some point in or around 47, probably of natural causes. There is no evidence at all to suggest that the marriage was unhappy and being widowed for a second time was not unusual in Rome, given the age gap in many patrician marriages. But Passienus doesn't seem to have had children from previous marriages and he had made a will leaving his fortune to Agrippina, leading Suetonius to suggest he was murdered. The historian claims that Passienus 'died through the trickery of Agrippina' (*periit per fraudem Agrippinae*), suggesting that she fooled him into ingesting poison to get her hands on his money.[18]

It's not clear when the accusation was first made, whether there were suspicions at the time or they began to circulate only after an identical allegation was levelled in relation to Agrippina's role in the death of her third husband, Claudius; if a woman acquires a reputation as a poisoner, innocent past events can be interpreted in a very different light. What can be ruled out is the far-fetched notion that she got rid of Passienus because she was already plotting to marry the emperor, who had a healthy young wife at the time. Even a woman who was developing as much political intelligence as Agrippina could never have envisioned the sudden vacancy that would be created by Messalina's murder a year or so later. She was probably already looking around for a third husband among Rome's patrician class when that extraordinary and totally unexpected opportunity presented itself.

A bust of Agrippina in the Museo Archeologico Nazionale in Naples shows an attractive woman with large eyes, even though part of her face is hidden by the heavy curls that were fashionable in the middle of the first century. In AD 52, three years after she married the emperor, we get a rare glimpse of Agrippina and Claudius at a public event. In a remarkable feat of engineering, a tunnel had been constructed through a mountain in central Italy to join the river Liris (Liri) to the Fucine lake (the lake was drained in the nineteenth century and no longer exists). Its completion was celebrated by a mock naval battle, with the emperor and empress presiding over the event. Agrippina arrived wearing a magnificent cloak in the Greek style, woven from gold thread (*chlamyde aurata*).[19]

She knew how to make the best of herself and her spectacular entrance with her husband was a fine piece of imperial propaganda. The celebrations for the opening of the tunnel were extravagant:

the staged battle on the lake involved 19,000 combatants, and the spectators were so delighted by it that the survivors were allowed to live. But a second display, an infantry engagement staged by gladiators on pontoons, ended in disaster when faulty construction caused a huge surge of water, sweeping everything away. Agrippina was furious and blamed Narcissus, who had been in charge of the tunnelling scheme, claiming he had skimmed money from the project. He hit back, accusing her of a 'feminine inability to control herself and overarching ambition' (*impotentiam muliebrem nimiasque eius spes*).[20] It attests to the continuing bad feeling between Agrippina and one of the most powerful figures at court, dating back to the marriage contest, when Narcissus backed a different candidate. He retained his influence with the emperor, but it's hard to believe that Agrippina felt anything but distaste towards the man who had orchestrated her predecessor's disgrace and murder. With good reason: Narcissus's retort following the lake disaster highlighted the question of her sex, no doubt reflecting wider disapproval of her assumption that she was her husband's equal.

Becoming the wife of a man who had divorced two wives and ordered the murder of a third had always been a high-risk strategy. Agrippina had risen to a position unparalleled in Roman history, joining her husband not just at ceremonial events but when he

conducted state business. Dio records her sitting on a nearby platform when Claudius received foreign ambassadors, an innovation he describes as 'one of the most remarkable sights of the time'.²¹ But Agrippina was a realist and she knew that her power depended entirely on the emperor, whose marital record showed him to be a selfish and fickle spouse. Seducing him was one thing, but meeting Claudius's sexual expectations would surely have jarred on a woman as reserved as Agrippina, and she was all too aware of his susceptibility to attractive women.

Agrippina's conduct after her marriage to Claudius is hard to defend if she played the role attributed to her by Roman historians, but it's a big 'if', as we shall see in a moment. The accusation that she got rid of other women because she was jealous (the accusation previously made against Messalina) seems wide of the mark, given that her marriage to Claudius was based on self-interest rather than genuine passion or even affection. Tacitus's suggestion that she was 'fierce in her hatreds' (*atrox odii*) is simply not consistent with the calculation that marked most of her transactions with other people;²² it makes more sense to see Agrippina's clearing out of potential rivals for her husband's wayward desire as a cold-blooded strategy that speaks volumes about the way her emotions had been blunted by the terrible series of losses she experienced as a young woman. It would have taken several generations of violent deaths to produce a woman like Agrippina, able to put aside normal human feelings in her single-minded determination not to meet the same fate as her female ancestors.

Even the ancient sources, with their habitual prejudice against women, tell the story in a way that suggests that she acted against other women not from personal motives but when she felt threatened. Dio claims, for instance, that she 'banished Calpurnia, one of the most prominent women – or even put her to death, according to one report – because Claudius had admired and commended her beauty'.²³ (It's clear from both Dio and Tacitus that this is not the Calpurnia mentioned in the previous chapter who was Claudius's concubine.) Agrippina certainly had reason to be wary of Lollia Paulina, who was one of the candidates Claudius had seriously considered as a possible fourth wife. Paulina's reputation as a great beauty has been mentioned earlier in this book, when it persuaded Caligula to summon her to Rome and marry her, making her briefly Agrippina's sister-in-law. The empress is said to have instigated proceedings against Paulina, accusing her of consulting astrologers and a statue of Apollo that supposedly had the gift of prophecy in an attempt to discover the likely outcome of Claudius's deliberations over his next marriage (behaviour described by one modern source as 'considered typical of would-be traitors'). As with Messalina's role in various prosecutions against prominent men and women, however, it is not clear whether Agrippina was the prime mover or provided cover for the emperor. Claudius prosecuted Paulina himself, describing her as a danger to the state, refusing to hear her defence and insisting that most of her vast property should be confiscated.

Paulina was exiled to an unknown destination, but it was a prelude either to murder or an enforced suicide. A tribune of the Praetorian Guard was sent after Paulina to coerce her into killing herself, cutting off her head and bringing it back to Rome; there's a suggestion that Agrippina had demanded it as a trophy, but it's much more likely that she wanted to be certain that her rival was dead.[24] What happened next was gruesome: the head was too decomposed to confirm Paulina's identity and Agrippina forced open the dead woman's mouth, recalling that her teeth had an unusual feature, and satisfied herself that she'd got the right woman.[25] It's a dreadful story, recalling the decaying body parts concealed in the bedroom in Syria where Agrippina's father died, and Dio's intention in telling it is to confirm her ruthless character. But it suggests that Agrippina was terrified of losing her hold over Claudius, something that speaks as much to her insecurity as to her lack of squeamishness.

Paulina's murder is one of a number laid at Agrippina's door by ancient historians. Dio says she became 'a second Messalina' and some modern historians agree, with Annelise Freisenbruch claiming that 'like Messalina, Agrippina chalked up a long list of victims during Claudius's reign'.[26] Guy de la Bédoyère has Agrippina 'allegedly having wealthy victims murdered' so she could steal their estates for her son, although he does at least frame it as an allegation.[27] Tacitus blames her for the execution of a former governor of Africa, Titus Statilius Taurus Corvinus, claiming that Agrippina persuaded Claudius to condemn him because she wanted to get her hands on the lavish gardens he owned. It is almost identical to one of the accusations against Messalina, who is supposed to have encouraged the condemnation of Asiaticus because she coveted *his* gardens, but the charges against Taurus were brought by the man who had been his deputy in Africa, who accused him of extortion and magic. Such allegations were common and Taurus anticipated a guilty verdict from the Senate by killing himself, something Tacitus attributes to his humiliation at being falsely accused.[28] (We will meet a woman called Statilia Messalina, who was either his daughter or his niece, later in this book.)

But the impulse to damage Agrippina by making her into a version of her despised predecessor appears to have counted for more than evidence in Roman historians' portrayal. Her biographer, Anthony A. Barrett, has compiled a list of nine murders or suicides laid at her door by ancient authors, something that would make her an even more successful serial killer than Robert Graves's Livia.[29] Once again, some of these were probably not murders at all (Agrippina's second husband Passienus), or were carried out by someone else (her stepson Britannicus, assuming that he was in fact poisoned). Even if these figures were correct, the imbalance between Agrippina's supposed 'victims' and the hundreds of men killed on the orders of Claudius is striking; it's the same double standard we witnessed earlier in this book, in relation to portrayals of Livia and Augustus. Barrett points out the absence of 'solidly identifiable victims' among the accusations against her, arguing that there were fewer executions *after* her marriage to Claudius than earlier in his reign.[30] He argues that it is 'difficult to avoid the conclusion that much of the impetus for this change for the better should be attributed to the influence and efforts of Agrippina', an assessment that runs counter to the popular view of the empress as a woman who murdered her way to the top.

What Agrippina certainly did do is work hard on behalf of her son, Lucius, eventually managing to displace Britannicus in the line of succession. Lucius was three years older than Claudius's son and closer to reaching the age of manhood, which gave him an advantage over Britannicus. Of course Agrippina was motivated by self-interest, because having honours heaped on Lucius was a way of extending her own power and influence, but she worked to that end with single-minded determination. Whether or not she had an affair with the freedman Pallas, whose advocacy on her behalf had been crucial during her campaign to marry Claudius, she was smart enough to maintain an alliance that played a vital role in positioning Lucius as the emperor's heir. With Pallas's support, Agrippina succeeded in having Lucius adopted into the Claudian family in AD 50 when he was twelve, bringing about the name change to Nero Claudius Caesar Augustus Germanicus, soon shortened to Nero, under which he would become notorious. She also secured the recall of Seneca from Corsica and appointed him tutor to the boy, a position that allowed the philosopher to become one of the future emperor's most trusted advisors. At the age of fifteen, Nero's position in the dynasty was confirmed by his marriage to Claudius's younger daughter, Claudia Octavia, who was thirteen or fourteen at the time.

The bad feeling between Agrippina and her first husband's sisters had by now been festering for more than a decade, and Nero's growing popularity with the Roman people ignited a contest between his mother and one of his paternal aunts, Messalina's mother, Lepida. There is no doubt that Lepida had survived dreadful experiences, including the murders of her third husband and her daughter, and she relished her influence over Nero, making a point of spoiling him while Agrippina treated him with severity and threats (*truci . . . ac minaci*).[31] With good reason, as it turned out: perhaps she had already recognised something in the boy, a resemblance to his vicious father, that worried her.

In a testimony to the fact that power was more important to her than anything else, however, Agrippina tried to quell her misgivings about Nero's character, for the time being at least. Her response to astrologers who warned her that her only son would rule Rome, but be responsible for her murder – 'Let him kill me, as long as he becomes emperor' (*atque illa 'occidat' inquit 'dum imperet'*) – sounds suspiciously prescient, suggesting it might be another later addition to Agrippina's biography – or the myths about her.[32] Tacitus's observation that 'she could give her son the empire, but she could not bear him as emperor' (*quae filio dare imperium, tolerare imperitantem nequibat*) is closer to the mark.[33] For the moment, however, Lepida stood in the way of her plans to remain the most important influence in Nero's life and Agrippina had had enough of her troublesome former sister-in-law. Lepida was accused of allowing gangs of her own slaves to run riot in southern Italy and of using magic against the empress, but if she expected the nephew she had indulged to stand up for her, she was sorely mistaken. Nero testified against her and Claudius did nothing to save his former mother-in-law. Lepida was sentenced to death.[34]

The year 54 was packed with sinister omens, including a comet, and a lightning strike on the memorial to Claudius's father, Drusus, that collectively seemed to predict disaster to the superstitious Romans.[35] No doubt such events happened all the time, but Roman historians are keen to create an atmosphere of foreboding in their account of events leading up to Claudius's death. The emperor made no secret of the fact that he had begun to regret marrying Agrippina and adopting Nero, hugging his own son, Britannicus, and urging him to grow up quickly. When his freedmen congratulated him on condemning a woman who had been on trial for adultery, he made a joke at his own expense, declaring that he was fated to marry wives who were 'shameless but not all unpunished' (*omnia impudica sed non impunita matrimonia*).[36] The Latin pun is all but impossible to reproduce in English but no one would have missed the reference to the murder of Messalina. Tacitus offers an even more ominous version of the same story, claiming that after he had been drinking heavily one day, Claudius blurted out that it was his destiny to suffer 'his wives' disgraceful behaviour' (*coniugum flagitia*) and then punish it.[37] The emperor was notably self-pitying, and he may well by now have been disillusioned with Agrippina, whose attentions during the marriage contest had concealed a much more formidable character than he anticipated. Her old enemy Narcissus fanned the flames, claiming that Agrippina's intrigues on behalf of Nero were as dangerous to the regime as Messalina's 'conspiracy' with Silius.[38] But the fact that Narcissus left Rome at this point to take a cure for gout in southern Italy, apparently at the suggestion of Agrippina, hardly suggests that everyone knew a crisis was looming.[39]

The allegation that Agrippina murdered her husband exists in several different forms. Most people believed that Claudius was poisoned, 'but when it was done and by whom is contested' (*ubi autem et per quem dato, discrepit*), Suetonius admits.[40] One of the strongest arguments against Agrippina being the guilty party is that by killing Claudius, she was eliminating her role as co-ruler of Rome, a position she had worked incredibly hard to attain. It's also striking that her alleged motive – her husband's reported rapprochement with his son Britannicus – is suspiciously similar to the story told about Augustus's secret visit to his grandson

Postumus shortly before his death. The sources can't even agree where the alleged poisoning took place, whether it was at a formal banquet on the Citadel with the priests, when Agrippina was not even present, or at a family dinner at which she served the emperor's food herself.

Tacitus says Agrippina secured poison from a convicted poisoner called Locusta and it was sprinkled on an 'exceptionally delicious mushroom' (*delectabili cibo boleto*) by the emperor's long-serving food taster, Halotus, who somehow managed to avoid ingesting anything harmful himself; Claudius had been drinking heavily, however, and the only effect of the poison was a sudden evacuation of his bowels. In this version Agrippina, horrified by the failure of her plan, called in Claudius's doctor, Xenophon, who was in on the plot, and got him to insert a feather dipped in a fast-acting poison down the emperor's throat.[41] Suetonius offers two different accounts, the first suggesting that Claudius was poisoned by Halotus while dining in Agrippina's absence, while the second implicates her directly; according to this latter version, she served Claudius with the poisoned mushrooms herself, with no mention of Halotus. There is no agreement about what followed either, whether the poison worked and Claudius died at dawn, or whether he vomited and had to be given a second dose during the night.[42] Dio has Agrippina taking quite a risk, eating from the mushroom dish herself and assuming that only the largest, which she encouraged Claudius to pick, had been contaminated by the poison.[43]

It might be argued that the timing of the emperor's death was convenient for Agrippina, if she was really worried about her deteriorating relationship with him. But Claudius was sixty-three years old and had repeatedly abused his body with bouts of overeating, heavy drinking and purging (Suetonius includes the gruesome detail that the second application of poison might have been administered via an enema). It's striking that Seneca doesn't mention poison at all in his satirical work *Apocolocyntosis*, a play on the words *colocynta* (pumpkin) and apotheosis, the process by which a human being becomes a god. The text, which was very likely written a couple of months after the emperor's death in October 54, describes his final hours and arrival in heaven (spoiler: Claudius doesn't actually turn into a pumpkin). In Seneca's version, the emperor became ill at midday while watching some comic actors and died within the hour. There is no reference to Agrippina or any suspicion of foul play.[44]

Indeed to twenty-first-century eyes, he was a prime candidate for a heart attack or a stroke, and a detail in Suetonius's account – that Claudius's first symptom was losing the power of speech (*obmutuisse*) – suggests the latter.[45] 'All the features are consistent with sudden death from cerebrovascular disease,' according to a paper published by two doctors in the *Journal of the Royal Society of Medicine* after assessing the available evidence.[46] Given the suspicion that attached by now to everything Agrippina did, however, she was bound to be accused of murder, although the number of individuals involved in the plot – not just Agrippina but Locusta, Halotus and Xenophon – is surprising; the more people who were in on it, the greater the risk that someone would talk.

Even if the consensus is that Claudius was taken ill during a typically excessive bout of eating and drinking, ancient and modern authors who insist on Agrippina's guilt are going far beyond the available evidence. The fact that she took swift action to ensure that Nero, not Britannicus, would be declared emperor tells us nothing; Agrippina's survival depended on her ability to think quickly and she knew it was vital to keep her husband's death quiet until she and her son were secure. Once Nero had been presented to the Praetorian Guard and hailed as emperor, the transition to a new reign would be smooth and her position safe – or so she thought. At thirty-eight, Agrippina had experienced more than most people endure in a lifetime, and had emerged in a position which even Tacitus, with grudging admiration, describes as 'unique to this day' (*unicum ad hunc diem exemplum*).[47]

Her son was still a teenager, adored by the populace but with little experience of affairs of state, and Agrippina had every reason to expect he would turn to her for advice and guidance. Either she had misjudged his character, however, or she failed to appreciate

the enormity of the change in her own circumstances. An emperor could be removed only by death, whether from natural causes or assassination, but previous reigns had demonstrated how easily an empress (or dowager empress in this case) could be sidelined. Within five years, Agrippina would be dead, murdered by a son who added matricide to the long list of crimes committed by the Julio-Claudian men. His father, Domitius, had been proved right about the boy's character, but even he could not have imagined that his and Agrippina's son would grow up to become a sexually perverse serial killer.

Matricide is an extreme form of domestic violence. It's also more common than most people realise: in 2020, fourteen women were killed by their sons in the UK according to figures collected by the Femicide Census, which compiles an annual record of all known cases of women murdered by men.[48] Sometimes the fatal assault is a single event, but in other cases it is a precursor to other crimes, including mass murder and sexual violence; one of the most notorious school shootings in the USA, the Sandy Hook massacre at a primary school in Connecticut in 2012, began with the perpetrator shooting his mother five times in the head as she lay in bed.[49] School shootings are rare in the UK, where guns are less easy to come by, but scarcely believable accounts of extreme domestic violence sometimes emerge in court; in 2021, for instance, a thirty-one-year-old man admitted strangling his grandmother, who was seventy-six, and raping her dead body twice at her flat in east London.[50]

Historians who question Nero's responsibility for the murder of his mother appear to be unaware of these patterns of behaviour, behaving as though matricide was a step too far even for someone as morally rudderless as the most notorious of the Julio-Claudian emperors. But it is clear from the ancient accounts that Nero's feelings towards his mother were an unstable combination of fear, resentment and desire. That he eventually adopted a series of stratagems to get rid of her, including staged 'accidents', should come as no surprise – or that the power struggle between them began not long after he succeeded his stepfather. 'It was I who made you emperor,' Agrippina once told Nero, not understanding that when she gave him the gift of absolute power, she fatally diminished her own.[51]

To begin with, things seemed to go well. When the Praetorian prefect asked Nero for a password for the first time after he became emperor, he replied 'the best of mothers' (*optimam matrem*).[52] Agrippina was allowed to attend meetings of the Senate on the Palatine, entering by a back door so she could listen to debates, concealed by a curtain, although it was a demotion from her more prominent role during the reign of Claudius.[53] A double relief found at Aphrodisias – a Greek city in what is now western Turkey with longstanding connections to the Julian family – reflects Agrippina's understanding of their relationship, showing her placing a laurel wreath on Nero's head. Agrippina is wearing a diaphanous gown, showing off her breasts and shapely waist, and she appears to have been transformed from a Roman matron into a deity, complete with a crown. Nero stares blankly ahead and it is reasonable to think he would have hated the image, even though it is an idealised version of him; in reality, he had a thick neck, pot belly and gangly legs.[54] The relief was a visual representation of the power imbalance between mother and son at the beginning of his reign, and he quickly found it intolerable.

A few months later, Nero was preparing to receive an Armenian delegation when he spotted Agrippina approaching the stage, intending to join him. She was used to sharing top billing with Claudius and expected the same treatment from her son, but Nero was furious. It was a fraught moment, according to Tacitus, who regarded Agrippina's conduct as an egregious example of lèse-majesté. A confrontation was averted by Seneca, whose fortunes had changed dramatically since Agrippina secured his recall from exile in Corsica. He urged the emperor to step down and greet his mother, disguising the snub as a gesture of filial affection (*specie pietatis*).[55] But Agrippina had misjudged both the strength of her own position and her son's willingness to share power, which would decline rapidly as his confidence grew.

What Agrippina did next was incredibly risky, and confirms that her championing of Nero had been governed by ambition rather than affection. Perhaps she was beginning to accept that her son was vain, foolish and cruel, and she had made a terrible mistake by giving him so much power; in AD 55, the year after Nero became emperor, Agrippina abruptly changed sides and began championing the interests of Claudius's son, Britannicus. She observed in Nero's hearing that the boy was now an adult (an arguable point since he was not yet fourteen, the youngest age at which a male Roman child was considered to have reached manhood) and the true heir to the empire. Resorting to threats, she announced her intention of taking Claudius's son to the Praetorians' camp, as she had done with Nero after the death of the late emperor. 'The daughter of Germanicus will be heard there!' she declared (*audiretur hinc Germanici filia!*).[56]

Agrippina was presenting herself as a kingmaker, but whether or not she seriously believed she could displace Nero, she had no opportunity to try it. Within weeks Britannicus was dead and suspicion inevitably fell on Nero. Of course, we have no proof either way, and the circumstances – the boy died at a banquet,

like his father – may have led contemporary observers to assume the worst. Like other men in the family, Britannicus suffered from epilepsy and his symptoms could be explained by a fatal seizure. He was cremated the same night, during a ferocious storm, which was said to show the gods' disapproval of the murder. In an almost throwaway remark, Tacitus makes the extraordinary allegation that 'a number of contemporary authors' claimed that Nero had repeatedly raped Britannicus several days before his death.[57]

Whether or not the boy was murdered, the fact that so many people believed it, and some even considered the young emperor capable of raping his stepbrother and indeed brother-in-law, shows that Nero was already regarded as a dangerous and volatile ruler. Agrippina, who was present at the dinner where her stepson died, now entered a period of her life in which she suffered one humiliation after another. Nero removed her image from Roman coins, took away her honours, deprived her of her bodyguards and forced her to move out of the imperial palace into the house once owned by her grandmother Antonia. She became the target of a campaign of harassment carried out by Nero's agents, who brought vexatious court cases against her while she remained in Rome and disturbed her sleep with shouts and jeers when she went to stay in a villa on the coast.[58] She was becoming dangerously isolated and her enemies circled, including a former friend, Junia Silana, and her former sister-in-law Domitia. Silana's connections with the Julio-Claudian dynasty stretched back to the reign of Tiberius, when her sister, Junia Claudilla, was the first wife of Caligula, and she had played a minor role in one of the greatest scandals of Claudius's regime when her husband, Gaius Silius, became the lover of Messalina. Silana had recently fallen out with Agrippina after the latter talked a young man, Titus Sextius Africanus, out of marrying her old friend, supposedly to prevent his inheriting Silana's substantial fortune. Silana and Domitia now joined forces in an attempt to bring down Agrippina, using informers who accused her of plotting to place a man called Rubellius Plautus – son of Julia Livia and grandson of Claudius's sister Livilla, which meant he had as strong a claim as Nero – on the throne.[59] The plot was badly timed and failed. But the fact that they were emboldened to do it shows how diminished the former empress's status had become.

One of the things Agrippina hadn't reckoned on, unsurprisingly considering Nero's age, was how easily she would be displaced as his confidante by other women. The young emperor was still married to Claudius and Messalina's daughter, Octavia, but he had no time for her and began an affair with a freedwoman called Claudia Acte. She was older than Nero, who was only seventeen when the relationship began, and originally from Asia Minor (Turkey). Her Latin name, Claudia, suggests she had been a slave in the household of the previous emperor, and she is identified in the *Octavia* as one of the slaves of his daughter, which was an added insult to the young empress.[60] This wasn't just snobbery, as Roman authors assumed, claiming that Agrippina resented the fact that a former servant (*ancillam*) was a rival for her son's affections.[61] She rightly feared she was losing her influence with Nero, while Octavia could only look on as her husband considered marrying her rival, even persuading some former consuls to swear falsely that Acte had royal ancestors.[62]

When Agrippina saw that her hostility to the woman was damaging her relationship with Nero, she supposedly changed tactics and offered to allow him to use her own bedroom for his extra-marital affairs. Nero was unimpressed and showed her who was boss in no uncertain terms, dismissing his mother's longtime ally Pallas from the court. In the event, his affair with Acte petered out after three years when he discovered a new erotic interest, a woman called Poppaea Sabina, whose mother of the same name appeared briefly in a previous chapter of this book. But his affairs provided the background to one of the most sensational stories about Agrippina, which is the claim that she was so desperate to regain her hold on Nero that she offered to have sex with him herself.

The story is told in different forms by Tacitus, Suetonius and Dio, although with significant caveats. Tacitus doesn't vouch for its authenticity, saying he found it in the lost work of Cluvius Rufus, who described a desperate Agrippina turning up several times towards the end of lunch, when Nero had been eating and drinking heavily, 'stylishly dressed and ready for incest' (*comptam in incesto paratam*); she is then supposed to have exchanged 'unrestrained kisses' (*lasciva oscula*) with her son in full view of his dining companions.[63] Tacitus admits that another author, Fabius Rusticus, claims that it was Nero who was eager to commit incest, a version backed up by Suetonius, who says it was well known that the emperor was 'desperate to have sex with his mother' (*matris concubitum appetisse*); he says that Nero had to be talked out of it by her enemies, who thought it would give Agrippina too much power.[64] Dio admits he doesn't know whether the allegation is true or 'invented', but both he and Suetonius add a detail that might explain how it arose: Nero had a mistress who resembled Agrippina and, according to Dio, he used to parade this woman in front of his friends, boasting that he was sleeping with his mother.[65]

It's a revealing anecdote in itself, suggesting either that Nero *was* physically attracted to Agrippina or wanted to shock his associates by pretending he was. If the former empress's reputation has been dealt a further blow merely by her son's cruel joke, however, it is a testament to the existence of an audience eager for every scrap of malicious gossip about the Julio-Claudian women. (It has to be said that mother–son incest is currently one of the most popular searches in internet porn, demonstrating its enduring power as a fantasy.) One obvious reason why such stories attached to Agrippina is that she had been accused of incest before, when her brother Caligula was said to have had sex with all three of his sisters, although there is no evidence that she agreed to it. In addition, her marriage to her uncle was technically incest, until the law was changed, and laid the groundwork for the claim that she was willing to sleep with close relatives to further her career. There is quite a difference between an uncle and a son, however, and Tacitus admits that people might have believed the story about Agrippina trying to seduce Nero because they regarded 'any sexual novelty as credible in such a woman' (*credibilior novae libidinis meditatio in ea visa est*).⁶⁶ It's a classic example of 'give a dog a bad name' and it doesn't just apply to ancient historians.

Tom Holland writes about rumours circulating in Rome that Agrippina 'had begun to make moves on [Nero], painted and dressed like a prostitute, whenever he was drunk'.⁶⁷ Holland admits that the story is unlikely to be true, in view of Agrippina's reputation for iron self-control, but it is the phrase 'painted and dressed like a prostitute' that sticks in the throat. The adjective *compta* simply means that Agrippina had taken care with her appearance; it could even be translated as 'elegant', without any implication of ostentation or vulgarity. The same question keeps on arising: why are ancient and modern authors alike so keen to associate the Julio-Claudian women with the commercial sex trade? It is true that Agrippina was sadly diminished from the days when she turned all eyes in a golden cloak, but even the torrid rumours about her in ancient Rome stopped short of portraying her as a prostitute.

What we do know is that by 58, when Nero had been emperor for four years, he was entirely estranged from Agrippina. She seems to have more or less retired from public life, spending a great deal of time at her country house in Tusculum (near modern-day Frascati), around 25 kilometres south-east of Rome, and at the villa she had shared with her first husband at Anzio. Nero's attempts to reduce her status and influence had worked, but even that didn't satisfy him – so much so that he decided to get rid of her. Even now, it is hard to credit that a young man of twenty would take the heinous step of arranging the murder of his own mother, but matricide is usually the final act of men who have spent years nurturing a sense of grievance; according to Tacitus, this was no momentary whim but a 'crime' Nero had been thinking about for a long time (*diu meditatum scelus*).⁶⁸ He rejected the option of using poison because of the suspicions attaching to Britannicus's death, and in any case it might not work, because Agrippina was by now fearful for her life and said to take antidotes regularly.[69] A more ingenious scheme was called for, preferably one that would look like an accident, and Nero was not short of ideas or accomplices.

His plot to murder Agrippina with a booby-trapped boat in the bay of Naples is one of the most fantastical anecdotes to have survived from the ancient world. The scheme was melodramatic, preposterous even, but entirely in keeping with Nero's love of theatre and illusion. Indeed, he seems to have had difficulty separating fantasy from reality more generally, his behaviour becoming so extreme that it suggests he had inherited the instability that afflicted previous generations of men on the Julian side of the family. Dio claims that the idea of using a collapsible boat to kill Agrippina came from watching a play in which just such a vessel appeared, falling apart to let out animals and then being put back together again.[70] The murder of his mother has all the hallmarks of a performance, complete with props and simulated displays of affection, in which Nero awarded himself a starring role.

There had been earlier schemes against Agrippina, including a plot to install a false ceiling in her bedroom which would collapse and kill her, but she was tipped off and it had to be abandoned.[71] Shipwrecks were common in the ancient world and the idea of his mother dying in one appealed to Nero, who was planning to celebrate the festival of Minerva – ironically, one of special significance to women – in Baiae, the seaside resort near Naples where many of the women in this book owned villas. Baiae is around 5 kilometres north of the naval base of Miseno, where one of Rome's two fleets was stationed at the time. It was commanded by another of Nero's old tutors, a freedman called Anicetus who loathed Agrippina. He was delighted to be asked to oversee construction of a boat which would fall apart, like the one Nero had seen in the theatre, and throw her into the sea.

In March 59, Agrippina was staying at Anzio. She was more than a little surprised to receive a friendly note from her son, inviting her to visit him in Baiae. Hoping he had had a change of heart, she agreed to meet him in the nearby town of Bauli (Bacoli), where she owned another villa. Her suspicions were lulled when he greeted her affectionately and invited her to a banquet at his house in Baiae hosted by one of his friends, the future emperor Marcus Salvius Otho. Accounts differ as to whether Agrippina travelled to Baiae in a litter or in a boat which was deliberately damaged on arrival so she could not use it for the return journey. But Nero gave her the place of honour at the banquet and showered her with gifts, hugging and kissing her when she said she needed to get back to Bacoli. 'For you I live and because of you I rule,' he is supposed to have said, supplying the acknowledgement she had craved for years.[72] In a horrifying glimpse into his character, he is said to have been in high spirits as he escorted his mother to the lavishly decorated ship that had been booby-trapped for the occasion. Tacitus says Nero gazed into Agrippina's eyes and embraced her, either because he was enjoying his own performance so much or because 'the final sight of his mother, who was about to die' (*periturae matris supremus adspectus*) touched his sentimental heart.[73]

It is to the *Annals* that we owe the fullest account of what happened next. It was a calm night, the sky above the bay glittering with stars, as the boat pulled away from the shore. Agrippina was accompanied by two friends, Crepereius Gallus and Acerronia Polla. They were relaxing on couches under a canopy, marvelling at the astonishing change in Nero's behaviour, when one of the sailors gave a signal. The roof of the canopy, which had been fitted with lead weights, fell in on the passengers, killing Crepereius instantly. The two women were saved by the raised sides of their couch, although Agrippina sustained a wound to the shoulder. The boat stayed afloat, however, and some of the crew who were in on the plot rushed to one side, trying to force it to capsize. Both women were tipped into the water where

Acerronia, imagining it would increase her chances of being rescued, made the fatal mistake of pretending to be Agrippina. She shouted to the sailors to save the emperor's mother, only to have them beat her to death with oars, poles and anything else that came to hand. It was a scene of pure horror, but probably one that preserved Agrippina's life. Injured and probably a little drunk, she would have seen her friend's blood spreading through the water as Acerronia's cries faded to nothing. With a great effort of will, Agrippina managed to remain silent and escape the notice of the crew as she struck out for the shore. (Did Nero not know that his mother was a strong swimmer? How on earth did he miss this vital fact?) She was picked up by a fishing boat and managed to get home to her villa at Bacoli.

Her situation was desperate. The 'accident' had happened close to land, with no high winds or rocks to explain the collapse of the boat. The events of the evening flashed through her mind, revealing Nero's affectionate words and gestures to be utterly false. Quick thinking as ever, she knew that her only chance of getting through the next few hours lay in pretending to believe that the whole thing was an accident. She summoned a freedman, Lucius Agermus (Agerinus in some versions), and told him to hurry to Baiae with a message that she had survived a disaster at sea. She instructed Agermus to reassure Nero that she wanted to rest and there was no need to visit her, even though she knew how worried he would be. Then she lay back on her bed and waited.

It was not yet morning, but Nero knew of the plot's failure before Agermus could deliver Agrippina's message. The emperor was in a state of abject terror, fearing that his mother might appeal to the army to rise in her defence or denounce him to the Senate. He had his advisers, Seneca and the Praetorian prefect, Sextus Afranius Burrus, woken up and appealed to them for advice. Not for the first time, three powerful Roman men gathered to plot the elimination of a defenceless woman, recalling the moment Claudius's freedmen discussed how best to get rid of Messalina. Ignoring everything he owed Agrippina, without whom he might have eked out his life in bitter exile, Seneca brazenly asked Burrus whether the Praetorian Guard would obey an order to kill her. Burrus, who had been appointed on Agrippina's recommendation eight years earlier,[74] was as disloyal and self-serving as Seneca, responding regretfully that the Praetorians would never agree to harm the daughter of Germanicus. Nero then summoned Anicetus, whom he blamed for botching the construction of the booby-trapped boat, and ordered him to finish the job. Anicetus immediately agreed to go to Bacoli and kill the emperor's mother, while Nero came up with a hastily improvised plan to deflect blame. When Agermus arrived moments later with Agrippina's conciliatory message, the emperor dropped a sword at the man's feet and shouted that the freedman had tried to assassinate him. He was thinking ahead, preparing a statement to the effect that his mother had killed herself after her plot to kill *him* was exposed.

In Bacoli, meanwhile, crowds were gathering on the beach, having heard about Agrippina's astonishing escape and eager to celebrate her survival; it shows she was still popular with ordinary people, despite her son's attempts to isolate her. In the villa, however, Agrippina was growing more anxious by the minute. It was barely any distance to Baiae, yet Agermus had not yet returned with Nero's response. Suddenly a column of soldiers arrived and began driving the crowds away from the beach. Agrippina heard them surrounding the villa, followed by the sound of the front door being broken down. Anicetus burst inside, pushing past every slave he came across, and made for the dimly lit bedroom where Agrippina had been trying to recover. The few remaining servants melted away and she was left with a single maid, who now ran from the room. 'Are you leaving me as well?' she pleaded to no avail (*tu quoque me deseris?*).[75]

Then she caught sight of Anicetus with two thugs close on his heels: Herculeius and Obaritus, a naval captain and a centurion respectively. She rallied, telling them that if they had come to check on her condition, they could report back to Nero that she was well; if they had come to kill her, however, she absolutely refused to believe her son was responsible. Was she still acting or trying to convince herself? She did not have to wait long to have her worst fears confirmed. The three men surrounded her bed. Herculeius hit her on the head with a club, while Obaritus drew his sword to finish her off. Agrippina summoned all her strength, pulled back her robe and pointed to the womb from which Nero had emerged. 'Strike my belly!' she cried out (*ventrem feri!*).[76] Blows rained down on her and she was hacked to death.

Agrippina's final words are stirring, defiant – and very likely invented. Domestic homicide is painful and messy, often involving a great deal more violence than is required to kill the victim (the modern term is 'overkilling'). Would she really have been conscious long enough, and had the presence of mind, to call out something that would resonate down the ages? Then there is the question of who could have heard and recorded any such declaration, given that the only people present were her assassins – unless her maid had managed to hide within earshot. The story of the collapse of the boat had spread like wildfire and Agrippina survived long enough to tell servants back at the villa what had happened. But she was alone with her killers and they are hardly likely to have repeated a story that shows her in such a positive light.

A slightly different version of the anecdote appears in Dio, who has Agrippina shouting, 'Strike here, Anicetus, strike here, for this bore Nero.'[77] But the earliest version of the story is to be found in the *Octavia*, where the chorus tells the story of the fake shipwreck and the assassination that followed. The playwright has Agrippina pointing to her womb and crying out, 'Here is where your sword must be plunged' (*hic est fodiendus*).[78] Even this version is not original, appearing to have been borrowed from a scene in Seneca's play *Oedipus*, which is based on the myth of the Greek king who killed his father and married his own mother. The Romans placed great store on having a 'good' death and historians wanted to portray the former empress meeting her end nobly, behaving with the courage expected of Augustus's last surviving great-granddaughter. Their accounts are dramatic, but they obscure the excruciating pain and paralysing fear experienced by victims of fatal domestic violence.

Nero, meanwhile, had spent a sleepless few hours at Baiae waiting for his hitmen to report back. When he got the news that his orders had been carried out, he insisted on rushing to Bacoli to see his mother's corpse for himself. Perhaps he wanted to be sure she was really dead, but Suetonius implies other motives, claiming that Nero examined her body closely, 'fondling her limbs' (*contrectasse membra*) and offering a running commentary on her appearance.[79] He was most likely putting on a performance, pretending to an indifference he did not really feel, but the scene is cold-blooded even for him. Dio paints an even more lurid scene, claiming that Nero demanded to have Agrippina's body stripped naked. 'I didn't know I had so beautiful a mother,' he is supposed to have said, lending credence to the anecdotes about his desire for his mother.[80] (Sexual arousal at the sight of a woman's dead body is not as unusual as people like to imagine.)

The death of such an illustrious figure in the dynasty as Agrippina would normally have been followed by a ceremonial funeral, and a place in the mausoleum built in Rome by her great-grandfather, Augustus. But the state of her corpse would have revealed too much about the circumstances of her death, and she was hastily cremated on a dining couch. Nero is said to have been haunted by guilt for the rest of his life, crying out that he was being hounded by his mother's ghost (*materna specie*) and the Furies.[81] We do not need to take these stories too seriously, however, because Nero's murder of his mother was not a one-off. His career in domestic homicide had just begun, as we shall see in the next chapter.

9

The Serial Killer

Domitia (*c.*8 BC or earlier–AD 59): elder sister of the emperor Nero's father and the empress Messalina's mother, Nero's aunt. **Poisoned**, aged 66 or older

Claudia Octavia (AD 39/40–62): daughter of the emperor Claudius and Messalina, first wife of the emperor Nero. **Forced into fake suicide**, aged 22 or 23

Poppaea Sabina (*c.*AD 30–65): second wife of the emperor Nero. **Kicked to death**, aged 35

Claudia Antonia (AD 30–66): elder daughter of the emperor Claudius, half-sister of Claudia Octavia, sister-in-law of the emperor Nero. **Murdered**, aged 36

Statilia Messalina (*c.*AD 35–post 69): empress of Rome, third wife of the emperor Nero, **date and cause of death unknown**

One of Nero's first actions after viewing his mother's corpse was to send a letter to the Senate claiming that Agrippina had been plotting to kill him.[1] He made her sex central to the denunciation, accusing her of wanting to share power (*consortium imperii*) with him and receive oaths of allegiance from the Praetorian Guard, an indignity she supposedly intended to impose on the Senate and the Roman people.[2] There was no evidence for any of it, but Nero or his adviser Seneca – who actually composed this egregious piece of victim-blaming – appealed to traditional ideas about womanhood to destroy public sympathy for Agrippina. It's impossible to overestimate the durability of Roman misogyny and the letter had the desired effect; while Nero was still in Baiae, officers of the Praetorian Guard came to congratulate him on his escape from the 'crime' planned by his mother (*matris facinus*).[3] His friends rushed to temples to give thanks for his survival, while the inhabitants of nearby towns followed suit. Nero even tried to suggest that a new, more merciful era had dawned, now his mother was out of the way, by announcing the recall from exile of a number of her 'victims', including the woman called Calpurnia who was banished – and, according to Dio, possibly put to death on Agrippina's orders – several years earlier.[4] (Dio's casual reference to the 'murder' of a woman who turned out to be alive a decade later shows the bias of ancient authors where Agrippina is concerned.) Nero also allowed the ashes of Lollia Paulina, who had briefly been the wife of his uncle Caligula, to be brought back to Rome and placed in a tomb suitable to her station. Nero was restless, nevertheless, unable to settle in the villa from which he had escorted his mother to her death. All sorts of fanciful noises are supposed to have been heard, including ghostly trumpets sounding in the hills and 'sobbing from his mother's grave' (*planctusque tumulo matris*).[5]

Nero wandered around Campania, afraid of returning to Rome, and when he could put it off no longer, he was mightily relieved to see cheering crowds turn out to greet him. He was even more reassured when his mother's statues were pulled down and senators fell over themselves to condemn her, while her birthday was declared a day of ill omen – the same humiliation imposed on her own mother by Tiberius twenty-six years earlier. Rome was now in the grip of a mentally unstable twenty-one-year-old whom no one dared oppose, openly at least, and the atmosphere seems to have resembled that of Stalin's Soviet Union, with public displays of servility undercut by dangerous (and hence anonymous) acts of rebellion. A piece of graffiti appeared around the city, adding Nero's name to a list of mythical matricides,[6] and a veil was thrown over a surviving statue of Agrippina with a message addressed to her son: 'I am embarrassed but you have no shame.'[7]

Nero was reassured by the realisation that he had got away with the brazen murder of his mother, however, and we know that a sense of impunity is vital to serial killers. When nothing happened, the emperor became bolder, putting another female relative in his sights. His paternal aunt Domitia was in her mid-to-late sixties, much older than his mother, and in poor health. She seems to have been genuinely fond of him, despite her long-standing animosity towards her former sister-in-law, but she also had substantial assets, owning magnificent homes in Baiae and Ravenna. Nero was on the lookout for an alternative to the seaside villa in Baiae that now held such dreadful associations with his mother's final night, and the prospect of getting his hands on his aunt's estate proved irresistible.

The opportunity presented itself on his return to Rome, when he heard that Domitia was confined to bed with severe constipation (*duritie alvi*). He turned up at her house on the pretext of paying his respects, bringing with him his usual retinue of sycophants and hangers-on. Domitia suspected nothing and was delighted to see him, propping herself up and stroking his cheek; she would be able to die happy, she told him, if she lived long enough to see him shave for the first time. (This was a milestone for Roman men and Nero introduced a new festival, the *Juvenalia* or games of youth, to mark the occasion of his own first shave in 59.) The emperor turned to his companions and pretended to make a joke, saying he had better shave instantly. But as soon as he left the sickroom, he summoned his doctors and instructed them to give Domitia an overdose of laxative – literally to 'purge the sick woman generously' (*ut largius purgarent aegram*). Nero did not even wait until Domitia was dead to seize her property, destroying her will so no one could argue with him.[8]

Gossip now added the suspicious death of Nero's aunt (*amitae necem*) to the killing of his mother, something that raises questions about the judgement of his latest mistress, Poppaea Sabina. It may be that Poppaea, who was around seven years older than Nero, mistakenly believed she could control a man who must have felt like an immature boy. (She was twenty-seven or twenty-eight when the affair began in 58.) But it is important to remember that habitual abusers of women, which Nero certainly was, are adept at shifting blame away from themselves. They are often charming in the early stages of a relationship, bombarding their next victim with presents and declarations of love.[9] Nero had wealth, power and status on his side, and it would not be surprising if Poppaea, whose troubled early life we shall hear more about in a moment, was taken in.

The anonymous author of the *Octavia* has the emperor showering Poppaea with gifts, some of them taken from his wife; when the fictional Octavia rails at Poppaea as Nero's 'arrogant mistress, glittering with trinkets taken from our house' (*superbam paelicem, nostrae domus spoliis nitentem*), she is describing a scenario that will be painfully familiar to women who've seen their partner's new squeeze wearing a familiar pair of earrings.[10] So will Nero's complaint, in the play, that he's the victim in the breakdown of his marriage because his first wife never loved him. 'My wife's spirit was never in harmony with mine' (*animusque numquam coniugis iunctus mihi*), the fictional Nero laments.[11] The playwright was privy to the emperor's inner circle and he may well be reflecting something Nero actually said to his friends, although it would not be surprising if Octavia was unable to conceal her distaste for him. Like other women who get involved with married men, Poppaea would have heard Nero's side of the story, not his wife's, and women who are forced into competition with each other rarely get to compare notes.

Of course, Poppaea gets a bad press from ancient historians. Dio accuses her of indulging in 'extremes of luxury' and having an obsession with her appearance, claiming that she bathed every day in the milk of 500 asses that had recently foaled.[12] The story seems to have originated with Pliny, who makes the improbable assertion that some women were in the habit of washing their faces with it 700 times a day, and that it was Poppaea who started the fashion. He also suggests she was so keen on donkey milk as a means of keeping her skin white that she used to travel with 'whole troops' of female asses.[13] (Feeding and milking a herd of this size would be quite an undertaking and we never hear where all these ruminants were supposed to be grazed.) Tacitus is frustrated by evidence that appears to contradict his hostile opinion of Poppaea, reluctantly admitting that she was beautiful, clever and charming to talk to; he even acknowledges that she rarely went out in public and, when she did, her face was usually veiled. But he warns us not to be fooled: while 'she put on a show of modesty, her behaviour was depraved' (*modestiam praeferre et lascivia uti*).[14] His condemnation of Poppaea is one of the most savage anywhere in the *Annals*, designed to bear out his contention that her 'conspicuous immorality' (*insignis . . . impudicitia*) was the source of 'a whole series of national disasters' (*magnorum rei publicae malorum initium fecit*).[15] Everything has to be twisted to fit that verdict, raising doubts about the veracity of much of what was written about her in the ancient world.

Ancient authors are not much interested in Poppaea's background. She can't have been born much later than the early 30s because her father, Titus Ollius, was a friend of Sejanus and killed himself after the prefect's execution in 31.[16] Archaeological evidence suggests that her mother's family was from Pompeii, where her ancestors were wealthy but plebeian. They had achieved prominence in Rome only very recently, when Poppaea's maternal grandfather, Gaius Poppaeus Sabinus, became a consul during the reign of Augustus. (We met her mother, the elder Poppaea Sabina, in Chapter 7.) The family had business interests and owned property in Campania, probably including a sumptuous villa at Oplontis, a small settlement on the bay of Naples which has since been covered by the modern town of Torre Annunziata. Oplontis is only 5 kilometres from Pompeii, and when Vesuvius erupted in AD 79 the villa was buried under six metres of ash, lava and mud. It remained hidden until the late sixteenth century, preserving much of its interior decoration, and it has only partially been excavated in the twenty-first. Its vast scale and ravishing frescoes indicate how wealthy Romans lived during Nero's reign, and if it did indeed belong to Poppaea, the style of the decoration suggests that she was a woman with exquisite taste.

The villa was around a century old when she inherited it, with many of the original frescoes intact, and she appears to have kept it as it was until an earthquake in 62 necessitated repairs; the internal walls are covered in brilliantly coloured paintings from the previous century, showing theatrical scenes and images from Greek and Roman myths. Deep reds and ochres, familiar from less grand houses in Pompeii, contrast with cooler forest scenes in the *viridarium*, an indoor garden reminiscent of the dining room in Livia's villa at Porta Prima. A colonnade surrounds a central courtyard, presenting plenty of opportunities for shade, and a swimming pool has been found in the garden. It is not difficult to imagine Poppaea drifting through the rooms on a hot day, stopping to watch a lifelike bird drinking from a stone basin or admire a peacock whose tail hangs over the frame of another wall painting. She may well have stayed in the villa with Nero in AD 64, two years after their marriage, when the couple visited Pompeii together and made offerings of jewels and gold to the city's patron goddess, Venus.

Poppaea's return to her maternal ancestors' home town as empress marked a remarkable turnaround in her family's fortunes. Both sides of it had been dogged by a series of scandals, beginning with the suicide of Titus Ollius. Poppaea was probably no more than a year old at the time and originally known as Ollia, the feminine version of her father's name, but it was changed to Poppaea Sabina after his death to reflect her relationship with her maternal grandfather. The younger and much more famous Poppaea is supposed to have inherited her mother's good looks, but it is not evident from surviving statues, which show a woman with chubby cheeks and heavy formal curls.

Like so many girls from prominent families in Rome, Poppaea was a victim of marriage to an older man while she was still a child; she was around fourteen when she was married to the prefect of the Praetorian Guard, a career soldier called Rufrius Crispinus. Three years into the marriage, her mother killed herself after being accused of adultery with the wealthy senator from Gaul, Decimus Valerius Asiaticus. The death of Poppaea's mother would have affected her more deeply than that of her father, whom she was too young to remember, but by the age of seventeen she had lost both parents to suicide. As well as being prematurely sexualised, she had a vivid example in her own mother of the risks faced by a Roman woman who lost her reputation. It is hardly surprising, after this experience, that Poppaea, from the beginning of her affair with Nero, was intent on persuading him to marry her. Tacitus's claim that she cared nothing for her reputation is surely wrong, but his observation that she was swayed neither by her own feelings nor anyone else's (*neque adfectui suo aut alieno obnoxia*) is plausible, given the losses and humiliations she had experienced.[17] Poppaea would not be the first Roman woman to cope with shame and violent death by cauterising her feelings, and while various men are described as being madly in love with her, there is little evidence that she reciprocated their affection. She and Nero's mother Agrippina are presented as deadly rivals, but they evidently shared an ability to suppress emotion.

Poppaea had a son with Crispinus but the marriage ended in divorce. It was of so little interest to Roman historians that the date was not recorded, and it is not clear either when she married her second husband, Otho. He was a couple of years younger than Poppaea, and if Nero cut an unprepossessing figure, it has to be said that his best friend was hardly an improvement. Otho was overweight, with bandy legs and improbably curled hair which was almost certainly a wig, while his self-indulgent personal habits led to accusations of effeminacy; he had his body hair plucked regularly and he used to rub his face with moist bread (*pane madido*) every day to slow the growth of his beard.[18]

It is not clear whether Poppaea was seduced by Otho, who then introduced her to Nero, or whether she was already having an affair with the emperor, who ordered Otho to marry her to provide cover. The consensus is the latter but Tacitus, who follows this version of events in his *Histories*, changed his mind in the *Annals*, which was written later.[19] Whether Poppaea had much say in the matter is open to question; Otho was a member of Nero's inner circle and they certainly were not averse to sharing the same woman, at the outset at least. In Dio's unvarnished version of events, Nero 'gave' Poppaea to Otho and the two men subsequently 'enjoyed her together'.[20] The thought of the petulant emperor and his vain friend passing Poppaea back and forth for sex is unedifying, but it evidently went on for quite some time.

The arrangement went wrong when Otho unexpectedly fell in love with Poppaea, becoming insanely jealous of her sexual relationship with Nero. One evening, when the messengers sent by the emperor arrived at Otho's house to collect Poppaea to spend the night at the imperial palace, they returned empty-handed. Nero reacted furiously, storming over to Otho's house where he fumed outside the bedroom door, alternatively pleading and demanding the return of his 'property' (*depositum*).[21] It was a catastrophic misjudgement on Otho's part: Nero retaliated by dissolving his marriage to Poppaea, who was forced into a second divorce. The emperor banished Otho from Rome, concealing the humiliation he felt at Otho's reneging on their arrangement by appointing him governor of Lusitania (Portugal and western Spain). A witty verse circulated in Rome, asserting that Otho had been exiled for adultery – but the adultery was with his own wife.[22]

This scandalous sequence of events demonstrates once again how elite Roman women were used by their male counterparts. Ancient historians portray Poppaea as petulant and controlling, threatening to return to Otho if the emperor did not get rid of his mother, but it seems unlikely that she had so much influence. In any case, it's clear that Otho and Poppaea were still married at the time of Agrippina's murder in March 59, something confirmed by the fact that Nero gave his friend a starring role in the plot to place his mother on board the booby-trapped boat. Otho willingly agreed to deflect suspicion by hosting a 'startlingly generous dinner for both of them' (*cenam utrique exquisitissimae comitatis*) in Baiae, which he would hardly have done if the bust-up over Poppaea had already ended his friendship with the emperor.[23] It is safe to assume that the terminal breach between the two men and Otho's divorce from Poppaea did not happen until later that year, which is Suetonius's version of events, and even then Nero was in no rush to divorce Octavia and marry his mistress.

What is certainly true is that this second divorce made Poppaea's situation a great deal worse, exposing her to the kind of malicious gossip relayed with lip-smacking relish in Roman histories. But ancient authors have another, undeclared motive for portraying Poppaea in the worst possible light, which is to highlight the contrast with Octavia. That the two women were rivals is not in doubt, but Nero had been abusing his young wife for years before he began an affair with Poppaea. Wives and mistresses are often in the same difficulty, trying to manage a superficially charming but selfish man, but they are encouraged to see each other as enemies. It's unlikely that Octavia and Poppaea recognised how much they had in common, each having suffered the tragic loss of both parents. But it left them isolated and at the mercy of powerful men, a fact usually overlooked in the rush to see them as polar opposites.

By the time Claudia Octavia married Nero, she had already witnessed the suicide of the first man she was supposed to marry and the murder of her mother, Messalina. The precise year of her birth was not recorded, so we can only estimate her age at important moments; Roman historians were more interested in her dynastic significance than her character or history. Tacitus says she was in her twentieth year in AD 62 but that would place her birth after that of her brother Britannicus, and we know he was the younger sibling. Octavia was engaged in childhood to Augustus's great-grandson Lucius Junius Silanus Torquatus, but the engagement was broken off in 48 after he was accused of incest with his sister, and Silanus killed himself a few months later. It is unclear how well Octavia knew Silanus, who was considerably older, but the end of the engagement made her available for marriage to her stepbrother Nero in 53 (the obstacle posed by that relationship was circumvented by Octavia's paper adoption into another patrician family). Two huge bereavements followed quickly: her father, Claudius, in 54, and her brother, Britannicus, in 55. The marriage was spectacularly unhappy, not least because of Nero's exceptionally unpleasant character, and the fact that Octavia was effectively sidelined by Nero's affair with her freedwoman Acte. His appalling conduct towards his wife seems to have been an open secret in Rome, although it barely finds its way into histories of the period.

Even so, the marriage is treated at length in the *Octavia* which, as we have already seen, offers a rare account of domestic abuse in the first century AD. It has strikingly modern touches, mirroring the way well-meaning friends and family members offer bad advice to women in violent relationships. Octavia's old nurse pleads with her to try to placate Nero, prompting an impassioned response from the empress: 'I would overcome cruel lions and savage tigers more easily than the fierce heart of this cruel tyrant' (*vincam saevos ante leones tigresque truces fera quam saevi corda tyranni*).[24] One of the drama's most unusual features is Octavia's frank acknowledgement of how sickening she found having sex with Nero, a reaction that was surely shared by many victims of child marriage in the period.[25] She appears to suggest that she could not bear to sleep with him after witnessing her brother's death, and it is certainly true that the marriage was childless. Even Nero's friends were appalled by his neglect of Octavia and criticised him to his face, according to Suetonius, prompting Nero to sneer that being the emperor's wife ought to be enough for her.[26] But the most telling detail of his abuse of Octavia appears in Suetonius's next sentence, where its significance appears to have been entirely overlooked. According to the historian, Nero made 'numerous failed attempts to strangle her' (*eandem . . . saepe frustra strangulare meditatus*). Suetonius doesn't explain how the emperor's assaults on his wife became known but strangulation leaves visible marks on the neck, which seems more likely than Octavia revealing something so intimate and shocking.[27]

Most modern authors take the phrase at face value, assuming that Nero was trying to kill his wife with his bare hands, even though he usually got other people to do his dirty work for him. That assumption needs to be challenged, and not just because Nero was bigger and stronger than Octavia. We know now that non-fatal strangulation, sometimes but not always for sexual purposes, is a common feature of domestic abuse. In 2021, when it became apparent that men were using a 'rough sex' defence in English courts after women had been killed or seriously injured, the law was changed to create a new offence of non-fatal strangulation; the UK government acted after research showed that some men were choking their partners or deliberately impeding their ability to breathe 'in an attempt to control or intimidate them'.[28] It is impossible to know whether Nero was sexually aroused by strangling Octavia, something that would fit with his perverted tastes, or whether his aim was to demonstrate dominance over her. But one of the most striking modern findings about non-fatal strangulation is its relationship to domestic homicide. Women who have been subjected to this kind of abuse are *seven times* more likely to be murdered by their partner.[29] And that is exactly what happened to Octavia.

Nero had repeatedly put off a decision to divorce Octavia until his hand was forced by Poppaea's pregnancy in AD 62. Suddenly Nero had the prospect of an heir and he seized it, covering up what he was doing by making a series of graceless accusations against his wife. First she was accused of being infertile, then she was supposed to have committed adultery with a slave, an Egyptian flute player called Eucaerus. The latter accusation was entirely out of character, given Octavia's awareness of her rank and lineage, so Nero resorted to having her slaves tortured under the supervision of the Praetorian prefect Ofonius Tigellinus. It backfired when most of the women refused to make false allegations against their mistress, insisting on her innocence even under torture. One of them, a slave called Pythias, turned the tables on Tigellinus, telling him that 'every female part of Octavia's body was cleaner' (*castiora esse muliebria Octaviae*) than his dirty mouth.[30]

But Nero pressed ahead with the divorce, marrying Poppaea only twelve days later, and vented his spleen against his now ex-wife by banishing her from Rome. In an ominous echo of what Tiberius had done to his grandmother Agrippina, the emperor had Octavia removed from the city under armed guard. Nero was a coward, however, and what happened next shook him to the core, namely the demonstrations mentioned in the introduction to this book. He had reckoned without the affection people felt for Octavia and they poured onto the streets in an echo of the protests that followed Augustus's banishment of his daughter Julia more than sixty years earlier. Nero hesitated, and even considered remarrying Octavia, something that inspired a delighted crowd to invade the palace precincts again, but the emperor changed his mind and the revellers were driven out by soldiers armed with swords.

Tacitus blames Poppaea for what happened next, claiming that she played on the emperor's anxieties and encouraged him to have his wife murdered. The historian portrays Poppaea as 'mad with fear' (*metu atrox*), prostrating herself at Nero's feet and claiming that her life was in danger from Octavia's supporters.[31] But the scene Tacitus describes is a reprise of an earlier one where Poppaea is supposed to have urged Nero to get rid of Agrippina, suggesting he was in danger from his mother and threatening to go back to Otho if he didn't act.[32] Both episodes play to the notion that the emperor was weak and unable to resist the histrionics of a manipulative woman, putting us firmly back in the territory of 'she made me do it'. Yet Nero's choice of an old accomplice – Anicetus, commander of the Roman fleet at Miseno and one of his mother's assassins – to deal with the Octavia problem once and for all suggests that the emperor was determined to rid himself of a wife he regarded as little more than a nuisance. He summoned Anicetus and offered him a stark choice: admit to adultery with Octavia or be killed himself. Anicetus did not hesitate, agreeing to 'confess' to a council of Nero's friends and even inventing titillating details that went beyond his brief. The scoundrel was duly packed off to Sardinia, where he lived comfortably in exile and died a natural death.

Octavia, meanwhile, faced a series of new and absurd charges. She was supposed to have seduced Anicetus in the hopes of raising an insurrection in the Roman fleet against her husband. She was also supposed to have become pregnant by Anicetus and procured an abortion, despite the fact that Nero had previously accused her of being infertile. Nero used these allegations as an excuse to exile her to Pandateria, to the old Augustan palace where several generations of Julio-Claudian women had been confined and murdered. It is hard to believe that she did not fall into despair on her arrival, accompanied by soldiers who watched her every move. Tacitus says as much, describing her as so convinced of her impending murder that she was 'already removed from life' (*iam vitae exempta*).[33] The expected death sentence arrived a few days later, although Nero insisted that the murder had to look like suicide. Octavia pleaded with her killers, pointing out that she had accepted her divorce from the emperor, but to no avail. Her hands were tied and her veins cut open. When her blood did not flow fast enough, the men forced her into a scalding hot bath. They waited until she was dead, cut off her head and took it back to Rome.[34]

If Poppaea now believed herself to be safe, she would be proved wrong. At first, things went well: her daughter, Claudia Augusta, was born the following year, in January of AD 63, and Nero showered his wife and child with honours. It was a rare moment

of optimism in his chaotic reign, but the infant died four months later; Nero declared the child a goddess, although he was once again without an heir. Just over a year later, one of the defining events of his reign took place, diverting his thoughts from the question of the succession. In the summer of AD 64, a hugely destructive fire broke out in Rome, burning for nine days and destroying almost three-quarters of the city. Tacitus describes it as a disaster (*clades*) and records harrowing scenes as the flames raced across flat areas of the city, surged up the hills and shot down again to ravage low-lying areas. The air was filled with the cries of terrified women (*lamenta paventium feminarum*), while the able-bodied tried to help the very young, elderly and disabled to escape the conflagration.[35] Choking smoke attacked their lungs and some people who had lost all their possessions sat down and died, along with others who hadn't been able to rescue their loved ones.

The emperor was absent from Rome when the fire began, staying in the villa at Anzio that used to belong to his murdered mother, and he was in no rush to return to the city. When he finally arrived, he threw open public buildings and constructed emergency accommodation for the homeless, but the damage – to Rome and to his reputation – had been done. A rumour swept the streets, claiming that the emperor had chosen to perform on his private stage at Anzio while the fire burned, singing a composition that compared modern disasters to the destruction of Troy (*Troianum excidium*).[36] It's the origin of the famous story that Nero fiddled while Rome burned, and he made things worse by shamelessly taking advantage of the space created in the city by the flames. According to Tacitus, Nero 'used the downfall of his country to build a palace' (*Nero usus est patriae ruinis exstruxitque domum*), unintentionally providing a symbol of his profligacy.[37]

The Domus Aurea (Golden House) consisted of a series of buildings stretching from the Palatine to the Esquiline hill, decorated with gold, precious stones and mother of pearl. An enormous pool was surrounded by a garden consisting of cultivated fields, woods and vineyards, where domestic and wild animals roamed. The palace's dining rooms had ceilings of panelled ivory (*cenationes laqueatae tabulis eburneis versatilibus*) that could be moved aside to shower Nero's guests with flowers or perfume from sprinklers.[38] Suetonius's surprising claim that the principal banqueting room was circular, and revolved day and night, has been confirmed by excavations at the site. In addition, the emperor could not resist installing a colossal bronze statue of himself in the entrance.

Such extravagance was the height of bad taste when so many people had lost their homes and livelihoods, and it's hardly surprising that they began to blame the emperor for the fire. Nero cast around for a scapegoat and lighted upon a relatively new sect, the Christians, who were rounded up and murdered in the most brutal fashion. This strategy rebounded on him because people pitied the victims, realising that they had been sacrificed to appease one man's savagery (*in saevitiam unius*) rather than for the public good.[39]

The following year, Poppaea became pregnant again. We do not know whether Nero had already begun to abuse her physically by then, although the fact that he repeatedly squeezed his first wife's neck hard enough to leave marks suggests he had. Domestic abuse often escalates when a woman is pregnant, enraging immature men who are used to being the centre of attention and resent their wives' need to put themselves first. One evening, when Nero returned home late from the chariot races, Poppaea remonstrated with him (*conviciis incesserat*). Suetonius says she was ill (*aegra*), suggesting that this second pregnancy was not going well, but Nero didn't care. He responded angrily, lashing out with a kick to her stomach that killed her (*ictu calcis occidit*).[40] The scene, as Poppaea collapsed in agony and bled to death, is almost too horrible to imagine.

The killing was the sole occasion in almost a century of abuse when a Julio-Claudian emperor personally carried out a domestic homicide. In modern terms, it would more likely result in a charge of manslaughter rather than one of murder, with the defence arguing that Nero had not intended to kill Poppaea, but the fact remains that he was responsible for the death of his wife and unborn child. The risk of serious injury to a pregnant woman who is attacked in this manner could hardly be more obvious, yet ancient and modern historians alike are willing to give Nero the benefit of the doubt. Tacitus describes the cause of the fatal assault on Poppaea as 'her husband's random fit of anger' (*fortuita mariti iracundia*), as though the whole thing was an unfortunate accident.[41] Indeed variations of the word 'accident' appear in some accounts, as though what happened to Poppaea was similar to someone stepping onto the Appian Way and being hit by a chariot. Dio says Nero 'leaped upon her with his feet while she was pregnant', but cannot say whether the emperor did it 'accidentally or intentionally'.[42] Mary Beard thinks it is pointless to debate whether Poppaea's death was a 'tragic accident or terrible domestic abuse'.[43] For some unaccountable reason, and with heavy-handed irony, Tom Holland describes the killing from Nero's point of view:

> He had never meant to kill Poppaea. It had been foolish of her to nag him, of course, especially when all he had done was to come home late one evening from the races. He had been tired, and pretty much bound to lash out; but even so, he should never have kicked her in her swollen stomach.[44]

It can't be said often enough that violence against women is *never* an accident, regardless of the perpetrator's intentions. The attempt to frame it as such in this instance is all the more perverse in the light of Nero's documented history of violence against his first wife. Men assault women because they can, because they are bigger and stronger and can't be bothered to control their emotions. The frequently cited fact that Nero mourned Poppaea extravagantly, burning huge quantities of perfume in her honour, doesn't tell us anything about his true feelings towards her; abusive men often display remorse, although it's usually mixed with a generous dollop of self-pity. We know that Nero couldn't bear to have her remains cremated, trying to preserve her corpse by having it stuffed with spices and embalmed. He gave her a state funeral, acting the role of chief mourner before Poppaea's body was placed in the Mausoleum of Augustus, but what happened next shows that his view of human beings was that they were essentially replaceable.

Nero ordered a search far and wide for someone who looked like Poppaea, was presented with a young freedman with a passing resemblance to his dead wife, and had him castrated. The emperor 'married' him at a ceremony in Greece and gave the unfortunate young man an obscene name, Sporus, which is a Latinisation of a Greek word meaning 'semen', or 'spunk'.[45] It is another example of Nero's omnivorous attitude towards domestic abuse, which encompassed male as well as female victims – and it's impossible not to marvel at the conclusions drawn from this bizarre series of events. Nero's 'grief', the preposterous funeral arrangements, even his 'marriage' to a male lookalike, are all taken as evidence of his love for Poppaea; Suetonius claims that Nero 'loved her passionately' (*dilexit unice*), while Dio talks about how much the emperor missed her following her death.[46]

Nero's supposedly warm feelings for Poppaea did not extend to her son from her first marriage, who was named Rufrius Crispinus after his father, the former Praetorian prefect; after her death, the emperor had his stepson drowned on a fishing trip because the boy was reported to have played at being a general and an emperor.[47] (The boy's father was exiled to Sardinia in the year Poppaea was killed, on the 'pretext' of a conspiracy but really because Nero hated her ex-husband, according to Tacitus. Crispinus committed suicide in 66, after hearing he had been sentenced to death.)[48] The emperor soon set about looking for a third wife, a pressing matter since he was nearing thirty and had no heir. His arrogance is demonstrated by the identity of the woman he now had in his sights, namely his former sister-in-law. Even in a family as used to intermarriage as the Julio-Claudians, it was an astonishing choice: Claudia Antonia was Claudius's daughter from his marriage to Aelia Paetina and hence the elder half-sister of Nero's first wife, Octavia.

Antonia was thirty-six in AD 66, when the emperor proposed marriage, and she had already been widowed twice. Both her husbands had died violent deaths: her first, Gnaeus Pompeius

Magnus, had a famous name in Rome but was stabbed to death while in bed with a male lover; the second, Faustus Cornelius Sulla Felix, came from another illustrious family and was the empress Messalina's half-brother, but he had been murdered on Nero's orders four years before the emperor's proposal to Antonia. Cornelius Sulla was accused of involvement in plots against Nero in 56 and again in 58, when he was exiled to Marseille, even though Tacitus claims he was too stupid to organise a coup; the historian says the emperor misread Cornelius Sulla's 'weak mind' (*socors ingenium eius*) as a form of cunning.[49] He languished there for four years until Nero sent assassins to burst in and kill him during dinner, taking his head back to Rome where the emperor joked that Cornelius Sulla's hair was prematurely grey (*praematura canitie*).[50] However Antonia felt about this second husband, whom she had married probably for dynastic reasons, she was now another Julio-Claudian woman who found herself alone and exposed. And Cornelius Sulla is unlikely to have been the only prominent citizen whose hair turned grey in the terrifying, unstable atmosphere of the final years of Nero's reign.

In 65, a conspiracy gathered pace to assassinate the emperor and replace him with a popular aristocrat called Gaius Calpurnius Piso, whom we met in Chapter 6 when Caligula abducted his first wife. The plot was betrayed but Nero saw it as an opportunity to get rid of people he no longer had any use for, including Seneca. The philosopher had asked to retire from public life three years earlier, aware that the emperor's current advisers were poisoning his mind against his former tutor.[51] There was no evidence that Seneca was involved in the Pisonian conspiracy, but Nero ordered a tribune of the Praetorian guard, Gavius Silvanus, to go to a house where Seneca was staying, six kilometres from Rome, bearing a death sentence. (Silvanus, who *was* one of the plotters, could not bear to deliver the news himself, so he chickened out and sent one of his staff officers.) Seneca's preparations for suicide are one of the great set pieces of the *Annals*, showing him obeying the tenets of his philosophy to the last, but it is also clear that he was curating his reputation. He remonstrated with his friends, pointing out that no one could have been unaware of Nero's cruelty (*saevitiam Neronis*) after the emperor had his mother and brother murdered (*matrem fratremque interfectos*).[52] This denunciation would have been rather more impressive if Seneca had not erased his own discreditable part in the slaughter of Agrippina.

Antonia's name came up in connection with Piso's conspiracy as well, but Tacitus dismisses the idea that she would have risked her life and reputation on such a reckless venture. Even so, a breath of suspicion may have been enough to convince Nero that Claudius's surviving daughter posed a threat, prompting the mad idea that he could neutralise the risk by making her empress now he was single again. The notion that Antonia would consider marriage with the man responsible for the murders of her half-sister and her second husband, and quite possibly that of her half-brother Britannicus as well, beggars belief. And while Antonia's appearance in Roman history is brief, it is impossible not to admire her courage; she refused Nero's offer of marriage, even though it was more in the nature of an order and she would have known the likely consequences. Nero reacted predictably, bringing spurious charges against her and having her executed.[53]

He turned next to one of his mistresses, a woman called Statilia Messalina, whose father or uncle, Titus Statilius Taurus Corvinus, made a brief appearance in Chapter 8. Ancient historians are not much interested in Statilia, leaving us in the dark about her background, although Guy de la Bédoyère believes she was 'intelligent and beautiful'; he also follows the consensus by suggesting she was a couple of years older than Nero.[54] Statilia already had a husband, Marcus Julius Vestinus Atticus, one of the consuls in 65, who had married her despite being aware of her relationship with the emperor. There is a curious echo here of the Nero-Otho-Poppaea triangle, although it is important to remember that neither woman had as much power or choice as the men. In this instance, however, it's clear that Nero loathed Vestinus and hoped he would be incriminated in the Pisonian conspiracy, as so many prominent men and women had been. When he wasn't, Nero resorted to using 'the brute force of an autocrat' (*ad vim dominationis conversus*) against his rival, sending a battalion of soldiers to Vestinus's house overlooking the forum. A dinner party was in full swing when they arrived – the emperor evidently enjoyed performative gestures – and Vestinus understood straightaway what was happening. He shut himself in his bedroom, summoned his doctor and had his veins cut open (*abscinduntur venae*). Rather than wait for death, Vestinus asked to be carried to a bath and had himself lowered into hot water to speed up the process. His guests, meanwhile, were not allowed to leave the house, apparently because it amused Nero to think about their terror as the evening tipped over into horror; the emperor gave the order for them to be released only when he decided they had been punished enough for their 'lavish consular feast' (*epulis consularibus*).[55]

Even if Statilia wasn't present at this bloodbath, she must have been scared out of her wits by such a brutal demonstration of her lover's pathological jealousy, and she was hardly in a position to refuse his proposal of marriage. Statilia thus became Nero's third wife and empress of Rome, probably in the summer of 66, although it must have crossed her mind that she might end up as the victim of a third uxoricide. The fact that she managed to outlive him is explained by a stroke of luck: Nero was overthrown only two years into their married life.

A successful strike against a Roman emperor needed the support of the army. In March 68, Gaius Julius Vindex, governor of east and northwestern Gaul, rebelled against Nero. He appealed to Galba – mentioned in Chapter 8, and by now governor of much of Spain and northern Portugal – to bring his legions and join him in a coup. Vindex killed himself after being defeated by forces loyal to the emperor at the battle of Vesontio in May, but there were growing calls for Galba to replace Nero. When the Praetorian prefect, Gaius Nymphidius Sabinus, declared for Galba, the emperor realised the game was up. He went into hiding at a villa on the outskirts of Rome owned by one of his freedmen, where he heard the news that the Senate had declared him a public enemy.[56] Nero killed himself with the help of his secretary, Epaphroditus, on 9 June AD 68, the sixth anniversary of Octavia's murder on Pandateria. He was thirty and had ruled Rome for almost fourteen turbulent years. He was subjected to *damnatio memoriae* after his death and his sumptuous palace barely outlasted him, stripped of its gold and precious jewels by looters; the bare rooms of the Domus Aurea were filled with earth and the site built over, disappearing from view until its accidental rediscovery in the late fifteenth century. Nero's widow, Statilia, seems to have taken no part in his funeral, leaving it to his former mistress Acte and two of his old nurses to carry his remains to the tomb of his father's family on the Pincian hill (now the site of the Borghese Gardens).[57]

Nero's demise had profound consequences for the Roman state. He had no children with Statilia and he had destroyed his only chance of producing an heir when he killed Poppaea, which meant that his death brought the period of Julio-Claudian rule in Rome to a close. A period of violent instability followed, known as 'the year of the four emperors', when three men – Galba, Otho and Vitellius – enjoyed brief reigns before Vespasian restored peace in December 69 and founded the Flavian dynasty. In a bizarre turn of events, Otho had declared his intention of marrying Nero's widow, Statilia, in what feels like belated revenge for being forced to hand Poppaea to the emperor a decade earlier. It would have made Statilia empress for a second time but, fortunately for her, Otho was defeated in battle with Vitellius's forces and killed himself before the marriage could take place. Ancient historians don't tell us what happened to Statilia after Otho's suicide, even though she stands out as a rare survivor of both Nero and his doomed dynasty.

It is impossible to ignore the symmetry: a historical period that began with what was in effect a rape, when Octavian abducted a pregnant woman from her husband, ended with the murder of another pregnant woman by his great-great-grandson. The Julio-Claudians had dominated the city's and the empire's politics for almost a century, producing some of the most extraordinary female figures in western history. But even they were no match, in the end, for the sexual predators and callous abusers who held all the power in first-century Rome.

10

The Long Shadow of Roman Misogyny

At first sight, Rome's early imperial history is a lesson in what happens to women in a society where they have few rights and protections. Even the most privileged, born into families that had enjoyed wealth and influence for centuries, were vulnerable to arbitrary and fatal abuse at the hands of male family members. Everyday life for poor women, non-citizens and slaves was much harsher, but it's clear that no woman was safe in a society that vested so much power in men. And the pivotal position of Rome in western culture, especially after the Renaissance, highlights a paradox: generations of influential men were educated to admire a culture that produced sublime works of art and literature without understanding that abuse of women was integral to the system. In the UK, a knowledge of Greek and Roman history was regarded as essential to a gentleman's preparation for public life, producing prime ministers, authors and artists who could find an ancient parallel for just about every occasion. In the twenty-first century, the former prime minister Boris Johnson is one of a handful of people who still peppers speeches and articles with classical quotations, but ancient Rome continues to fascinate.

What it tells us about the status of women has been overlooked, however, and it's important to draw the correct conclusion. It would be easy to argue that the mistreatment of women in the early Roman empire shows the importance of legal protection in women's lives, which is obviously the case, but it also tells us *why* that law is sorely needed. Women were abused and murdered on a horrifying scale in ancient Rome, not because of something unique to its culture, but because there was nothing to stop men behaving badly. A wife who was beaten or raped by her husband had no redress, something that's been addressed in the modern world by a raft of laws that supposedly protect women. But laws are useful only if they are enforced, ensuring that barriers to justice for women – all women, including those who are poor, not white, and disregarded by the criminal justice system – are dismantled. In the twenty-first century, that still isn't happening in one crucial respect, which is the failure to confront and punish violence against women. There are countries, such as Iran and Afghanistan, where women have very few rights and are under the control of theocratic governments that direct every aspect of their lives. Modern democracies, by contrast, have criminalised rape, physical assault and controlling behaviour, but the laws are so poorly enforced as to be close to useless.

If that seems harsh, it's because the misogyny that allowed women to become victims of extreme male violence 2,000 years ago hasn't gone away, despite frequent assertions from politicians, lawyers and police officers that such behaviour is intolerable. In the UK, between two and three women are killed each week, more than half of them by current or former partners. The figure is similar in Italy, where the killing of a twenty-two-year-old student, allegedly by an ex-boyfriend, prompted thousands of people to pour onto the streets in 2023 in protest against yet another femicide.[1] There have been similar demonstrations in France, yet excuses are still being made for men who kill intimate partners, as they were when powerful Roman men murdered their wives. The new law to make non-fatal strangulation a stand-alone offence in England and Wales, mentioned in the previous chapter, was introduced after an outcry about the number of violent abusers who claimed that women *wanted* to be asphyxiated – and juries believed them.

The sheer extent of domestic abuse is staggering: around 1.4 million women are victims in England and Wales each year, according to the government's own crime survey.[2] Many of those cases aren't reported to the police, either because women are afraid of their partners or have no confidence in the authorities, but official records show almost 900,000 recorded crimes involving domestic abuse each year. Not even 10 per cent lead to prosecutions and fewer than 40,000 offenders were convicted in the twelve months to March 2023, confirming that you don't have to be a Roman emperor to get away with terrorising women. The numbers are even worse when it comes to sex offences, where almost 200 women report a rape to the police in England and Wales *every day*, yet the conviction rate is below 2 per cent.[3] The overwhelming majority of men who commit rape in this country will never be punished, and the lack of any effective sanction means that the criminal justice system is *creating* serial rapists. Police and prosecutors are defensive, claiming that rape cases are difficult to prove, while politicians take refuge in ordering one inquiry after another. Feminists have long argued that the quality of investigations has been undermined by misogyny *within* police forces, which means that victims may find themselves being interviewed by detectives who share the attitudes of their attackers. In 2023, following the rape and murder of a young woman by a serving police officer two years earlier, an inquiry found 'institutional' misogyny in the country's biggest force, the Metropolitan Police Service.[4]

Some forms of violence towards women have in effect been decriminalised, to a point where we find ourselves almost as unprotected as Roman women, who had no hope of seeing abusers in powerful positions stopped and punished. It represents a massive failure to recognise and root out hostile attitudes to women which have been tolerated for centuries. This book is intended, in part, as a reminder that those attitudes towards women are not new, and that ancient Rome is one of the earliest and best documented sources. The stereotypes used by Roman authors – nagging wives, bossy mothers, ungrateful daughters – are familiar to us today. Even the most flagrant abuse of women has been normalised, so much so that the billionaire paedophile Jeffrey Epstein got away with targeting vulnerable teenage girls for years, apparently without raising suspicions among his powerful friends and acquaintances. 'It is . . . said that [Jeffrey] likes beautiful women as much as I do, and many of them are on the younger side,' Donald Trump remarked archly in 2002.[5] In 2016, just before that year's presidential election, a tape emerged of Trump boasting about assaulting women in 2005 but it didn't stop him being elected to one of the most powerful positions in the world.[6] Nor were his supporters put off in 2023 when a jury decided he had sexually abused a writer, E. Jean Carroll, in the changing room of a department store in New York during the 1990s – and lied about it afterwards.[7]

In the same year, Dior renewed its multi-million-dollar contract with the film star Johnny Depp, whose former wife, the actor Amber Heard, had accused him of domestic violence. Three years earlier, Depp lost a libel action against a British newspaper when a judge found that Heard, who is almost a quarter of a century younger than her more famous ex, had told the truth about twelve of fourteen alleged incidents of domestic violence. Evidence shown to the court included a series of text messages in which the *Pirates of the Caribbean* star indulged in violent fantasies, including one where he expressed the hope that Heard's 'rotting corpse' was decomposing in the trunk (boot) of a car. In another, he fantasised about drowning her and burning her body. 'I will fuck her burnt corpse afterwards to make sure she's dead,' he wrote to a friend. A couple of years later, Depp sued in a US court after Heard described herself as a victim of domestic abuse, without naming him, in an article in the *Washington Post*. The actor won the case and Heard was trolled mercilessly, accused of being a liar and received death threats.[8] Depp's career has since flourished, with other actors and musicians queueing up to support him, while Heard is reported to have paid her ex $1 million in damages.[9]

When the emperor Augustus vilified his daughter and granddaughter as 'ulcers and sores', he was employing a tactic so frequently used by abusers that it now has an acronym. DARVO stands for 'deny, accuse, reverse victim and offender', and it has been used time after time by woman-haters who are determined to portray *themselves* as victims. Nothing will change until we stop allowing violent men to define their behaviour as a reaction to intolerable provocation, as the emperor Tiberius did when he pursued a vendetta against his former wife Julia and her children 2,000 years ago. None of this is an argument for ditching the study of Classics; I wish more girls had the opportunity I was given to discover the extraordinary world of ancient Rome. But it is to suggest that much more sceptical attitudes are needed towards a civilisation that was simultaneously sophisticated and brutal, especially towards women. Imagine what the empress Agrippina might have achieved if she had been a man, able to exercise power without having to depend on a husband or a son. The dynasty's women have been belittled precisely *because* their role was so central to its survival, something their menfolk didn't want to acknowledge. It would have died out without Augustus and Scribonia's daughter Julia, who towers over this book – and Roman history – like a female colossus. That's why I'm going to make the not entirely mischievous suggestion that the dynasty should be renamed the Juli*a*-Claudians, in recognition of women who deserve to be as well known as the men who used and abused them.

ACKNOWLEDGEMENTS

My love of Latin was instilled by two outstanding teachers, Mrs Anstey and Miss Hunt. They taught Latin in the days when we knew next to nothing about our teachers' lives outside lessons, so I never found out Mrs Anstey's first name. She taught me at the Girls' Grammar School in Stevenage, which I left when I was in the fifth form, but I knew Enid Hunt better because she took me though A level Latin at Basingstoke High School for Girls. There were only four of us in the class and I won the sixth-form prize for Latin, a *Cassell's Latin Dictionary* that I used for my translations of Roman authors when I was researching this book.

The idea of writing about the Julio-Claudian women began to germinate in 2021, when I visited the British Museum's *Nero* exhibition with my friend Beverly Byrne, who shared my scepticism about attempts to rehabilitate one of history's most flagrant abusers of women. The book started to take shape while I was staying at the seventeenth-century farmhouse in Sussex owned by two lawyer friends, Naomi Cunningham and Tim Pitt-Payne KC. A conversation with Katie Hawks in their kitchen helped develop my ideas, and I also appreciated being able to talk about ancient history with Cherry Lavell in front of Naomi's not-quite-so-ancient Aga. My agent, Caroline Michel, grasped what I wanted to do as soon as I told her my ideas; I couldn't have written the book without her support and the enthusiasm of Arabella Pike at William Collins. Kit Shepherd's copy-editing was meticulous and illuminating. Several of my friends spent a couple of years listening to me recite the many wrongs done to Roman women: I'd like to thank Lynn Shepherd, Lynn Pilgrim, John Pilgrim, Mary-Ellen Field, Caroline Coon, Sean Kelly, Barbara Hayes, Anita Bennett, Heather Finlay, Paola Diana, Jacqueline Faridani, Siobhan Coughlan and Diana Bentley for their patience. They provided endless encouragement and I hope they're happy with the outcome.

ENDNOTES

Introduction

1 'Understanding and Addressing Violence against Women: Femicide', World Health Organization information note, 29 September 2012, p. 1.
2 M. D. T. De Bienville, MD, *Nymphomania, or, A Dissertation Concerning the Furor Uterinus*, trans. Edward Sloane Wilmot (London: J. Bew, 1775).
3 *Nero: The Man behind the Myth*, British Museum, London, 27 May 2021–24 October 2021, curated by Thorsten Opper and Francesca Bologna.
4 *Octavia* 931–57. The play was traditionally attributed to Seneca but is no longer believed to be by him as it refers to events after his suicide in AD 65. It's also strikingly sympathetic to women, unlike the views expressed elsewhere by the philosopher. Its authorship remains one of the most tantalising mysteries from the ancient world.

1: The *I, Claudius* Effect

1 Some authorities believe the figure is Livia but the official guide to the Ara Pacis argues that chronological evidence supports the idea that it's Julia. See Orietta Rossini, *Ara Pacis* (2006; Milan: Mondadori Electa, 2012), p. 69.

2   Cicero, *Pro Caelio* 16.38.
3   Ibid. 20.49.
4   Ibid. 8.16.
5   Velleius Paterculus, *Roman History* 2.93.
6   Ibid. 2.74.
7   Suetonius, *Nero* 51.
8   'The Real Wicked Witch of Rome', *Daily Mail*, 10 May 2021.
9   Robert Graves, *I, Claudius* (1934; London: Penguin, 2006), pp. 67–8.
10 Ibid. pp. 130–1.
11 Robert Graves, *Goodbye to All That* (1929; London: Penguin, 2000), p. 237.
12 'How Writer Robert Graves' FIVE Lovers and His Bizarre Web of Sexual Intrigue Made His Steamy Novel I, Claudius Look Like a Tea Party', *Daily Mail*, 9 August 2018.
13 Mary Beard, *SPQR: A History of Ancient Rome* (London: Profile, 2015), p. 314.
14 Cassius Dio, *Roman History* 54.16. Translations from the Greek of Cassius Dio's *Roman History* are from the Loeb Classical Library edition, translated by Earnest Cary (9 vols, Cambridge, MA: Harvard University Press, 1914–27).
15 Sarah B. Pomeroy, *Goddesses, Whores, Wives and Slaves: Women in Classical Antiquity* (New York: Schocken, 1975), p. 164.
16 The philosopher Aristotle and the physician Hippocrates placed it at fourteen, while archaeological evidence from southern Italy in pre-Roman times suggests it might have been even later, between fourteen and sixteen. See Alessia Bareggi et al., 'Puberty in Pre-Roman Times: A Bioarchaelogical Study of Etruscan-Samnite Adolescents from Pontecagnano, Southern Italy', *International Journal of Osteoarchaeology*, vol. 32, no. 5 (2022), pp. 1114–29.
17 Guy de la Bédoyère, *Domina: The Women Who Made Imperial Rome* (New Haven and London: Yale University Press, 2018), p. 36.

2: Surviving Augustus

1. Cassandra N. Ramar and W. R. Grimes, 'Perineal Lacerations', *StatPearls*, 26 June 2023.
2. Cassius Dio, *Roman History* 48.44.
3. Tacitus, *Annals* 5.1.
4. Suetonius, *Augustus* 62.
5. Tacitus, *Annals* 1.10.
6. For a discussion of the use of *ducere* as a euphemism for having sex with a woman, often a prostitute, see J. N. Adams, *The Latin Sexual Vocabulary* (London: Duckworth, 1982), p. 174.
7. Suetonius, *Augustus* 69.
8. Robert Graves, *I, Claudius* (1934; London: Penguin, 2006), p. 20.
9. Tom Holland, *Dynasty: The Rise and Fall of the House of Caesar* (London: Abacus, 2016), p. 47.
10. Anthony Blond, *A Scandalous History of the Roman Emperors* (1994; London: Constable, 2000), p. 88.
11. Adrian Goldsworthy, *Augustus: From Revolutionary to Emperor* (London: Weidenfeld & Nicolson, 2014), p. 163.
12. Elaine Fantham, *Julia Augusti: The Emperor's Daughter* (Abingdon: Routledge, 2006), p. 17.
13. Ibid. p. 149 n. 12.
14. Suetonius, *Tiberius* 14.
15. Velleius Paterculus, *Roman History* 2.75.
16. Suetonius, *Tiberius* 6.
17. Velleius Paterculus, *Roman History* 2.72.
18. Suetonius, *Tiberius* 6.
19. Ibid.
20. Suetonius, *Augustus* 62.
21. Ibid. 79.
22. Ibid. 27.
23. Ibid. 67.
24. Ibid. 62.

25 Ibid.
26 Suetonius, *Augustus* 69.
27 Ibid.
28 Anthony Hirsh, 'Male Subfertility', *BMJ*, vol. 327, no. 7416 (20 September 2003).
29 Allan Massie, *Augustus* (London: Sceptre, 1987), p. 99.
30 Holland, *Dynasty*, p. 47.
31 Gaius Suetonius Tranquillus, *The Twelve Caesars*, translated by Robert Graves (Harmondsworth: Penguin, 1957), p. 84.
32 Suetonius, *Augustus* 62.
33 Ibid. 69.
34 Ibid. 63.
35 Cassius Dio, *Roman History* 58.2.
36 Laura Doyle, *The Surrendered Wife: A Practical Guide for Finding Intimacy, Passion, and Peace with a Man* (New York: Simon & Schuster, 2006).
37 Cassius Dio, *Roman History* 54.19.
38 Tacitus, *Annals* 1.10.
39 Suetonius, *Gaius (Caligula)* 23.
40 Cassius Dio, *Roman History* 53.33.
41 *Annals* 2.41.
42 Tacitus, *Annals* 1.3.
43 Cassius Dio, *Roman History* 55.32.
44 Tacitus, *Annals* 1.6.
45 Cassius Dio, *Roman History* 57.3.
46 Tacitus, *Annals* 1.6.
47 Suetonius, *Augustus* 99.
48 Tacitus, *Annals* 1.5.
49 Cassius Dio, *Roman History* 56.30.
50 Graves, *I, Claudius*, p. 132.
51 Suetonius, *Tiberius* 50.
52 Cassius Dio, *Roman History* 57.12.
53 Suetonius, *Tiberius* 51.

3: Unfortunately, She Was a Nymphomaniac: Part I

1. Cassius Dio, *Roman History* 67.14.
2. Suetonius, *Augustus* 65.
3. Propertius, *Elegies* 4.11, Cornelia to Paullus.
4. Cassius Dio, *Roman History* 55.13.
5. Elaine Fantham, *Julia Augusti: The Emperor's Daughter* (Abingdon: Routledge, 2006), p. xi.
6. Mary Beard, *SPQR: A History of Ancient Rome* (London: Profile, 2015), p. 379.
7. Adrian Goldsworthy, *Augustus: From Revolutionary to Emperor* (London: Weidenfeld & Nicolson, 2014), p. 401.
8. Tom Holland, *Dynasty: The Rise and Fall of the House of Caesar* (London: Abacus, 2016), pp. 135–6.
9. Anthony Blond, *A Scandalous History of the Roman Emperors* (1994; London: Constable, 2000), pp. 96–7.
10. de la Bédoyère, *Domina*, p. 135.
11. Anthony A. Barrett, *Agrippina: Sex, Power, and Politics in the Early Empire* (New Haven and London: Yale University Press, 1996), p. 20.
12. *Annals* 1.53.
13. Macrobius, *Saturnalia* 2.5.9.
14. Velleius Paterculus, *Roman History* 2.100.
15. Cassius Dio, *Roman History* 55.10.
16. Suetonius, *Augustus* 65.
17. Fantham, p. 89.
18. Tacitus, *Annals* 1.53; Annals 3.24.
19. Seneca, *De Beneficiis* 6.32.
20. Cassius Dio, *Roman History* 55.10.
21. Suetonius, *Tiberius* 7.
22. Ibid.
23. Suetonius, *Tiberius* 10.
24. Suetonius, *Tiberius* 11.
25. Pliny, *Natural History* 29.27.

26 Madison Brazan, 'Controlling Their Bodies: Ancient Roman Women and Contraceptives', *UTSA Journal of Undergraduate Research and Scholarly Works*, vol. 4 (2018), p. 10.
27 Tacitus, *Annals* 1.53.
28 Macrobius, *Saturnalia* 2.5.6.
29 Fantham, p. 86.
30 Cassius Dio, *Roman History* 55.10.
31 Pliny, *Natural History* 7.45.
32 Tacitus, *Annals* 3.24.
33 Seneca, *De Brevitate Vitae* 4.
34 Suetonius, *Augustus* 65.
35 Fantham, p. 23.
36 Fantham, p. 26.
37 Macrobius, *Saturnalia* 2.5.2.
38 Juvenal, *Satires* 6.434–7.
39 Suetonius, *Augustus* 64.
40 Ibid.
41 Macrobius, *Saturnalia* 2.5.7.
42 Ibid. 2.5.3.
43 Ibid. 2.5.5.
44 Cassius Dio, *Roman History* 54.6.
45 Fantham, p. 66.
46 Beard, *SPQR*, p. 378.
47 Suetonius, *Tiberius* 7.
48 Ibid.
49 Tacitus, *Annals* 1.53.
50 Macrobius, *Saturnalia* 2.5.8.
51 Suetonius, *Augustus* 65.
52 Cassius Dio, *Roman History* 55.10a.
53 *Roman History* 2.102.
54 Ibid. 55.13.
55 Macrobius, *Saturnalia* 2.5.4.
56 Suetonius, *Augustus* 65.

57 Suetonius, *Augustus* 101; *Tiberius* 50.
58 Cassius Dio, *Roman History* 56.32.
59 Cassius Dio, *Roman History* 55.13.
60 Suetonius, *Augustus* 19.
61 Tacitus, *Annals* 1.53.
62 Ibid.
63 Cassius Dio, *Roman History* 57.18.
64 Tacitus, *Annals* 1.53.

4: Women Without Men

1   Suetonius, *Augustus* 23.
2   Ibid. 28.
3   Ibid. 86.
4   Suetonius, *Claudius* 26.
5   Suetonius, *Augustus* 19.
6   de la Bédoyère, *Domina*, p. 101.
7   Tom Holland, *Dynasty: The Rise and Fall of the House of Caesar* (London: Abacus, 2016), p. 146.
8   Suetonius, *Augustus* 72.
9   Pliny, *Natural History* 7.16.
10 Holland, *Dynasty*, p. 150.
11 Tacitus, *Annals* 3.24.
12 Ibid.
13 Ovid, *Tristia* 2.207.
14 Ovid, *Tristia* 2.103–8.
15 Suetonius, *Augustus* 65.
16 Tacitus, *Annals* 4.71.
17 Orietta Rossini, *Ara Pacis* (2006; Milan: Mondadori Electa, 2012), p. 78.
18 Tacitus, *Annals* 1.33.
19 Ibid. 6.25.
20 Ibid. 1.69.
21 Ibid.

22 Tacitus, *Annals* 2.75.
23 Suetonius, *Gaius (Caligula)* 1.
24 Tacitus, *Annals* 2.69.
25 Ibid. 2.71.
26 Ibid. 2.72.
27 Suetonius, *Gaius* 1.
28 Tacitus, *Annals* 3.1.
29 Tacitus, *Annals* 3.2–3.3
30 Suetonius, *Tiberius* 52.
31 Tacitus, *Annals* 3.16.
32 Ibid. 4.8.
33 Suetonius, *Gaius* 30.
34 Tacitus, *Annals* 4.17.
35 Ibid. 4.52.
36 Ibid.
37 Ibid.
38 Tacitus, *Annals* 4.53.
39 Ibid. 4.54.
40 The villa and its destruction are mentioned by Seneca in his essay *De Ira (On Anger)*, 3.21.
41 Tacitus, *Annals* 4.60.
42 Suetonius, *Tiberius* 53.
43 Tacitus, *Annals* 5.3.
44 Suetonius, *Tiberius* 64.
45 Ibid. 54.
46 Ibid.
47 Suetonius, *Tiberius* 53.
48 Ibid.
49 Ibid.

5: The Woman Who'd Had Enough

1   The term *damnatio memoriae* is modern but covers a whole range of sanctions used in ancient Rome, from removing

names from official lists, to disfiguring portraits and celebrating the anniversary of the subject's death with a public festival.
2. Tacitus, *Annals* 4.3.
3. Tacitus, *Annals* 3.3.
4. Suetonius, *Claudius* 30.
5. Ibid.
6. Ibid. 33.
7. Tom Holland, *Dynasty: The Rise and Fall of the House of Caesar* (London: Abacus, 2016), p. 237.
8. Suetonius, *Claudius* 3.
9. Tacitus, *Annals* 4.60.
10. Suetonius, *Gaius (Caligula)* 24.
11. J. N. Adams, *The Latin Sexual Vocabulary* (London: Duckworth, 1982), p. 198.
12. Suetonius, *Gaius* 24.
13. Cassius Dio, *Roman History* 59.11, 59.3.
14. Anthony A. Barrett, *Agrippina: Sex, Power, and Politics in the Early Empire* (New Haven and London: Yale University Press, 1996), p. 54; Annelise Freisenbruch, *The First Ladies of Rome: The Women behind the Caesars* (London: Jonathan Cape, 2010), p. 123.
15. *Caligula with Mary Beard*, BBC2, 2013.
16. Guy de la Bédoyère, *Domina: The Women Who Made Imperial Rome* (New Haven and London: Yale University Press, 2018), p. 171.
17. Jane M. Rudd and Sharon D. Herzberger, 'Brother-Sister Incest – Father-Daughter Incest: A Comparison of Characteristics and Consequences', *Child Abuse and Neglect*, vol. 23, no. 9 (1999), pp. 915–28.
18. Peter Yates and Stuart Allardyce, *Sibling Sexual Abuse: A Knowledge and Practice Overview* (Ilford: Centre of Expertise on Child Sexual Abuse, 2021), pp. 6, 8.
19. Tacitus, *Annals* 2.26.

20 Ibid. 1.29.
21 Ibid. 1.76.
22 Ibid. 2.44.
23 Cassius Dio, *Roman History* 57.13.
24 Ibid. 57.14.
25 Tacitus, *Annals* 4.3.
26 Suetonius, *Tiberius* 52.
27 Tacitus, *Annals* 2.84.
28 Ibid. 3.34.
29 Suetonius, *Tiberius* 62.
30 Tacitus, *Annals* 4.8.
31 Ibid. 4.10.
32 Ibid. 4.8.
33 Ibid. 4.11.
34 Barbara Levick, *Tiberius the Politician* (Routledge, 1976), p. 161.
35 Velleius Paterculus, *Roman History* 2.127.
36 Tacitus, *Annals* 4.39.
37 Ibid. 4.39–40.
38 Suetonius, *Tiberius* 65.
39 Flavius Josephus, *Jewish Antiquities* 18.182.
40 Cassius Dio, *Roman History* 58.10–11.
41 Suetonius, *Claudius* 27.
42 Cassius Dio, *Roman History* 58.11.
43 Tacitus, *Annals* 4.3.
44 Suetonius, *Tiberius* 62.
45 Cassius Dio, *Roman History* 58.11.
46 Tacitus, *Annals* 6.2.
47 Suetonius, *Tiberius* 76.
48 Suetonius, *Tiberius* 73.
49 Tacitus, *Annals* 6.50.
50 Cassius Dio, *Roman History* 58.26.
51 Tacitus, *Annals* 6.46.
52 Suetonius, *Gaius* 29.

53 Ibid. 23.
54 Cassius Dio, *Roman History* 59.3.
55 Suetonius, *Gaius* 23.

6: The Misogynist's Apprentice

1   Suetonius, *Gaius (Caligula)* 15.
2   Ibid. 12.
3   Ibid. 22.
4   Ibid. 50.
5   Ibid.
6   Suetonius, *Gaius* 23.
7   Cassius Dio, *Roman History*, 59.1.
8   Ibid. 27.
9   Ibid.
10 Ibid. 50.
11 Ibid. 54.
12 Ibid. 22.
13 Ibid. 60.
14 Mary Beard, *SPQR* (Profile, 2015), pp. 395 and 396.
15 Ibid. 45.
16 Tom Holland, *Dynasty* (Little, Brown), p. 301.
17 Ibid. 46.
18 Suetonius, *Gaius* 50.
19 Ibid. 36.
20 Cassius Dio, *Roman History* 59.3.
21 Suetonius, *Tiberius* 43.
22 Suetonius, *Tiberius* 44.
23 Ibid. 43.
24 Tacitus, *Annals* 6.51.
25 Ibid. 6.1.
26 Ibid. 6.1. From John Jackson's note, p.154 of the Loeb edition.
27 Suetonius, *Tiberius* 57.
28 Ibid. 45. J. N. Adams, *The Latin Sexual Vocabulary* (London:

Duckworth, 1982), p. 200, cites this use of *inludo* with reference to 'different types of insulting or sexual act [*sic*]'.
29. Cassius Dio, *Roman History* 58.22.
30. Suetonius, *Tiberius* 42.
31. Tacitus, *Annals* 6.20.
32. Suetonius, *Gaius* 10.
33. Ibid. 51.
34. Tacitus, *Annals* 6. 20.
35. Suetonius, *Gaius* 11.
36. Ibid. 23.
37. Ibid. 33.
38. See Chapter 1 for Claudilla as an example of teenage mothers dying in childbirth.
39. Suetonius, *Gaius* 12.
40. Tacitus, *Annals* 6.45.
41. Cassius Dio, *Roman History*, 59.1.
42. Ibid. 59.10.
43. Suetonius, *Gaius* 26.
44. Suetonius, *Gaius* 25.
45. Pliny, *Natural History* 9.58.
46. Suetonius, *Gaius* 25.
47. Juvenal, *Satires* 6.614–15.
48. Suetonius, *Gaius* 25.
49. Suetonius, *Life of Passienus Crispus*.
50. Tom Holland, *Dynasty: The Rise and Fall of the House of Caesar* (London: Abacus, 2016), p. 287.
51. Mary Beard, *SPQR: A History of Ancient Rome* (London: Profile, 2015), p. 396.
52. Seneca, De Consolatione ad Helviam (*Consolation to Helvia*) 10.4.
53. Flavius Josephus, *Antiquities of the Jews* 19.205.
54. Suetonius, *Gaius* 24.
55. Cassius Dio, *Roman History* 59.11.

56 Suetonius, *Gaius* 24.
57 Ibid.
58 Suetonius, *Gaius* 29.
59 Ibid. 37, 39.
60 Ibid. 56.
61 Ibid. 58.
62 Ibid. 59.
63 Cassius Dio, *Roman History* 59.30.

7: Unfortunately, She Was a Nymphomaniac: Part II

1 MIT Libraries DOME website, catalogue entry for photograph of a statue of Messalina holding Britannicus (Musée du Louvre MR 280, Ma 1224).
2 Juvenal, *Satires* 6.117–32.
3 Desmond Morris, *The Naked Woman: A Study of the Female Body* (London: Jonathan Cape 2004), pp. 20, 153.
4 Suetonius, *Claudius* 37.
5 For the use of *tentigo* to refer to a male erection, see J. N. Adams, *The Latin Sexual Vocabulary* (London: Duckworth, 1982), p. 103.
6 Pliny, *Natural History* 10.83.
7 'Empress Messalina – Nymphomaniac', *Imperium Romanum*, 18 November 2021.
8 Nathanael Richards, *The Tragedy of Messalina, Empress of Rome*, II.ii.39.
9 Suetonius, *Claudius* 26.
10 See Annelise Freisenbruch, *The First Ladies of Rome: The Women behind the Caesars* (London: Jonathan Cape, 2010), p. 127. Guy de la Bédoyère (Domina p. 195) thinks she was about twenty-three in the year she died, which would make her around thirteen at the time of her marriage to Claudius. Barbara Levick suggests she was fourteen or fifteen in her biography of Claudius (2nd edn, p. 63).
11 Suetonius, *Claudius* 17.

12 Ibid. 33.
13 Ibid.; Tacitus, *Annals* 11.29–30.
14 Suetonius, *Claudius* 27.
15 Ibid. 36.
16 Cassius Dio, *Roman History* 60.18.
17 Ibid. 60.28.
18 Ibid. 61.31.
19 Suetonius, *Claudius* 29.
20 Ibid. 38.
21 Ibid. 39.
22 Ibid. 29.
23 Ibid. 37.
24 Cassius Dio, *Roman History* 59.19.
25 Cassius Dio, *Roman History* 60.8.
26 Cassius Dio, *Roman History* 60.8.
27 Seneca, *Octavia* 944–6; Suetonius, *Claudius* 29.
28 Cassius Dio, *Roman History* 60.18.
29 Ibid. 60.27.
30 Ibid. 60.14.
31 Suetonius, *Claudius* 37.
32 Tacitus, *Annals* 11.37.
33 Josephus, *Antiquities of the Jews* 19.1.20.
34 Her daughter of the same name is much more famous, becoming empress after marrying Claudius's successor, Nero, in AD 62.
35 'Abuse is exacerbated by an attitude among some professionals that these children are "*troublesome*", "*promiscuous*", "*criminals*" or "*slags who knew what they were getting themselves into*" – rather than extremely vulnerable young people in need of support': All-Party Parliamentary Group for Runaway and Missing Children and Adults, 'Report from the Joint Inquiry into Children Who Go Missing from Care', June 2012, p. 7.
36 de la Bédoyère, *Domina* p. 190.

37 Tacitus, *Annals* 11.28.
38 Cassius Dio, *Roman History* 60.28.
39 See p. 108.
40 Tacitus, *Annals* 11.26.
41 Seneca, *Octavia* 257–72.
42 Tacitus, *Annals* 11.26; Cassius Dio, *Roman History* 61.31.
43 Tacitus, *Annals* 11.27.
44 Ibid. 11.28.
45 Ibid. 11.30.
46 Ibid. 11.31.
47 Ibid. 11.31.
48 Ibid.
49 Tacitus, *Annals* 11.32.
50 Ibid. 11.34.
51 Ibid.
52 Tacitus, *Annals* 11.37.
53 Ibid. 11.35.
54 Ibid. 11.35.
55 Ibid. 11.36.
56 Ibid. 11.37.
57 Ibid. 11.37.
58 Ibid. 11.38.
59 Ibid.
60 Tacitus, *Annals* 11.37.

8: The Last Woman Standing

1 Suetonius, *Claudius* 26.
2 Ibid.
3 Tacitus, *Annals* 12.5.
4 Ibid. 12.5–6
5 Ibid. 12.7.
6 Ibid. 12.64.
7 Cassius Dio, *Roman History* 61.33.

8   Tacitus, *Annals* 12.7.
9   Guy de la Bédoyère, *Domina*, p. 155.
10 Suetonius, *Nero* 5.
11 Tacitus, *Annals* 6.47.
12 Suetonius, *Nero* 6.
13 Ibid.
14 Ibid.
15 Suetonius, *Galba* 21.
16 Ibid. 5.
17 Quintilian, *Institutio Oratoria (Orator's Education)* 6.1.50.
18 Suetonius, *Life of Passienus Crispus*
19 Tacitus, *Annals* 12.56.
20 Ibid. 12.57.
21 Cassius Dio, *Roman History* 61.33.
22 Tacitus, *Annals* 12.22.
23 Ibid.
24 Ibid.
25 Cassius Dio, *Roman History* 61.32.
26 Annelise Freisenbruch, *The First Ladies of Rome: The Women behind the Caesars* (London: Jonathan Cape, 2010), p. 141.
27 de la Bédoyère, *Domina*, p. 211.
28 Tacitus, *Annals* 12.59.
29 Anthony A. Barrett, *Agrippina: Sex, Power, and Politics in the Early Empire* (New Haven and London: Yale University Press, 1996), p. xxi.
30 Ibid. pp. 104–5.
31 Tacitus, *Annals* 12.64.
32 Ibid. 14.9.
33 Ibid. 12.64.
34 Suetonius, *Nero* 7.
35 Suetonius, *Claudius* 46.
36 Ibid. 43.
37 Tacitus, *Annals* 12.64.

38 Ibid. 12.65.
39 Cassius Dio, *Roman History* 60.34.
40 Suetonius, *Claudius* 44.
41 Tacitus, *Annals* 12.66–7.
42 Suetonius, *Claudius* 44.
43 Cassius Dio, *Roman History* 61.34.
44 Seneca, *Apocolocyntosis* 2.
45 Suetonius, *Claudius* 44.
46 V. J. Marmion and T. E. J. Wiedemann, 'The Death of Claudius', *Journal of the Royal Society of Medicine*, May 2002.
47 Tacitus, *Annals* 12.42.
48 *Femicide Census 2020* (2020), p. 8.
49 'Adam Lanza Hated His Mother He Shot Dead Because He Thought "She Loved the Students at Sandy Hook More Than Him"', *Daily Mail*, 28 December 2013.
50 'Killer Who Choked Grandmother to Death and Repeatedly Raped Her Corpse Faces Jail', *LBC*, 22 February 2022.
51 Cassius Dio, *Roman History* 61.7.
52 Suetonius, *Nero* 9.
53 Tacitus, *Annals* 13.5.
54 Suetonius, *Nero* 51.
55 Tacitus, *Annals* 13.5.
56 Ibid. 13.14.
57 Ibid. 13.17.
58 Suetonius, *Nero* 34.
59 Tacitus, *Annals* 13.19.
60 *Octavia* 104–5.
61 Tacitus, *Annals* 13.13.
62 Suetonius, *Nero* 28.
63 Tacitus, *Annals* 14.2.
64 Suetonius, *Nero* 28.
65 Ibid.; Cassius Dio, *Roman History* 62.11.
66 Tacitus, *Annals* 14.2.

67 Tom Holland, *Dynasty: The Rise and Fall of the House of Caesar* (London: Abacus, 2016), p. 381.
68 Tacitus, *Annals* 14.1.
69 Ibid. 14.3.
70 Cassius Dio, *Roman History* 62.12.
71 Suetonius, *Nero* 34.
72 Cassius Dio, *Roman History* 62.13.
73 Tacitus, *Annals* 14.4.
74 Ibid. 12.42.
75 Ibid. 14.8.
76 My account of Agrippina's murder closely follows Tacitus's version, *Annals* 14.4–8, which is the most detailed one we have.
77 Cassius Dio, *Roman History* 62.13.
78 *Octavia* 368–72.
79 Suetonius, *Nero* 34.
80 Cassius Dio, *Roman History* 61.14.
81 Suetonius, *Nero* 34.

9: The Serial Killer

1 Tacitus, *Annals* 14.10.
2 Ibid. 14.11.
3 Ibid. 14.10.
4 Ibid. 14.12.
5 Tacitus, *Annals* 14.10.
6 Suetonius, *Nero* 39.
7 Cassius Dio, *Roman History* 62.16.
8 Suetonius, *Nero* 34.
9 Sandra Horley, former chief executive of Refuge, has written a book about the stratagems abusers use to draw unsuspecting women into controlling relationships: *Power and Control: Why Charming Men Can Make Dangerous Lovers* (London: Vermilion, 2002).
10 *Octavia* 125–6.

11 Ibid. 537.
12 Cassius Dio, *Roman History* 62.28.
13 Pliny, *Natural History* 28.50.
14 Tacitus, *Annals* 13.45.
15 Ibid.
16 Ibid.
17 Ibid.
18 Suetonius, *Otho* 12.
19 Tacitus, *Annals* 13.45; *Histories* 1.13.
20 Cassius Dio, *Roman History* 62.11.
21 Suetonius, *Otho* 3.
22 Ibid.
23 Ibid.
24 *Octavia* 86–8.
25 Ibid. 108–10.
26 Suetonius, *Nero* 35.
27 Ibid.
28 'New Non-Fatal Strangulation Offence Comes into Force', Ministry of Justice press release, 7 June 2022.
29 Nancy Glass et al., 'Non-Fatal Strangulation Is an Important Risk Factor for Homicide of Women', *Journal of Emergency Medicine*, vol. 35, no. 3 (2008), pp. 329–35.
30 Tacitus, *Annals* 14.60.
31 Ibid 14.61.
32 Ibid. 14.1.
33 Ibid. 14.64.
34 These dreadful events are described in detail by Tacitus, *Annals* 14.64.
35 Ibid. 15.38.
36 Ibid. 15.39.
37 Ibid. 15.42.
38 Suetonius, *Nero* 31.
39 Tacitus, *Annals* 15.44.

40   Suetonius, *Nero* 35.
41   Tacitus, *Annals* 16.6.
42   Cassius Dio, *Roman History* 62.27.
43   Mary Beard, *SPQR: A History of Ancient Rome* (London: Profile, 2015), p. 429.
44   Tom Holland, *Dynasty: The Rise and Fall of the House of Caesar* (London: Abacus, 2016), p. 421.
45   Suetonius, *Nero* 28.
46   Ibid. 35; Cassius Dio, *Roman History* 62.28.
47   Ibid.
48   Tacitus, *Annals* 15.71 and 16.17.
49   Ibid. 13.47.
50   Ibid. 15.57.
51   Ibid. 14.53.
52   Ibid. 15.62.
53   Ibid.
54   de la Bédoyère, *Domina*, p. 265.
55   Tacitus, *Annals* 15.68–9.
56   Suetonius, *Nero* 49.
57   Ibid. 50.

10: The Long Shadow of Roman Misogyny

1   'Mass protests in Italy after student stabbed 26 times', *Daily Telegraph*, 26 November 2023.
2   'Domestic Abuse in England and Wales Overview', Office for National Statistics bulletin, 24 November 2023.
3   'Rape Offences at Highest Recorded Level', *BBC News*, 21 July 2022.
4   Baroness Casey of Blackstock, 'Baroness Casey Review, Final Report: An Independent Review into the Standards of Behaviour and Internal Culture of the Metropolitan Police Service', March 2023.

5 'Trump Called Epstein a "Terrific Guy" Who Enjoyed "Younger" Women before Denying Relationship with Him', *Washington Post*, 8 July 2019.
6 'Transcript: Donald Trump's Taped Comments about Women', *New York Times*, 8 October 2016.
7 'Despite Being Found Liable for Attack, Trump Claims E. Jean Carroll Made "False Accusations" against Him', *NBC News*, 10 March 2024.
8 'Depp v Heard: How Has Online Abuse of Amber Heard Become Acceptable?', *Sky News*, 1 June 2022.
9 'Amber Heard settles defamation case with Johnny Depp', *Guardian*, 19 December 2022.

LIST OF ILLUSTRATIONS

PLATES

Garden fresco, Livia's Villa (Bridgeman)

Livia as a young woman (Adam Eastland / Alamy)

Julia the Elder (Musée Saint-Raymond / Didier Descouens)

Cameo of Tiberius (Sailko / Museo archeologico nazionale)

Agrippina the Elder (INTERFOTO / Alamy)

Antonia as a priestess of Augustus (Penta Springs Ltd / Getty)

Cameo of Livilla as Ceres with her twin sons (Staatliche Museen zu Berlin, Antikensammlung / Johannes Laurentius)

Messalina holding Britannicus (Masterpics / Alamy)

Messalina, Aubrey Beardsley (Artgen / Alamy)

Agrippina the Younger (funkyfood London – Paul Williams / Alamy)

Nero and Octavia (Henry Lillie Pierce Fund / Museum of Fine Art, Boston)

Poppaea Sabina (IanDagnall Computing / Alamy)

Title page, M. D. T. De Bienville, MD, *Nymphomania, or, A Dissertation Concerning the Furor Uterinus*, translated by Edward Sloane Wilmot, 1775. Wellcome Collection, London

Family group showing main characters in the Julio-Claudian dynasty. Marble frieze, Ara Pacis Augustae, late first century BC. Museo dell'Ara Pacis, Rome (Science History Images / Alamy) 12

Penguin Modern Classics cover, Robert Graves, *I, Claudius*, 2006 22

Marble head of Livia, late first century BC. British Museum, London (© The Trustees of the British Museum) 45

Marble head of Augustus, early first century AD. British Museum, London (© The Trustees of the British Museum) 45

Marble funerary statue of Marcus Claudius Marcellus, late first century AD. Musée du Louvre, Paris (Luisa Ricciarini / Bridgeman) 48

Livia holding a bust of Augustus after his death. Sardonyx cameo, early first century AD. Ephesos-Museum der Antikensammlung, Vienna (Bridgeman) 50

Marble head of Livia in later life, early first century AD. State Hermitage Museum, St Petersburg (Album / Alamy) 52

Palace of Augustus, Ventotene (Pandateria) (author's photo) 56

Marble head of Tiberius, early first century AD. British Museum, London (© The Trustees of the British Museum) 65

Silver denarius (coin) showing Julia with her sons Gaius and Lucius, minted in Rome, 13 BC. British Museum, London (© The Trustees of the British Museum) 72

Marble bust of Marcus Vipsanius Agrippa, first century BC, Paris, Musée Du Louvre (NPL – DeA Picture Library / Bridgeman) 75

Marble head of Lucius Caesar, late first century BC. Museo Arqueológico Provincial, Cuenca (Album / Alamy) 79

Marble head of Gaius Caesar, early first century AD. British Museum, London (© The Trustees of the British Museum) 80

Marble head of Agrippa Postumus, late first century BC. Musée Saint-Raymond, Toulouse (Didier Descouens) 84

Marble head of the younger Julia, late first century BC. Archäologische Museum, Innsbruck (https://www.flickr.com/photos/184393744@N06) 90

List of Illustrations

Marble bust of the elder Agrippina, early first century AD. Archaeological Museum, Istanbul (NPL – DeA Picture Library / Bridgeman)   98

Marble bust of Germanicus, early first century AD. Getty Villa Museum, Los Angeles (The Getty Center)   98

Germanicus with three of his children. Cameo, early first century AD. British Museum, London (© The Trustees of the British Museum) 102

Head of the elder Agrippina wearing a laurel wreath. Sardonyx cameo, mid-first century AD. British Museum, London (© The Trustees of the British Museum)   111

Marble head of Antonia, early first century AD. Palazzo Massimo alle Terme, Rome (Marie-Lan Nguyen)   117

Bronze bust of the elder Drusus, late first century BC. Museo Archeologico Nazionale, Naples (cestmoi.ca)   118

Sardonyx cameo (damaged) of Drusilla or Julia Livilla, mid-first century AD. British Museum, London (© The Trustees of the British Museum)   121

Marble bust of the younger Drusus, early first century AD. Musée Saint-Raymond, Toulouse (Album / Alamy)   124

Bronze sestertius (coin) showing Livilla's sons Tiberius and Germanicus Gemellus as infants, minted in Rome AD 22/23. British Museum, London (© The Trustees of the British Museum)   126

Marble equestrian statue of Caligula, early first century AD. British Museum, London (© The Trustees of the British Museum)   140

Miniature green chalcedony head of Drusilla or Julia Livilla, mid-first century AD. British Museum, London (© The Trustees of the British Museum)   155

Nicolai Abildgaard, *The Dying Messalina and Her Mother*. Oil on canvas, 1795–8. Statens Museum for Kunst, Copenhagen (piemags / SMKM / Alamy)   165

Aubrey Beardsley, *Messalina and Her Companion*. Ink and watercolour on paper, 1895. Tate Gallery, London (ARTGEN / Alamy)   166

Marble head of Claudius, mid-first century AD. British Museum, London (World History Archive / Alamy)   168

Claudius and Messalina in a chariot drawn by serpents. Sardonyx cameo, mid-first century AD. Cabinet des Médailles, Bibliothèque Nationale de France, Paris (GRANGER – historical picture archive / Alamy) 169

Messalina with her children, Claudia Octavia and Britannicus. Sardonyx cameo, mid-first century AD. Cabinet des Médailles, Bibliothèque Nationale de France, Paris (Clio20) 187

Claudius and Agrippina facing her parents, Germanicus and the elder Agrippina. Sardonyx cameo (the Gemma Claudia), mid-first century AD. Kunsthistorisches Museum, Vienna (INTERFOTO / Alamy) 195

Marble head of Agrippina the younger, mid-first century AD. Museo Archeologico Nazionale, Naples (Dea Picture Library / Getty Images) 202

Bronze statue of Agrippina the younger as empress, mid-first century AD. Museo Archeologico Nazionale, Naples (Marie-Lan Nguyen) 203

Marble bust of Nero, mid-first century AD. Museo Archeologico Nazionale, Cagliari (Paolo Certo / Alamy) 212

Marble statue of a boy in a toga, thought to be Britannicus (Fabrizio Garrisi) 215

Marble head of Poppaea Sabina, mid-first century AD. Palazzo Massimo alle Terme, Rome (Adam Eastland Art + Architecture / Alamy) 233

Bust of Otho. Galleria degli Uffizi, Florence (Stefano Baldini / Bridgeman) 234

Marble bust of Claudia Octavia, mid-first century AD. Cleveland Museum of Art, Cleveland 237

Silver drachm (coin) showing Nero and Poppaea Sabina on opposite sides, minted in Antioch (Antakya), AD 62/63. British Museum, London (© The Trustees of the British Museum) 241

The Domus Aurea, Rome (BackyardBest / Alamy) 243

Marble statue (damaged) of Claudia Antonia, mid-first century AD. Domus Romana, Rabat, Malta (M66DJE / Alamy) 246

Marble bust of Statilia Messalina, Musei Capitolini, Rome (https://www.flickr.com/photos/184393744@N06) 248

INDEX

All places are in Rome, unless stated otherwise.

Abildgaard, Nicolai 165
Acerronia Polla, Agrippina the Younger's friend 221–2
Actium 11, 69, 74, 99
Adams, J. N. 122
Aelia Paetina, Claudius' second wife 193, 194, 246
Aelius Sejanus, Lucius 107, 111, 112, 120, 121, 126–31, 134, 231
Aemilia Lepida, daughter of Julia the Younger 82, 87, 91, 92, 97
Aemilius Lepidus, Marcus 33, 122, 157
Aemilius Lepidus, Paullus 57
Aemilius Paullus, Lucius 91–2, 93
Afranius Burrus, Sextus 222–3

Agermus, Lucius 222, 223

Agrippa (Marcus Vipsanius) 49, 74–6, 79, 88, 150
    marriage to Claudia Marcella Major 74
    marriage to Julia the Elder 12, 56, 61, 73, 76, 77
Agrippina the Elder 88–91, 98–114
    Augustus and 149
    childhood 56, 76
    children 25, 87, 124, 129, 139
    exiled 55, 113
    family deaths 197
    marriage to Germanicus 18, 82
    death 8, 148
Agrippina the Younger 193–226
    childhood 112
    autobiography 18, 110
    Caligula and 155–6, 157, 175
    Claudius and 27
    marriages 122, 154
    Nero and 158, 227–9
    Poppaea and 234, 240
    portrayals 202, 213–14
    statues 204, 228, 229
    death 8, 236
Albucilla 198–9
Alfidia 32, 34

Alliaria 85
Andromeda 93
Anicetus 220, 223–4, 240
Annaeus Seneca, Lucius
  accounts 19, 63–4
  on Augustus 69
  on Caligula 154–5
  on Claudius 210–11
  Julia Livilla and 175–6
  on Julia the Elder 68, 163
  Nero and 207, 214, 222–3, 228
  Piso and 247–8
  works 3, 225
Antonia 2, 115–24, 130, 133–4, 136–7, 174, 248
Antonius, Iullus 62, 68, 69, 72, 74, 78, 81
Antonius, Lucius 35, 48, 56, 59, 73, 75, 79, 80, 81, 84
Antyllus (Marcus Antonius) 71
Apicata 128, 131, 132, 133
Ara Pacis Augustae (Altar of Augustan Peace) 12, 73, 97
Arruntius, Lucius 199
Asiaticus (Decimus Valerius) 177–8, 206
Asinius Gallus, Gaius 76, 113, 125
Atticus (Marcus Julius Vestinus) 249
Audasius, Lucius 84–5
Augustus (Gaius Octavius) 16–17, 89–98
  Julia the Elder and 8, 56–86
  legislation under 11, 12, 25, 102, 114, 172–3
  marble bust 45
  marriage to Claudia Pulchra 39–40, 41
  marriage to Livia 2, 3, 29–40, 43–7, 49–53
  marriage to Scribonia 29–30, 41–3
  planning dynasty 162
  private papers 18, 42, 44
  Tiberius and 100, 109
  Ventotene and 55

Baiae 15, 220–3, 225, 228, 229
Bacoli 220–2, 223, 225
Barrett, Anthony A. 60, 122, 206–7
Beard, Mary 60, 76, 122–3, 142, 154, 244
Beardsley, Aubrey 166
Blessed, Brian 21
Blond, Anthony 31, 60, 120
Britannicus 160–1, 214–16
  childhood 170, 181, 188, 209, 237
  line of succession 176, 207
  death 219
British Museum 5–6, 45
Brutus (Marcus Junius) 32–6

Caelius Rufus, Marcus 15–16
Caesonia, Milonia 138, 143, 153, 159, 173
Caligula 122–4, 134–6, 139–44, 148–59, 218
  childhood 103, 106
  Claudius and 173, 198
  Incitatus (horse) 6
  on Livia 47, 149
  'mad' emperor 80, 108, 111–12
  marriage 26, 173
  nickname 100
  statues 139–40, 159
  'three daggers' plot against 157, 175, 199
Callistus 174, 184, 194
Calpurnia 204–5, 228

Index   287

Calpurnia ('concubine') 170, 185
Calpurnius Piso, Gaius 152, 247–8
Calpurnius Piso, Gnaeus 102, 103–5
Capri 53
Carroll, E. Jean 255
Cassius Longinus, Gaius 32, 33, 35, 122
Cassius Longinus, Lucius 133
Catullus 15
Cercina (Kerkennah), Tunisia 85
Chaerea, Cassius 158
child marriage 25–7
Cicero, Marcus Tullius 15–16, 33
Cinna Magnus, Gnaeus Cornelius 44
Claudia Acte, Nero's mistress 217, 237, 250
Claudia Antonia, Claudius' daughter 193, 227, 246–8
Claudia Augusta, Nero's daughter 241
Claudia Marcella Major, Augustus' niece 74
Claudia Octavia, Nero's wife 8, 161, 170, 182, 188, 207, 217, 227, 236–41, 250
Claudia Pulchra, Augustus' first wife 15, 28, 39–41, 43, 69
Claudia Pulchra, Publius Quinctilius Varus's widow 109
Claudius 160–92, 199–211, 213–17
   Antonia and 134
   disabilities 44, 119–21
   Drusus the Younger and 105
   marriage 25, 27, 159, 193–7
   See also *I, Claudius* (Graves)
Claudius, Appius 62
Claudius Marcellus, Marcus 20–1, 47, 72, 74–5
Claudius Nero, Tiberius 18, 28–37, 51, 121, 148

Claudius Pulcher, Appius 32
Claudius Thrasyllus, Tiberius 151
Cleopatra 13, 22, 35, 71, 162, 163
Cleopatra ('concubine') 170, 185
Cleopatra Selene 13
Clodia Pulchra 15–16
Clodius Pulcher, Publius 15, 39, 104
Cluvius Rufus, Marcus 17–18, 154, 155
Conopas 93
contraception 67
Cornelia 57, 71, 91
Cornelius Scipio 62
Cornelius Sulla Felix, Faustus 247
Crassus (Marcus Licinius) 33
Crepereius Gallus 221
Crispinus, Quinctius 62
Crispinus, Rufrius 233, 234, 246
Crispinus the Younger 245–6

damnatio memoriae (non-person) 116, 134, 159, 167, 250, 266
DARVO ('deny, accuse, reverse victim and offender') 256
de la Bédoyère, Guy 27, 60, 93, 123, 180, 198, 206, 249
Depp, Johnny 255–6
Diana, Princess 58, 59
Dio, Cassius
   on Agrippina the Younger 196, 204–5, 210, 224
   on Apicata 131
   on Caligula 122, 135, 144
   on Calpurnia 228
   Drusus the Younger and 125
   on Gaius 79, 81
   history of Rome 19
   on Iullus Antonius 68
   on Julia Livilla 176
   on Julia the Elder 81, 84, 86

Dio, Cassius (*cont.*)
  on Livia 43–4, 47, 50
  on Livilla 133
  on Messalina 167, 177, 180, 183
  on Nero 218, 220, 225
  on Poppaea 235, 244
  on Sabinus 171
  on shortage of women 26
  on Tiberius 49, 147
Dio of Alexandria 15, 16
Domina (2021 TV series) 20–1
Domitia, Nero's aunt 201, 216, 227, 229–30
Domitia Lepida, Messalina's mother 167–8, 191, 193, 196, 199, 208
Domitian 18, 55
Domitius Ahenobarbus, Gnaeus 198–9, 212
Domus Aurea (Golden House) 242–3, 250
Doyle, Laura 44
Drusilla the Younger, Caligula's daughter 153
Drusus, son of Germanicus 106–7, 109, 112, 113
Drusus (Marcus Livius) 32
Drusus, son of Livia
  childhood 29, 31, 72, 76
  marriage and children 2, 91, 98, 116, 118–19, 208
  death 21, 51, 66
Drusus, son of Tiberius 104–6, 124–8
  Germanicus and 100, 101, 102
  marriage 119
  poison plot against 131, 133
  death 127, 148

Egypt 102
Elephantis 145

Ennia Thrasylla, Caligula's lover 138, 150–1
Epaphroditus 250
Epstein, Jeffrey 255
Eucaerus 239
Eudemus 133
Evodus 190, 191

Fantham, Elaine 31, 60, 63, 71
femicide (definition) 1, 8
Flavia Domitilla, Domitian's niece 55
France 253
Freisenbruch, Annelise 122, 206
frescoes 2, 145, 232
Fulvia 17, 35, 69, 99, 104, 164, 196

Gaius Caesar 79–81, 141
  childhood 12, 38–9, 48, 59, 73, 75
  marriage 78, 91, 119
  death 48–9, 84
Gaius Caesar (Caligula) *see* Caligula
Galba (Servius Sulpicius) 200, 250, 251
Gallius, Quintus 38
Gallus, Cestius 147
Gardens of Lucullus 178, 187, 188, 190–1
Gennari the Younger, Benedetto 22
Germanicus 82, 91, 98–114, 139, 152, 200
Germanicus Gemellus 126, 127
Goldsworthy, Adrian 31, 60
Grant, Michael 16
Graves, Robert 20–4, 42
  I, Claudius 20, 21–2, 24, 31, 47, 51, 116

Hadrian 18
Halotus 210, 211

Index

Heard, Amber 255–6
Herculeius 224
Holland, Tom 31, 42, 60, 93, 120, 142, 154, 219, 244

I, Claudius (Graves) 20, 21–2, 24, 31, 47, 51, 116
infanticide 96
Italy 253

Jackson, John 146
Johnson, Boris 7, 252
Josephus, Flavius 130, 154, 155, 177
Julia Drusilla, Caligula's sister 112, 138, 148, 153, 155–6, 159
Julia the Elder, Augustus' daughter 2–4, 15–16, 54–87
  biographies of 31
  Caligula on 149
  childhood 30, 41
  Drusus the Younger and 125
  exiled 8, 43, 55, 70, 78–81, 189
  marriage to Agrippa 47, 60–1
  marriage to Marcellus 27
  marriage to Tiberius 58, 65–7, 107, 146
  portrayals 12, 21, 72–3
  final days 86–7
Julia Livia, Tiberius' granddaughter 8, 121, 126, 160, 176–7
Julia Livilla, Caligula's sister 99, 103, 112, 122, 155–8, 160, 175–7, 194
Julia the Younger, Julia the Elder's daughter 56, 59, 82, 83, 88–97
Julio-Claudian women 1–9
Julius Caesar (Gaius) 17, 28, 32, 33, 37–8, 56, 140
Julius Vindex, Gaius 250
Junia Claudilla, Caligula's first wife 26, 138, 150, 216

Junia Silana, Caligula's sister-in-law 216
Junius Silanus, Decimus 94–5, 96, 97
Junius Silanus, Marcus 150, 151, 177
Junius Silanus Torquatus, Lucius 237
Juvenal (Decimus Junius Juvenalis) 4, 19, 71, 153, 161–2, 163–5, 166

Khan, Sadiq 7
Knüpfer, Nicolaes 165

Levick, Barbara 128
Livia Drusilla, Augustus' wife 20–1, 29–40, 42–7, 49–53
  Caligula on 47, 149
  children 2, 147
  first empress 173
  Germanicus's death 105
  Julia the Elder and 67, 72, 82
  Julia the Younger and 97
  'Livia's Garden' frescoes 2, 3
  marble head 45
  marriage to Augustus 3, 58, 70–1, 83
  marriage to Tiberius Claudius Nero 28, 51
  servants 93
  death 121
Livia Orestilla, Caligula's second wife 138, 144, 152
Livilla, daughter of Antonia 21–2, 106, 115–22, 124–34
  cameo 116–17
  marriage to Drusus the Younger 105, 107, 124–8
  marriage to Gaius 27, 78, 119
  death 8, 133–4, 194

Livius Drusus Claudianus, Marcus 32, 33–4
Locusta 210, 211
Lollia Paulina, Caligula's third wife 138, 152–3, 193, 194, 205–6, 228
Lusius Geta, Lucius 185
Lygdus (eunuch) 127, 133

Macrobius 61, 67, 73
Maecenas, Gaius 44, 75
Marius, Sextus 147
Mark Antony (Marcus Antonius)
  Augustus and 60
  letters 18
  marriage 30, 163
  children 13, 69, 71
  military general 11, 33, 34–5, 36, 102
  Scribonia and 42
Marsyas 64, 68
Massie, Allan 41
matricide 212–13
Memmius Regulus, Publius 152
misogyny, legacy of Roman 252–6
Mnester 180, 189–90
Morris, Desmond 163
mortality, perinatal 26

Naevius Cordus Sutorius Macro, Quintus 135, 136, 150, 151, 198
names, female 12–13
names, male 12–13
Narcissus 174, 184, 185, 187–8, 189, 190–1, 194, 203, 209
Nero (Claudius Caesar Drusus Germanicus) 8, 25, 142, 158, 182, 199–200, 207–9, 213–26, 227–51
Nero Julius Caesar 106–7, 109, 111–13, 139

Nero exhibition, British Museum (2021) 5–6, 257
Nicholson, Nancy 23
Nymphidius Sabinus, Gaius 250

Obaritus 224
Octavia 2, 71, 72
Octavia (play) 8, 181–3, 224–5, 230–1, 237–8
Octavian *see* Augustus
Ollius, Titus 231, 233
Oplontis, Naples 232
Ostia 183, 185–7
Otho (Marcus Salvius) 221, 234–6, 240, 251
Ovid 95–6, 97

Palazzo Massimo 1–2
Pallas 174, 184, 194, 207, 217
Pandateria (Ventotene), Pontine island 54–6, 70, 78, 113, 241, 250
Parrhasius 145
Phibbs, Geoffrey 23
Phillips, Siân 21
Phoebe 63
Pianosa island 83
Pinarius 38
Plancina 103, 104
Plautia Urgulanilla, Claudius' first wife 131, 170–1
Plautius, Aulus 169
Plautius Rufus, Publius 92
Plautus, Rubellius 216
Pliny the Elder 67, 68, 93, 164–5
police forces 254
Polybius 171–2, 184
Pomeroy, Sarah B. 26
Pompeius, Sextus 35–6, 41
Pompey the Great 33, 35, 246–7

Pontine islands 54–5, 112, 139, 176
Poppaea Sabina the Elder 178, 232, 233–4
Poppaea Sabina 217, 227, 230–6, 239–41, 243–6, 250–1
Poppaeus Sabinus, Gaius 232
Postumus (Marcus Agrippa) 21, 49, 51, 56, 82–3, 84–5, 86, 97, 210
Propertius 57, 162
prostitution 14
Pulman, Jack 20, 22
punishments, for women 8
Pythias 239

Quinctilius Varus, Publius 89, 109

Reggio di Calabria 81–2
Riding, Laura 23–4
Rusticus, Fabius 218

Sabinus (soldier) 171
Sallustius Passienus Crispus, Gaius 154, 200–1, 206
Sandy Hook massacre (2012) 213
Scribonia, Augustus' second wife 41–3, 86–7
    Julia the Elder and 57, 62, 70, 77, 78, 81
    marriage to Augustus 28, 29–30
Sempronius Gracchus, Tiberius 61, 62, 67, 85
Sextus Africanus, Titus 216
Silius, Gaius (father) 108
Silius, Gaius (son) 178, 180–1, 184–5, 186, 189, 216
Silvanus, Gavius 247
Sosia Galla 108, 109
Sporus 245
Statilia Messalina, Nero's third wife 227, 249–50, 251

Statilius Taurus Corvinus, Titus 206, 249
strangulation, non-fatal 238–9, 253–4
Suetonius (Gaius Suetonius Tranquillus)
    accounts 19
    on Agrippina the Elder 112
    on Agrippina the Younger 209
    on Antonia 136
    on Audassius 84–5
    on Augustus 63
    on Caesonia 153
    on Caligula 122, 140, 143, 148, 151, 155, 157
    on Claudilla 150
    on Claudius 170, 173, 175, 194, 210, 211
    on Domitius 198
    on Galba 200
    on Julia the Elder 77
    on Livia 37
    on Messalina 164, 167
    on Nero 218, 225, 238, 245
    on Passienus 201
    on Poppaea 243–4
    on Tiberius 36, 147
    on Vila Iovis 145
    De Vita Caesarum 18
    Life of Augustus 42, 44, 47, 50, 92–3, 96
'sugar daddy' websites 179

Tacitus, (Publius Cornelius) 46–8, 49–50
    accounts 17–18, 19
    on Agrippina the Elder 99, 100, 109–10, 112
    on Agrippina the Younger 195, 196, 204, 206, 208, 210, 212, 214

Tacitus, (Publius Cornelius) (*cont.*)
  on Albucilla 198
  on Antonia 248
  on Augustus 30, 68, 94
  on Caligula 154
  on Claudius 170, 209
  on Cornelius Sulla 247
  on Crispinus 246
  on Drusus the Younger 127
  Germanicus's death 105
  on Julia the Elder 31, 61, 63
  on Livilla 116, 132, 134
  on Messalina 167, 180, 183, 187, 188, 190, 192
  on Nero 215–16, 217–19, 221, 242
  on Octavia 236–7
  on Poppaea 231, 234–5, 240, 244
  on Rome's fire 241–2
  on Sejanus 129
  on Taurus 206
  on Tiberius 85, 109, 145–6
  on Tiberius Gemellus 136
Terentia 44
Thebes (Luxor), Egypt 102
Theodorus of Gadara 146
Tiberius 16–17, 34–6, 129–36, 144–51
  Agrippina the Elder and 100–2, 106–14
  Agrippina the Younger and 197–8
  Antonia and 130
  Augustus and 49, 51
  Caligula and 124, 132, 139
  on Capri 110, 129, 144
  Drusus the Younger and 125
  Germanicus's death 105
  Livia and 21, 34, 52–3
  marriage to Julia the Elder 2–3, 56, 58, 65–7, 72, 76–8, 84–7
  marriage to Vipsania Agrippina 88, 97, 125
  death 198
Tiberius Gemellus 107, 126–7, 129, 132, 134–5, 136, 141
Tigellinus, Ofonius 239
Traulus Montanus, Sextus 190
Tremirus island 95, 96
Trump, Donald 255

Ulysses (character) 47

Valens, Vettius 172, 186
Valeria Messalina, Claudius' third wife 160–92
  Asiaticus and 206
  Juvenal and 4, 19
  marriage to Claudius 159
  portrayals 165, 169, 187
  death 8
Valerius Messalla Barbatus, Marcus 167
Velleius Paterculus 17, 47, 62, 81, 99, 128
Vestal Virgins 155, 187, 188
Vibidia 187, 188, 191
Villa Iovis, Capri 144, 145–6, 148–9
Vinicius, Lucius 72
Vinicius, Marcus 176–7
Vipsania Agrippina, Tiberius' wife 76, 88, 125, 146
Virgil 44
Vitellius, Aulus 251
Vitellius, Lucius 194

Xenophon 210, 211